TRUE

TRUE

The Autobiography of
Martin Kemp

ORION

First published in 2000 by
Orion Media
An imprint of The Orion Publishing Group Ltd
Orion House
5 Upper St Martin's Lane, London WC2H 9EA
in association with
Northern & Shell plc, proprietors of OK! Magazine
The Northern & Shell Tower
City Harbour
London E14 9GL

A CIP catalogue record for this book
is available from the British Library.

ISBN 0 75283 264 6

Typeset at The Spartan Press Ltd,
Lymington, Hants

Printed in Great Britain

Contents

Acknowledgements

Writing this book has been one of the hardest, the most painful and yet the most pleasurable things I have ever done. There are so many people to thank who have made it possible.

My children, Harley and Roman, without their love and support, I would have fallen apart.

My brother Gary, who gave me the encouragement to write my story and who also gave me the 'Mac' that pushed me on my way.

Rob and Kath, whose enthusiasm and help I will always be thankful for.

Nicola, whose opinions were so important during times of doubt.

Derek Webster at AIM for turning my dream into reality.

Steve Dagger to whom I will always be grateful.

Trevor Dolby at Orion for guidance and experience.

My mum and dad, for always being on the other end of the phone with the answers to all my questions, and who taught me how to be a good parent.

And of course, Shirlie whose love and endless devotion is the centre of my world and without whom everything is worthless.

Lastly, to all my friends who have unknowingly helped me write this book and who have filled my life with colour.

Enjoy

The Price

'So . . . let's cut the formalities and have a look at your holiday snaps, shall we?'

I stood up, my legs slightly buckled at the knees, already expecting the worse. I couldn't look at Shirlie and see the fear in her eyes, I had enough of my own to deal with. My mouth was dry and I needed a drink as Dr C switched on the X-ray viewing screens that hung on the wall next to his desk. He clipped the first huge scan to the table. I remember how amazing it was to see inside my head for the first time and finally realize that my teachers were wrong when they called out, 'Is there nothing between your ears, Kemp?'

'There's the little fellow,' said Dr C in his soft Irish accent.

To me it all looked like a big grey mess, rather like a jelly fish that I trod on when I was a kid on a family holiday in Southend . . . but to him it was a little fellow. I found the old trick quite reassuring. Quite comforting.

I looked over at Shirlie, who by now I could feel shaking as she stood next to me. It was a strange moment, it was as if for the first time in our twelve years together we were both alone, both locked up in our own emotions that were whizzing around our bodies like some cheap fairground ride.

'You have a lump on the back of your head.'

I knew that, I had been able to see the thing clearly growing for the past month.

I had been out in Canada working on an episode of the *The Outer Limits*, playing a scientist who comes up with a formula for everlasting life. In the end, as always, it all goes horribly wrong and the scientist starts to deteriorate at an alarming speed. For the end sequence I had to wear a bald cap . . . My lump stuck up in the air like one of Fred Flintstone's, as if I had just been hit on the head by Barney's bowling ball. I ate my lunch in my trailer alone, looking at my strange eruption in the mirror.

'And you have one in the centre of your brain, but we will come back to that in a while.'

'Two lumps?' I said.

'Yes . . . but the other one is much deeper down. We'll come back to that.'

It was hard trying to hold myself together after that. I could feel my hands start to sweat and my stomach do a 180-degree turn. This wasn't what I wanted to hear.

Poor Shirlie was looking as sick as I felt. At times like this I would always try and be strong for both of us, always say things like 'Don't worry . . . it'll be all right' or 'It'll sort itself out . . . wait and see' – the sort of things everyone says when they know full well that there's trouble ahead. I couldn't do anything, I was struggling to keep myself from fainting.

I never heard the rest of what Dr C was saying. I was battling to remain upright, although looking back on it I had every right to sit down.

'Come and sit down . . . Can I get you both some water?'

Christ, was it that obvious? I thought I had done a good job in being brave up until that moment Dr C went through the side door in the corner of the office leaving Shirlie and me alone, looking at each other. I could see the tears in Shirlie's eyes, falling from what was to be my tower of strength . . . I thought at the time just how pretty she looked.

Dr C came back into the room with our two small paper cups of water. He sat behind his desk, and then said softly:

'Well, it's not cancer.'

'It's not?'

I tried to remain as calm as was possible but just hearing that word sent a shiver up my spine.

'How are you fixed tomorrow?'

'Why?' What a stupid question!

'We're gonna need to get that thing out as soon as possible.'

'Tomorrow sounds good,' I said.

I was in bits, I didn't know whether to laugh or cry. I wanted to ask about the other tumour that he nonchalantly spoke about, the one deeper inside my brain, but I didn't know if my tongue could pull itself away from the sides of my mouth . . . or my head could stop spinning for long enough for me to get the words in place. I heard Shirlie's broken voice.

'How? . . . I mean . . . why?'

'That's something I can't answer, I'm afraid. There seems to be no reason why these things pop up or who they choose to pop up on. They seem to be rather like a cold sore, some of us are more vulnerable than others.'

'I see.'

'Look go home, get some rest and I'll see you in the morning.'

Shirlie wiped her eyes as she stood up and pulled her coat around her tiny shoulders.

'OK, we'll see you tomorrow then.'

She slipped her hand inside mine and squeezed it gently.

'Come on.'

As we walked out of the office I said the strangest thing to Dr C.

'Thank you.'

Thank you for what! The fact that I had two brain tumours in my head? Within the next twenty-four hours this stranger would be sawing away at the part of my body that held my darkest secrets. Or maybe I was saying thank you so that he would think that I was a nice guy, so that he might make a better job of it.

The door to the office closed. I couldn't help thinking that it was a door closing on our future, on our dreams, on everything we wanted and had spoken about together, and on our past; the incredible roller-coaster ride I had been on for the last fifteen years.

The next thing I knew we were in the lift going back down to the car-park. Has anyone ever said that life is funny? I guess they have . . . but I never realized just how hysterical it could all get. Ever since I could remember I considered myself one of the lucky few, born with a silver spoon in my mouth, but when that spoon starts to tarnish, boy does it taste bad.

I couldn't sleep much that night. My head seemed to be bursting with pressure. As I lay in the darkness I felt my lump, I traced a small ring around the outside of it with my finger, the whole of my skull seemed to be out of shape; it seemed to start about three-quarters of the way up the back and lean over to the right-hand side. What a mess.

Was I going to die? The question rolled around in my brain every couple of minutes. I didn't just have the one tumour, I had two. Whoever was trying to kill me off had definitely hired a professional.

Was I going to die? I wasn't scared of death, but I was petrified of leaving behind my children and letting them grow up and face the world without me . . .

Was I going to die? Who knows, it was out of my hands. I'd certainly lived a lifetime of experiences already, maybe my time was up.

I stared out of the bedroom window and into the darkness that had fallen over Hampstead Heath. I could see the sun starting to break through and find its way between the cracks in the clouds. I looked back at Shirlie who was fast asleep on the bed. She looked peaceful. I wanted to wake her, I wanted to talk to her, I needed to shake these horrible thoughts out of my head, but I didn't want to put them into hers. I knew she wouldn't be getting a lot of rest over the next few days . . . I let her sleep.

*

That morning the traffic on the roads was unusually quiet, and we seemed to make our way through town and up to the hospital far too fast. We parked the car outside the National Hospital in Queen Square. The sign above the door says 'Hospital for Neurosurgery' and my heart raced. It was only then that it hit home: my God, brain surgery. It's something we laughed at in school – 'Oi, you need brain surgery.' Well, here I was.

Shirlie and I got out of the car, put our money in the meter and checked in at reception.

'Ah . . . Mr Kemp . . . not doing any more records?'

'No.'

'I loved your band.'

'Thanks.'

'Me and the wife had the band play that song of yours five times at our wedding . . . What was it called?' He tried to hum the chorus.

'Ha, ha, ha, ha . . . I know this much is . . .

'True!' I said.

'That's the one.'

He pushed the form out in front of me . . . and then four small pieces of green notepaper.

'Sign down the bottom of the pink form . . . and, if you don't mind, put your autograph on these for me – the nurses have been waiting for you to come in all day.'

For some strange reason I felt embarrassed to be there. Embarrassed that I should be checking into a brain hospital. In fact my embarrassment overtook my fear. It was so strong, I was glad to sign his autographs and leave the office.

We took the stainless steel elevator to the top floor and were met by a little Irish nurse called Linda. I was trying to smile, but my legs were far too heavy and my stomach felt like it was going to throw out its belongings there and then. I could feel some of the young nurses look at me out of the corner of their eyes. I was glad to get into my room.

'This is your room, Mr Kemp.' She opened a small door on the left. 'And your bathroom . . . of course there's a bedpan by the side of your bed.'

Christ, a bedpan, I never thought of that. How could I ever use that? Some of these nurses had probably come to see me in concert, or at the cinema, maybe even sent me fan mail as kids. I mean some of them were definitely at the right age to have been Spandau fans or Duranies. How on earth could I hand over a steaming hot bedpan? I could feel myself start to sweat just thinking about it.

I caught Shirlie out of the corner of my eye, her poor face. I think she would have been happier if this whole nightmare was happening to her.

What am I worrying about? Tomorrow they are going to cut my head in half, and I'm worrying about where I'm going to go to the toilet!

I felt the lump on top of my head. It felt rounder, bigger than it did before. Maybe it was growing faster now. I wanted to get this thing out of my body as quickly as possible, but shit, I had two lumps; the second one, that was deep inside my brain, we hadn't even discussed yet.

A few friends came to see me that evening. We laughed and joked as they tried desperately to change the subject. We seemed to spend far too long discussing whether or not Take That were 'over' and who was kissing who in *Coronation Street* the previous week. Claire, a sweet redhead who has been a friend of mine and Shirlie's for years and who owns a hairdresser's in Radlett, came in to shave my head. I felt almost guilty as she went about the task, I mean it was hardly a nice soul boy wedge I was after. I could have had the hospital butcher do the same job without asking her to make the journey into town, but I'm glad she did. At least she cut it off with feeling.

As my hair fell to the floor, the room fell silent as my lumps and bumps became exposed. It was like being on trial for murder and the prosecution having just put their eyewitness in the dock. It was all over, the evidence said it all. I felt like a condemned prisoner about to make his last walk. If it wasn't for the 'Nil by mouth' notice that was hung above my bed, it wouldn't have surprised me if someone had knocked on my door to offer me my last supper.

I couldn't believe this was happening to me. I couldn't believe that I was the focal point of this horror story. It was all I could do to stop myself from getting up out of the chair and wishing someone else good luck and promising that I would be in tomorrow with the fruit, chocolates and *OK* magazines. I didn't want to be the one left behind in that room to face the silence.

The time seemed to race past. It's amazing just how slowly time goes when you're waiting for Christmas or your summer holidays to come, and how quickly it can move at moments like this. Pretty soon my friends all said good night, everyone kissed my cheek and said good luck and then walked out into the corridor to wait for Shirlie, to give us those last few moments alone.

'Are you going to be OK?' Shirlie whispered. She knelt down beside the hospital chair that I was sitting in and folded her arms across my knees. She held my hand and stroked my fingers. This wasn't a time to kiss, the moment weighed far too much.

'Yeah, of course I will.'

I could see the bottom of her eyes fill with tiny pools of water as she spoke to me.

'Don't worry.'

'Of course not.'

'I'll be there when you wake up.' Shirlie stood up and walked over to the heavy swing doors before she turned back to me and smiled one last time . . . 'And take the pre-med . . . you'll enjoy that.'

I was left on my own for the first time, in that weird half-light of hospital rooms, to contemplate the whole ridiculous situation. Only two days ago I was lifting more weights and running further in the gym than I had ever done, fitter than I had been for years. Maybe in some strange way, fate was preparing me for the marathon ahead, making me run that extra mile, lift that extra pound, building up my strength, physically, before I climbed over the ropes and into the ring with my opposition.

I drifted off and quickly fell into my own private world. I had a dream that my teeth started to fall out one by one, and I was desperately trying to keep them in as I was in the middle of filming a big movie and had to shoot an important scene in the morning with Madonna. I had heard just how fussy she was about teeth.

There was my usual plane crash dream in there as well. This dream always pops up at times of stress, when my world becomes too complicated and I can't put things into order. I'm in the cabin of a 747 (first-class, thank God!), and we're flying so low over people's homes that I can see through their windows and into their lives.

In the first home I can see a young couple having sex on the sofa. The lights are dim and I can hear 'Lets Get It On' playing on the stereo. It's not sexy, but the love coming from them is so tangible and so intense that I find it impossible to look away.

In the second home, there's a group of young kids playing with a Ouija board, their fingers on a glass that is starting to rise from the centre of the board and float in mid air under its own power. This house smells dusty, as if it needs a good clean. The scene sends an uncomfortable shiver up my spine, I try desperately to look away before they catch me watching them, but the attraction is too strong, I'm mesmerized by the moment and continue to look.

The last house I pass I can see the clearest of all. There's a woman in a flowered dress ironing piles of fresh washing that's been stacked up on one end of the ironing board. A cigarette burns in the ash tray on the white formica shelf behind her, filling the room with smoke. It's not the usual horrible nicotine stench but a warm comforting smell that seeps into my body and makes the thought of my imminent danger fade away. There's a man at the back of the room, sitting in front of a television while white noise flashes up on its screen. The man is too tired from his hard day's work to do anything about the interference, but he sips on a hot cup of tea and smiles at the woman as she does her house work. Neither one of

8

them notices the aeroplane go by as we search for a place to crash. The plane plunges up and down several times before the effort to keep it aloft fails.

The plane doesn't explode as it hits the ground, but it breaks into hundreds of tiny pieces, throwing me clear, allowing me to float in the air long enough to realize that the home I was looking at in detail moments earlier as the plane made its descent was mine thirty-five years ago, and the man and woman were my mother and father.

At some point my dreams all seemed to blend into one. Madonna was flying the plane and laughing at me as she called out of the window, 'How can I work with you? . . . You haven't got a tooth in your head.' I tried to close my mouth as my teeth crumbled away behind my lips, trying in vain to keep them in place. I watched the plane crash behind me as I continued my usual journey to safety.

'Mr Kemp . . . Mr Kemp, do you want to pop these into your mouth?'

I was back in the land of the living, and the little Irish nurse was offering me two blue tablets. She looked tired, it had obviously been a hard night.

'It's six o'clock . . . Take these, they'll help you relax, it's just a pre-med.'

I wasn't sure if I wanted to pop them into my mouth. I wondered if I should stay awake for as long as possible. I mean, this was the biggest day of my life – shouldn't I be aware of what's going on around me? Shouldn't I be able to communicate for as long as possible?

'They won't send you to sleep, just relax you.'

What the hell? I took the two blue tablets and pretty soon felt a wave of relaxation flow through my body. The first release I had had since Dr C broke the news yesterday afternoon.

My bed started to move, and lights flashed in my eyes as they wheeled me down the corridor and into the lift, down into the bowels of the hospital. The lights reminded me of walking on stage at the Live Aid concert ten years before. I got to the front of the stage where the sight of one hundred thousand screaming people hit me. It's a rush that flies through your body and up into your brain like the medication that was flowing through there at that very moment.

Paul McCartney had just come off stage, where he had sung 'Let It Be'. As I got to the front, I noticed that his handwritten lyrics were still sitting on top of his grand piano. I didn't see who put them into their grubby pocket, but I wished I was a little quicker.

'Martin . . . MARTIN, we're going to look after you, try not to worry.'

I thought it was a little too late for that. I recognized Dr C's soft voice. I couldn't get my head up off the pillow to look at him, it felt as if someone was holding me down.

'We're just going to send you to sleep, you'll just feel a little prick in your arm.'

I knew I only had a few seconds left as I started to fall into the centre of a giant swirling whirlpool.

'Say hi to my brain,' I said. Finally the whirlpool took me down into its vast vortex.

A grey swirling mass of memories seemed to flow around me. Pictures of my life seemed to bounce around inside my head as Dr C began his work. There were many pictures hung in gilt frames around the walls of the twister. It was stranger than words can express, but I was sure that Dr C was inside my head, already pulling on some of the nerves inside my memory banks, triggering off these wonderful thoughts.

I had nothing else to do but to explore the corners of my mind and bring back to life memories of my childhood that I thought had somehow evaporated over the years. I felt myself crying as those incredible memories, those tingling thoughts and smells came flooding back.

My thoughts soon became a quest, a quest to find the answer to the question that Dr C couldn't answer in his surgery yesterday . . .

How, when and – most of all – why? Why me? When did the 'little fellow' decide to pop up and take a hold on my meninges? There must have been something, a single moment that started its growth. Stress, alcohol, drugs – they had all been part of my hectic life, part of my growing up inside the world of rock-and-roll with Spandau Ballet and trying to establish myself as an actor. The movie *The Krays* had given me an incredible platform to launch into the second half of my life. A new career put aside for when my face starts to wrinkle and my hair starts to fall out and the screaming fans decide to stop camping outside my front door.

There had to be a moment I could hang this problem on. I don't think I could handle the ambiguity, the sense of not knowing why. Dr C began his work and cracked open the casing of my soul, allowing the fresh air to rush in for the very first time.

1961.
138 Rotherfield Street

The small Georgian building in Islington was home for the first fourteen years of my life. I was born there in 1961, in my mother's bedroom on the second floor. It was just outside the sound of Bow bells, so if that's the criterion for being a cockney then I suppose I just missed out. Gary had been born in St Bartholomew's Hospital exactly two years earlier and defiantly held on to that distinction, of which I was always envious.

My birth was difficult, and my mother and I were taken into hospital moments later. I had turned a nasty shade of blue apparently, and for several moments they thought that I wasn't going to be stopping for long.

For years I suffered a recurring dream about those very first moments of struggle. It was horrible, some nights I would wake up in a cold sweat in the middle of the dream and not want to go back to sleep in case I was thrown back into it. I would get up and wait until the morning sun threw some light into my room before I could even think about going back to my bed.

In the dream I'm in the dungeon of a medieval castle. It's dark, lit only by one flaming torch that hangs on a distant wall. It smells damp and the sticky humidity is making me sweat. All I can hear is the sound of dripping water and the echo of my shoes as I walk down a flight of stone steps.

At the bottom there are no doors or windows, just a black murky pool of water with what looks like a dark blue oil slick moving around on top of it. I watch the pattern it creates, enjoying the way the oil moves around, as it gets sucked up by larger formations further along the water.

I know the way out of this building, I have to go into the dark waters and swim under the surface to reach a tunnel at the other end. I'm not frightened at this point because I've had the dream so many times that it has become almost routine. But as I sink into the blackness of the water, I start to realize that there are dead bodies floating around me, clinging on to me, slowing me down. My sense of fear is overpowering, I struggle for air as I become completely caught up in floating limbs.

The thought of giving in hits me like a ton of bricks. I want to stop swimming and float freely with the rest of the bodies. The effort needed to reach my destination seems impossible. My stomach twists and turns and I feel sick as the water starts to creep up my nose and into my lungs.

I force myself on and only just make it to the tunnel at the other end. I eventually swim through the red-brick tunnel and out to the other side, lifting myself up into the fresh air.

The dream hasn't returned since I made the connection with my birth.

I was a late talker, only putting together my words at three and a half. My brother did all the talking for me. If I wanted a sausage, Gary would ask for one for me. If I wanted to get out of my pram and try to walk, Gary would ask for me. In fact, if I needed anything, Gary would ask for me, he was always by my side and ready to help, no matter what the task. One of my first memories is that of Gary dancing around my high chair singing, 'Martin wants a poo poo, Martin wants a poo-poo.' It might have been the first song he ever wrote.

Our house was small, but built over four floors. It was used as a rent collection station, so we always had strangers standing in line in the front passage, arguing through the small glass slatted window that was built into the passage wall about late payments or the state of repair of their property. The floor below, the basement, was completely derelict, with rotten floorboards and mice that ran in and out of the wall joists trying to avoid the small piles of poison that were always there. There was no electricity in the basement, so it was always in complete darkness and it had that smell of dampness and rotten wood that hung in the air like clouds of grey fungus. I hated it. So many of my childhood nightmares revolved around that one place.

Our toilet was outside. To get to it I would have to take down my small torch and go past the basement at the bottom of the house, take the catch off the back door and run across the yard. I was always brave going out, but on the way back I would run up those stairs as quick as I could, never looking to see what was lurking over my shoulder or trying to catch my ankles.

The toilet was in one corner of our yard. In the other corner was a huge old brick air-raid shelter that took up what little space there was. The shelter was filled with old rusty bikes, cans of dried-up paint and giant prehistoric spider webs that clung on to an old tin bath that hung from a hook on the wall. It was scary, but not in the same league as the basement. The things that were in there were dirty but incredibly interesting, you never knew what you might find. During the hot summers I would explore the depths of the shelter, hoping to find some money that might have been stashed away when the Germans dropped their bombs. My mum would call out of the kitchen window, two floors up, 'Get out of there, it's dangerous.'

The toilet itself was always crawling with spiders. Daddy-long-legs would hang from the cistern that was high up on the brick wall behind me, throwing scary shadows from the bare light bulb that swung in the breeze. Some nights I was so cold that I would freeze as fast as the pipes around my head as I sat with my shorts around my knees and my carefully folded piece of newspaper in my hand. Through all of this, it never crossed my mind once that we were poor. It seemed to me we had everything we needed.

The top floor of the house was taken by my cousin Vivian, her Cypriot husband Harbi, whose Turkish music would filter down the staircase on Sunday mornings, and their two children, Alan, who was my age, and Radji, who came along a few years later.

We lived on the middle floor. There were two bedrooms, a living-room and the smallest kitchen you could imagine. The strangest thing is that there were no doors separating the landings. One of the rent payers downstairs could have walked into any room. Still I suppose people really did leave their street doors open in those days.

The house was right next door to the Duke of Clarence, a big old public house whose sign actually creaked in the wind outside my room on those windy North London nights. They were my first strains of music. We would also be treated to our regular dose of 'Roll out the Barrel' and 'On Mother Kelly's Doorstep' every Saturday night. It was a nice way to fall asleep, to the sound of people enjoying themselves, singing at the top of their beer-filled lungs. Even the odd fight outside at closing time didn't break up the warm feeling that still lives with me today.

By the time I was six, Gary and I had our own separate beds. His was on the other side of the room, pushed up against the opposite wall. As we lay there in the dark, he would terrify me with stories of how a hand was hiding under my bed and was creeping up my blankets. My mum would always take me into her bed and cuddle me to sleep, while poor Gary had to face his monster on his own. The nights that Gary didn't scare me I had to make up a different excuse to get into her bed. I remember that feeling of warmth and safety as if it was yesterday, the smell of heat coming from my mum as she put her arm around me, and the sound of my dad breathing on the other side of their enormous bed.

To feel loved and protected like that is a wonderful thing. Even today, if I have just woken from a bad dream, Shirlie will put her arm around me in the same way my mother did all those years ago and I will be back to sleep in moments with the nightmare behind me. No matter how old we get, sometimes we all need that feeling of safety and someone to tell us that it's all going to be all right.

It was while sitting on the step outside The Duke of Clarence, with my bottle of Coke in one hand and a bag of crisps resting between my legs, that I first heard the name 'Krays' being spoken. Two old-timers were leaning up against the outside wall with their pints of black and mild clutched in their bony hands, speaking of the twins in whispers as their roll-ups drooped out of the side of their mouths and the ash fell down their dark wool suits.

'The Krays will be up soon . . . You watch the place clear out then.'

My dad worked in a print shop at the Angel, Islington. He had been there since he was a small boy, mostly working for next to nothing, as most people did in those days. The smell of ink and hard work was the most comforting thing in my world as my dad would sit me on his lap when he came home every night at six o'clock. My dad is an incredibly artistic man, very good with his hands. He can paint, draw, decorate and make things out of wood that could compete with the best. When Gary and I were younger it was almost to the point of embarrassment. We were asked at school to make a hat for the Easter parade. My dad came up with this working model of a windmill with hopping clockwork chicks and revolving sails and sent me back to school on the Monday with this masterpiece balanced on my tiny head.

On Saturday mornings my dad would take me to work with him and let me watch him run the huge print machines that gripped the wooden floors like monstrous dinosaurs waiting to be fed with sheets of pure white paper. He would make me cups of hot milky coffee, let me draw with his best pens and explore the empty factory as he got on with his work. There was no one else around, just me and my dad – we were a team and I loved it. I would always bring home with me some paper clips or a ball of string that no one would miss, or if I was lucky a coloured felt-tip pen. These things meant the world to me and I put them under my bed, in a special place next to my toys.

My dad's grandfather was the local blacksmith, an honest, hardworking man who would drop sweets on the pavements as he walked along for the local children to find. He died suddenly from a blood clot on the brain after he was kicked in the head by one of the horses in his yard. Even in my desperate quest for the reason behind my tumours, I couldn't think for a moment that this had anything to do with my own problem. Surely this couldn't be hereditary, although it makes me wonder now whether it was just a blood clot he died from: maybe there was something more than they realized. There was no such thing as an MRI brain scan in those days, so we don't really know if his problem started even before he was kicked by the horse. A blood clot on the brain could just as easily be caused by an oversized tumour hidden away deep in the centre of the brain. Maybe I'm clutching at straws, but it's an idea.

My mum was the perfect mother. In between her cooking and ironing she taught Gary and me our reading, writing and arithmetic, way before we went to school. I saw my mother cry more than once because she couldn't afford to buy us new shoes or a new coat for the winter, but she never dreamed of taking even a part-time job away from us until we were well settled into our schools.

Mum would always have dinner ready so that we could all sit down together around the kitchen table and eat. When she finally did take a part-time job, it was as a machinist, working from home. The living-room would be piled high in unfinished garments and reels of cotton. The sound of that machine rocked me to sleep like my mother herself. Her handiwork came in useful years later when she would make shirts for me that I would wear on *Top of the Pops*.

We would always take my nan, my mum's mum, out in the car with us on Sunday afternoon trips to the country or down to Southend for the day. The car would be filled with smoke from her filterless 'Weights' – she couldn't have the window open for fear of a draught on her legs. The only fresh air allowed into the car was when we had to stop every thirty minutes to let her out to use the toilets.

I loved my nan. She used to say that I looked German, and I would click my heels, give a German salute and march around her tiny flat in Hoxton. Nan spoke in that wartime cockney accent that has now almost disappeared.

'There you go, I told you . . . What did I say?'

'Don't be silly,' my mum would say, trying to hold back a smile. 'He's having you on.'

'I don't care what you say . . . Look at those blue eyes . . . He got it in him I tell ya!'

I just carried on marching around the room as my nan blew out yet more clouds of thick grey cigarette smoke.

Mum and Dad worked hard, they cared for us, taught us everything they could, were proud of us and taught us how to love . . . and be loved. They were the best and, thank God, still are!

Just after my seventh birthday, my mum took me to the small drama club across the road from where we lived, The Anna Scher Children's Theatre. It was held in the community hall that sat in the heart of a block of flats called Benthem Court. The flats had a reputation of being one of the rougher areas of the district, the place you never wanted to take as a short cut . . . Even though the entrance to this giant red-brick castle was right across the road from the sanctuary of my street door, I had never once dreamed of walking over the drawbridge and into the mouth of the monster. As we got closer to the flats my heart was pounding, for I could see other children walking towards the club. What if I knew any of them? What if any of my school friends saw me holding hands with my mum? What if any of them were girls? I quickly made out to cough, so I could retrieve my hand from my mum's grasp as if I was going to cover my mouth as she had taught me.

We made it to the entrance of the community centre, up the stairs, through the two green swing doors and into the large hall. It smelt of jumble sales and dust and stale cigar smoke, but the sun was streaking in through its large windows on either side and on to the wooden floor, giving it a magical ambience. The place was filled with the ghosts of wedding receptions and school plays . . . I wanted to turn back.

Anna held out her hand to say hello, and I buried my face firmly into my mum's left buttock, the old ostrich technique that I had always found quite effective. It stayed there until I could hear Anna's voice booming out from the centre of the hall, starting the lesson.

'OK, let's start with our warm-up exercises . . . I want you all running around the room in an anti-clockwise direction.'

We sat down at the back of the room on two canvas chairs. I got my first look at Anna Scher. She had long blonde flowing hair and a pretty face that was framed by a short fringe, and wore a long, flowing, flowered skirt and a small white jumper that was tight around her arms. As she moved around the room with the children, there seemed to be no difference in age, no difference in enthusiasm. She didn't look like their teacher, she looked more like their friend, an equal, and definitely someone I could trust.

My mother and I watched for an hour and a half of what seemed to be pure magic. Children without any inhibitions, dancing, pretending to be grown-ups, using boxes of wigs and hats to dress up in, and at the end of it being praised with the type of enthusiasm that to this day I have only ever seen Anna Scher exude. As the lesson went on, my shyness became smiles and my smiles turned into laughter at the children's performances. I couldn't wait to pay my ten pence next Thursday and join in.

Tuesday and Thursday evenings came and went for the next eight years. In that time I spent with Anna she taught me a lot more than just the basic skills of acting. She taught me important lessons for life. Her big saying was 'Never forget your three P's – Professionalism, Punctuality and Point of Focus', which I have never forgotten. With the drama lessons I picked up a confidence and charisma that children of that age usually lack, which got me through school and prepared me for job interviews that were going to be a big part of my life.

'Two-nil.'

They were the first words I ever spoke in front of a camera. Gary and I were chosen to appear on a children's TV show called *Jackanory*. We were coming out of Highbury Stadium, the home of my beloved Arsenal football team, when someone stopped us to ask the score.

'Oi . . . you two, do you know what the score was?'

'Two-nil,' I said.

'Has the game finished?'

'Yeah, we're on our way home,' Gary replied.

If you'd blinked you would have missed us; it was one of those, but we were down on celluloid for the first time.

I never had any nerves whatsoever when I was a kid. I would just turn up, play the part and leave. I wish I had that ability now – it would make life so much easier. Who's to say that my tumours haven't developed as a result of years of stress, years of suppressed nerves at having to perform to the high standard that I set myself at a very early age.

By the age of ten I had a 'CV' to rival the best:

Jackanory *1972*
The Edwardians *1972*
Mind Where You Are Going *1972*
Katherine Mansfield *1973*
Scribble. *1973*
The Tomorrow People *1973*
Oranges and Lemons. *1973*
Dixon of Dock Green. *1973*
Rumpole of the Bailey *1975*
Jackanory *1975*

My final year with Anna brought me my biggest role as a child actor.

I had won the part in a BBC production called *The Glittering Prizes* with Tom Conti and Nigel Havers. I was to play a young boy who like myself had dreams of becoming England's answer to George Best. The shooting in Ipswich went well until the last day . . . the day I had been dreading.

It was a post-match shower scene with fourteen young boys completely naked in an old Victorian communal shower. We had just come in from a mud soaked school football pitch and had made our way into the changing-rooms.

I was dreading taking my clothes off in front of the cameras. Undressing in front of the doctor was always hard for me, but this was going to be a nightmare.

'OK, everyone strip off,' came the command from the assistant director. I looked around. The tension was so thick that you could have cut the air with a knife.

'Come on . . . we haven't got all day.'

Some of the boys who had been standing at the front of the pack started to take off their dirty clothes and pull down their muddy white shorts.

'OK, turn on the showers.' I could tell that the assistant director wasn't enjoying this, he wanted to get this shot done and the boys back into their clothes as quickly as he could. Then he turned to me.

He spoke in a softer voice, as if he was giving me the respect of a star.

'Martin . . . are you ready?'

I was anything but ready for this, I had butterflies in my stomach, my face was purple and my knees had evaporated into jelly. I looked around once again. The room seemed to be packed with onlookers, people who had nothing to do with the scene.

I closed my eyes for a moment and thought about Anna's three P's, two of them being professionalism and point of focus. I had made a good job of the part, I was pleased with the work I had done so far on the job and was as proud as anyone could possibly be when the director rubbed my head and said 'Well done'. I couldn't let them down now. I knew that if I didn't want to do this particular

21

scene I shouldn't have taken the role in the first place. I tried to focus on the task and then with a giant sigh pulled down my shorts. The assistant director went back to his loud, commanding voice as he spoke to the room.

'OK, let's do it . . . let's shoot.'

The water from the showers could only be luke warm, as the steam would have caused too much condensation for the cameras to handle. The boys tried to cover themselves as best they could as they shivered under the water.

I was lucky in one respect: I didn't have to get into the showers. My job that day was to stand up from a bench I was squatting on, face my bare bottom into camera and calmly piss on the poor boy sitting next to me. Now any man will tell you it's hard enough trying to get the thing to work in a urinal when you're standing next to someone and whistling 'Land of Hope and Glory', let alone with a camera trained on your bottom waiting for you to perform.

During the afternoon I had been given several bottles of juice, a can of coke and a giant bottle of my favourite creme soda to get me ready for my oncoming ordeal. I wasn't looking forward to it but I knew there was no way out, it had all gone too far. Afternoon tea was served around four, it was the usual cucumber sandwiches with no crusts and jam doughnuts all displayed on what looked like my dad's old decorating table. By the time that was over, I would have given anything to take the job in hand and find a quiet corner to wee up against, but somehow I held it back.

Now, when everything was ready and the boy sitting next to me was carefully placed within shooting distance, the director called 'Action'. They waited . . . and they waited . . . and they waited. The assistant director whispered to me, 'Martin, the cameras are rolling . . . you can do it now.'

I tried to relax and to breathe deeply as Anna had taught me, but my bowels had committed first-degree mutiny. They had quite simply stopped taking commands from my brain, and who in their right mind could blame them?

Each time the director called 'Action' and I tried to relax and concentrate as Anna had taught me, the whole thing got worse. The longer it went on, the more he called out 'Action', the harder it became.

The director, Waris Hussein, then had this idea that he would stand to the side of me, out of shot, and try his hand at the task. I was so pleased when the same mental block that had fallen on me now afflicted him. The whole thing was becoming a farce.

By now some of the boys were suffering from wrinkled skin, as they had been in the shower for nearly an hour. At this point a prop man came up with a small contraption. They were going to pour orange juice down a pipe that a continuity girl would hold next to me, just off camera.

The director called out for one last time: 'Action.'

I had never been so embarrassed, I wanted to get home and get a hug from my mum. I just wanted to get this whole thing over and put my clothes back on. I made a promise to myself as I watched the orange juice flow down the clear plastic pipe: I never wanted to act again . . . ever.

They got their shot in the end, and I went to the toilet to relieve my bursting bladder.

I never wanted to set my eyes on any of those people ever again.

I was thirteen. I had the ball on the half-way line. My legs were covered in mud from the soaking wet school football field and my breath froze as it poured from my lungs and out into the cold damp air. I had run myself into a state of near exhaustion that particular Saturday morning, looking for a goal to keep our side in the match. Just then a gap opened up in front of me. I could see a clear path from where I was to the opposition's goalmouth, all I had to do was to run the remaining ten yards and send the ball past the keeper and into the net. The celebrations were already ringing around my head. It wasn't such a hard task, I had been playing football for my school side for the past year and had run the same distance with the ball many times before. I loved all sports, but football was my passion.

The previous night I had been up until late, dyeing my football boots bright blue and lining the inside with an imitation fur lining. They looked great, but every time I kicked the ball my boot would come off, flying ten yards ahead of me like some deadly kung fu weapon. I had to make up for it, and here was a golden opportunity.

My head was down and my heart pushed my legs into the sodden ground below my feet. My redesigned boots tried everything to stick in the mud, but the field ahead of me was clear apart from the goalie at the other end. This was a chance that had to be taken. My toes gripped the insides of my boots, desperately trying to keep them on as I carried on running.

My dad was there as usual. He always came to the school football matches, no matter what the weather, to cheer me on and to take me home afterwards. I could always hear him calling my name and shouting encouraging words across the pitch. I would play my heart out for him, trying to make him proud of me, trying to score that winning goal.

As I ran towards the goal and through the open field, things seemed unusually quiet. I couldn't hear my dad or any of the other fathers over in their usual position by the gate. I lifted my head for another look at goal. Suddenly I heard the sound of someone chasing me. I prepared myself to be tackled from behind and pushed the ball a few more yards ahead.

'Bootball . . . bootball!'

What the hell was that? I looked up at the goalie, who was starting to run off his line and back to the changing-room hut. He had a look of horror on his face that I hadn't witnessed before.

'Bootball . . . Bootball.'

Something weird was going on – who *was* that behind me? As much as I didn't want to let my side down I had to check it out and take a look, even though it would slow me down.

'Bootball . . . bootball . . . I love bootball.'

I looked over my shoulder – and saw an extraordinary apparition.

On the next plot of land along Woodside Avenue was a mental hospital, a huge Victorian building with a red tiled roof and giant white clock tower that threw an enormous shadow over the pitch in the summer months. One of its inmates had found a way out and was right on my heels. He was wearing a white linen straight-jacket with his arms tied behind his back and a smile on his face that said it all . . . Freedom! Even though it was only momenta-rily.

I quickly moved off to one side, side-footed the ball to him and let him have the honour of putting it into the empty goal. His celebrations were short-lived however, as two men in their white coats came out to get him and took him back through the hole in the fence. It was a shame we lost, but I'm glad he scored.

I was always quite tall for my age, always towering over the rest of the class. In some ways, being tall was a godsend, as it kept me out of school fights and any bullying that was going on between the higher and lower years. I was almost six foot by the time I was thirteen. Six foot and as skinny as a drain pipe. The day I started at my secondary school, wearing my new school uniform and carrying my new leather brief-case, I stuck out like a sore thumb. There were kids in my class that were practically half the size of me, but thank God there was one other tall kid in the class room called David Turner, with whom I made friends.

Thanks to our height, by the time David and I were fourteen we were already managing to bluff our way into the cinemas in Holloway Road to see X-rated movies like *Enter the Dragon* and *The Godfather*, starring Marlon Brando.

It was while we were watching *The Godfather* one afternoon that a huge storm broke outside the cinema. It was a storm from hell, and every thunderclap rocked the Victorian foundations of the Hollo-way Road Odeon. At first I thought it was all part of the movie, as every bang seemed to land in an appropriate place, during a gunfight or a garrotting or over the top of an explosion. Half-way

25

through the movie, I felt a drop of water land on my head. It landed on my forehead and made its way down the bridge of my nose before dropping off and falling into my lap. I looked up, and water was pouring in through the cracks in the ornamental ceiling. It was surreal, it was raining on the screen and raining in the cinema at the same time – the best surround sound I have ever experienced.

The old couple next to me started to notice the water coming in through the light sockets on the side walls.

'Fuck me . . . it's fucking raining in here.'

CRASH! . . . Another loud thunderclap rocked the old building. A few people screamed and literally jumped out of their seats – they had had enough. The movie was good, but not that good.

CRASH! . . . The screen went black and then any remaining lights in the cinema went out.

CRASH! . . . The storm was right above us. It sounded even louder in the darkness of the giant, cavernous, black room.

The room was silent for a moment, and then there was the flicker of a torch and the sound of an old man's voice.

'Can you make your way out of the cinema as quickly as possible.'

You could just make out his gold epaulets and his white moustache as he shone his regulation torch down the aisle. He tried to stay calm.

'You can collect your readmission tickets from the desk downstairs.' Shit! . . . I had only just managed to get the courage up to buy the ticket in the first place. I was still only fourteen, four years short of the required age for an X film, and now I had to go and ask for another one. I kept my head low as I walked down the stairs. I mean I was tall, but my face still hadn't grown a whisker.

'This way . . . quick as you can,' said the old boy.

We moved out of our seats and along the aisle. The water was still dripping on our heads, and the thought of the whole roof collapsing did cross my mind once or twice. The old man called out again.

'Come on . . . let's go!'

I followed the crowd down the stairs and pretty soon I was

standing in front of the woman I had fooled an hour earlier. I tried to keep my head down and concentrate on something completely different. I noticed a giant mole on her cheek, it was just above her lip and had several thick black hairs poking out like some satellite floating freely in orbit. I felt sorry for her, I couldn't help but marvel as she swapped my chewed-up blue ticket for a brand new one.

CRASH! . . . The storm was back, and this time a wave came crashing through the doors and hit the backs of my legs, nearly knocking me off of my feet. I turned around, and beyond the glass doors I could see that the whole of Holloway Road was flooded. In fact it was waist high in water. My mind was in a panic. On the news, only the night before, I had seen a man in a dark three-piece suit saying alarming things. He spoke in a well-bred parliamentary voice and obviously knew what he was talking about. His prediction frightened me – he spoke like Nostradamus himself.

'POLITICIAN'

Yes we cannot carry on like this, just hoping that this catastrophe just won't happen. That the problem will all just disappear . . . nothing was built on hope. Hoping is just not good enough. All Londoners are responsible for our destiny . . . We have to do something about it, and now, while we still have a London to save. This is a real threat to life as we know it. The Thames flood barrier must be finished . . . and fast, before we all go under.

CUT TO. HOLLOWAY ROAD. EXT. WET.

Now I thought the worst. I had every right to, I was just about to dive off the high step of the cinema and into the Holloway Road. This wasn't an everyday occurrence.

I looked over to one side, where a few of the local kids were charging drivers fifty pence a time to push their cars on to a small patch of high ground that was around the side of the cinema. An old woman was being carried over a man's shoulder, the fact that her grey underwear was on show to the world being the least of her worries. There were women carrying children above their heads, men carrying their wallets, and everyone around was in complete and utter shock.

I started to swim in the filthy water that was sending my crotch soggy. I had seen enough, I was worried sick as I thought of home. I couldn't believe it – the whole of London under water. No more Arsenal, no more football . . . what was life going to be like from now on? Would we all have to live on boats? North London hardly had the same charm as Venice. The whole concept was just too alarming to consider.

Cardboard boxes, fruit and veg from the local grocer's and general household rubbish started to drift past, and the thought of rats started to cross my mind. I had always hated those things. I felt sick with worry. I wanted to get home, no matter what kind of state I would find it in. I wanted to see my mum, my dad, Gary. I wanted to sit in front of the electric fire and watch *Crossroads*. I didn't want this – this was scaring me.

I swam a little further, down towards the old tube station which is just under the bridge. Those poor people down by the train tracks! How many must have died? I hated the idea of crashing into a floating corpse.

Just then, as the monumental, dark, heavy skies started to part and beams of white sunshine started to break through the clouds, I noticed that the water was starting to shallow out. One hundred yards on, in fact, there was no water at all, it was completely dry. Because Holloway Road was built on a giant dip, sloping down-wards from each end towards its centre, all the water had collected there, right in front of the cinema.

I caught the bus the rest of the way home, and as I sat there in my soaking wet clothes the other passengers, who hadn't realized what had happened, looked at me as if I was mad. I tried to ignore their strange looks as I gradually dried out next to the window. I was so relieved. How and why? Didn't even cross my mind.

I had never been as happy to get home that evening in all the years I had been alive. My mum made me a cup of tea with some hot toast, put my feet up on the couch in front of the electric fire, and then went over to the television and put on *Blue Peter*. Just then I felt that I didn't want to be eighteen and go to any more X-rated movies. Fourteen seemed like a good age, and I thought I would make the most of it while it lasted.

It was 1978, the Sex Pistols had sold out, and I had left school two years earlier with a disappointing two O levels. This left me earning ten pounds a week from standing on street corners handing out free magazines to stressed-out women as they appeared from the darkness of the subterranean tube stations. The only antidote I had for this situation was to dream; it was the only way I could possibly retain some self-respect and some dignity. All those years at a grammar school, all those hours of homework, and there I was handing out free *Miss London* magazines with the rest of a failed generation.

I spent most of my time at school looking out over the grey London skyline dreaming of a free magic ride that would take me to stardom. It was partly because Anna Scher had showed me that there was more to life than a nine to five job, and partly because I was never that great academically – I found most lessons boring and far too hard to follow.

The only lesson I really enjoyed was geography, and that was because I had a crush on the teacher, Mrs Woodford, who was also my class teacher. She was only a small woman, but had a fiery temper, a wonderful smile and what looked to me at the time like mountainous breasts. Her soft blue eyes shone out from underneath her curly brown fringe and seemed to light up when your marks were above sixty per cent. In the mornings she would always leave a trail of sweet perfume in the air as she passed by your table. I always felt she had an extra moment for me and would look at me with a slightly bigger smile than she had for the rest of the class. She made those dark mornings with overcast skies slightly brighter for me as she called out the daily register, and as I worked out my excuses for not having done my homework.

While I stood outside those train stations with my bundle of magazines in the cold and sometimes pouring rain, the one thing I dreaded more than anything in the world was bumping into old class-mates who might be on their way to work. What would I say? What would I do? I hadn't achieved anything apart from a pocketful of dreams. They would most likely be settled into some secure bank job and wearing the suit and tie to go with it.

I was positive though. I knew that my time would come. I knew that destiny was going to be kind to me, that I wouldn't be out in the cold for long.

On Saturdays I worked in a fruit and veg shop in Essex Road, owned by a lovely couple called Slim and Doll Barnard. It was literally two minutes' walk from our house on Rotherfield Street, and I loved working there. Slim was a big man who only just recently passed away. He would sing from the moment he opened the shutters to the moment the tills stopped ringing out the tune of money. There was one song that he knew was my favourite, and he would sing it at the top of his lungs as I carried on serving some of the old faces with their potatoes and greens for the Sunday roast.

When my old wedding ring was new and each dream that I dream came true.
I remember with pride the day you were my bride, what a beautiful picture you made by my side.
Even though silver crowns your hair, I can still see the gold ring that's there.
Loves old flame, it's still the same, since the day I changed your name,
When your old wedding ring was new.

That song was sung more than once at after-show parties with Spandau, when the Jack Daniels had flowed and the Bollinger had all gone and the Yamamoto designer jacket had been thrown into a crumpled heap in the corner.

Working in the fruit shop and the *Miss London* magazine job were giving me some pocket money, but I really needed to earn something that resembled a wage. I was at an age where I wanted to hang out with my friends at the local pub and not have to sip on one pint of beer the whole evening.

It was my dad who got me my first real job, working as an apprentice in a print factory. The place was only small but filled with hundreds of wooden trays of metal type faces. The brick walls that surrounded the work area were painted a prison blue, and the fluorescent lights that were hung from every corner of the room gave everyone a pale grey complexion.

The one blessing was that the place was quiet. It had to be, as a lot of concentration was needed to tie together thousands of individual letters into huge metal pages ready to be laid into the bed of the printing presses.

I was thankful for the wage I was earning, but the longer I spent there the more my dreams of making something of myself faded. I knew I had to escape, and quickly, before I became trapped in that life cycle and unable to get out. It frightened me to think that I would be locked up in that print shop for years to come, but the longer I spent in there the more likely it started to seem.

The council had finally moved us out of Rotherfield Street, away from the outside toilet and the derelict basement that had fuelled my childhood nightmares, and just around the corner to Elmore Street. Our new house was huge and spread over five floors, with a separate flat below us that was rented out to a sweet old woman with white hair and a walking frame. To us, the new house was a mansion, and for the first time in our lives we had an indoor toilet that smelt of pot-pourri and air fresheners. Most importantly of all, we had our own street door. I had never seen my mum and dad quite as happy as the day we moved in there. I'll never forget their faces as we walked in for the first time and closed the door behind us.

The new house even had a bathroom. Previously my dad had taken Gary and me over to the public baths in Theberton Street every other Sunday morning while my mum would be cooking the roast. I hated it in those white enamel baths, calling out for more hot water every five minutes and finding orphaned pubic hairs floating in the water. The new house was only two minutes' walk away from the old one, but it felt as though we were living on a different planet.

One morning I closed the street door behind me as usual. It was a cold morning and the damp wind felt like a brick wall as it pushed at the back of my green nylon duffel coat and inside the edge of my fur-trimmed hood. The sky was overcast, and it smelt like rain that morning. It had been hard work getting out of my bed because the night before we had been at a Guy Fawkes night and I had drunk a few beers around the giant fire that we had built with our next-door neighbours in an empty garden a few doors along.

Elmore Street wasn't a main road, most of the time it was quiet, but cars tended to cut through it at a frightening speed – these were the days with no speed bumps and no sleeping policemen. The road had a small bend in it just before it straightened up outside our house, but you could clearly see the cars turning off Essex Road and taking their short cut through to Dalston. I looked at my watch as I stepped out of my house. Every minute was accounted for in those early mornings as I made my way to work, and the day was a complete disaster if I reached there even two minutes early.

I made my way down the garden path and out of the gate and started to cross the road. The wind was rattling around in my eardrums, creating a small whistling sound, when I saw a car coming down the road towards me. It wasn't anything unusual, by now I had seen a thousand cars take that same route. It wasn't speeding, there was nothing out of place, everything was just as it always was, but this time, for some reason that still haunts me, I heard a voice in my head. It was quite clear and quite urgent. It wasn't my voice, it was older, thicker, a voice that had experience layered into its warm tones. It said, 'Go back to your house – that car isn't going to turn.'

I didn't hesitate, I walked straight back behind the wrought-iron gate and watched as the car came straight down the road as promised, without making the turn, and smashed into the parked car where I had been standing . . . Without a doubt it would have killed me.

My mum threw open the top-floor window and my neighbours came out of their houses and we all watched the driver make his exit and run off up a side turning, disappearing into the early morning drizzle.

It wasn't until I arrived for work that I stopped to think about the voice in my head. It wasn't scary, it didn't frighten me, it had obviously saved my life. Whoever or whatever it was, it was on my side. I thought back to a game that Gary and I had played with an Ouija board when we were kids, with my brother and a friend of ours who had recently lost his dad. He obviously saw it as some kind of telephone.

The glass started to move, and once we had all got past the stage of giggling and trying to find out the identity of the person who was pushing it around the board, it began to spell out a message, letter by letter: 'THIS IS MARTIN'S GUIDE . . . MY NAME IS LEN'

My heart missed a beat and I jumped up off the floor. My parents had always warned me about playing with the Ouija board, about interfering with the unknown, and now it was picking me out of the crowd. It played on my mind for weeks. I wanted to ask my mum and dad if they had known someone called Len who had died recently, but I didn't want to let them know that I had been playing with the Ouija board. It was scary, I played the moment over and over again in my head, trying to work out how the glass had moved. I was sure that no one had pushed it, and seconds before it had made its way around the board it had felt as though it weighed a ton under the tip of my finger.

Could the voice in my head have been that of the spirit who called himself my guide all those years ago? Or was it my subconscious tuning in to that of the driver when he obviously fell asleep behind the wheel? I'll never know, but whoever it was, I'd just like to say thank you.

'Good morning Mart. Could you make the lads the tea, sweep the floor then go and see Larry – he's got a job for you.'

On the wall next to the kitchen was a picture of my face that one of the men had carefully drawn. The likeness was uncanny. Every teenage spot and boil that I had in that year was meticulously drawn on to it, and every cold sore that appeared would be represented by a piece of crusty bread roll. I made the fifteen cups of tea and carried it out on an old tin tray that buckled up on one side. 'Tea's up,' I shouted above the sound of the radio, on which Simon Bates was introducing yet another suicidal 'Our Tune'.

I could tell from the tension in the air that something was brewing. It was time for yet another apprentice wind-up . . . and yet another apprentice response.

'Larry, your tea.'

'Ah good, put it over there. Then I want you to go into the metal shop and ask those miserable bastards for a long weight.'

'OK.'

'Go on then.'

'Can't I drink my tea first?'

'Didn't you have breakfast? No go and ask him for the weight first.'

Long weights were the bars of metal that were melted down in the furnace to produce the type fonts – this was before the computer age.

I walked over to the machine room and opened the heavy double doors. The noise hit me like a ton of bricks, and the intense heat from the furnace and the smell of liquid metal made the place a living hell. I screamed at Jack, the deaf old guy who had been locked away in there most of his life, 'CAN I HAVE A LONG WEIGHT?'

'WHAT?'

'I WANT A LONG WEIGHT!'

'OK.'

And there I stood for another hour while they all laughed at their joke. Of course what I had asked for was 'a long wait'. I didn't mind playing along, it was better than working. I caught them looking at me through the glass panel in the door that was permanently steamed up. They had rubbed away a small circle in the condensation and were taking it in turns to take a look and laugh at me. I felt so stupid, not because I had fallen for their childish prank – I hadn't for one moment – but because I couldn't believe that was all I was worth. Someone to play those pathetic tricks on, to be treated like the print-room jester. My heart sank as I stood there and caught glimpses of the men outside the doors. Is that what I was going to be when I passed my apprenticeship in four years' time? Is that what I was working towards? Could that possibly be all I was worth? I had only been there a few months and I had already had enough.

The one Christmas I spent there, they told me that it was tradition that the new apprentice would stand on the main work-bench at the end of the room, called 'the stone', and sing a Christmas carol to the whole firm. By the time Christmas Eve came and the Babycham adverts had been running for well over a month and the streets outside were a foot deep in snow, I knew every word of 'Good King Wenceslas' by heart, and by now I had become used to making a dick of myself for their amusement. I sang every verse at the top of my voice, and by the end of it had them joining in.

After work finished that day, everyone went around the corner to the local pub, The Lord Nelson, a big old Victorian watering-hole on Old Street, where they found the greatest pleasure in watching me drink myself into a stupor with pints of 'lager top'. Most of the afternoon's drinking and crude jokes disappeared into a blur as I drank pint after pint of Mr Nelson's best. They were trying to get me drunk and I was trying to prove that I was a man.

I looked down at my watch. The hands said two o'clock. My head was spinning and my stomach was trying to escape from the confines of my body. The next thing I knew, I could hear the voice of an old man. This was a voice that had seen too many years of Players' cigarettes and Johnnie Walker's whisky and had been pushed to its limits on the local football terraces more than once.

'Son . . . what are you doing here?'

'What?'

'What are you doing here?'

I looked up. I was sitting on the floor. In front of me was this old, grey-haired security guard in a blue uniform with lots of badges and silver buttons.

'What are you doing here?'

Judging by the smell wafting up my nostrils, I had obviously been sick. I looked around. I could see piles of toasters and hi-fi systems, all in their boxes, stacked neatly on wooden pallets.

'How did you get in here?'

I managed to get myself to my feet and brush myself down.

'Where am I?' I said.

'You're in Argos's warehouse. Now, how did you get in here?'

He was obviously asking the wrong person, I had completely lost the last two hours. The old grey guard must have taken seasonal pity on me, because he showed me the door.

'Now you be careful, young man. Take this as a warning. Next time I'll call the cops.'

God knows how I got home that day, but it wasn't until Boxing Day supper that I could get anything into my mouth.

For nine months the days went slowly by as I learnt the trade and went to fetch chicken lip sandwiches at the local café. Then I saw light at the end of my escape tunnel.

My brother was working at the time with a small band that he had put together with some school friends. Gary and another young kid named Steve Norman played guitars. I knew Steve better than the others. I had seen him around my house, and he and Gary would play along to Kinks records in Gary's bedroom when my mum and dad were out. He was a good-looking kid and friendly with it.

John Keeble, a small dark-haired boy, played drums. He seemed to be older than the rest, even though his height said otherwise. The first time I ever saw John he was sitting behind a drum kit playing with Gary and Steve. I have never seen anyone more comfortable sitting on a tiny drum stool than that boy was that day.

The singer was a tall, lanky kid named Tony Hadley, whose dark hair flopped over his brown eyes and whose Roman nose hadn't quite settled into his long face. He seemed too awkward to be a singer, his long legs seemed to trip him up far too often, and his roots were more pub boy than Elvis. But he could sing – he had the gift. It wasn't quite sent from God yet, but if he worked on it you could tell that he could expect a delivery.

A small boy with a bad case of teenage skin played bass. His name was Richard Miller. His bass guitar looked as though it was two sizes too big, but he still looked kind of cool in a funny sort of way. He reminded me of Bruce Foxton, the way he played his instrument with a plectrum instead of using his fingers to bang out the notes. He was a nice kid and was always smiling, showing his over-sized teeth and reacting to Steve Norman's natural ability to make people laugh.

They called the band 'The Gentry', and they played the small pub circuit – The Greyhound, The Hope and Anchor and The Pinder of Wakefield.

After I finished my day's work at the print shop I used to help them carry the equipment into the pubs and help set it up on the small stages. I would have given anything to be up there with them. To this day I can't remember wanting anything as much as I wanted the chance to pick up a guitar and plug it into an amp and be part of that band.

I could play guitar, but very badly. I had played in a small school punk band of my own called The Defects, but never ventured past the three chords that were required to play songs like 'Cut Your Throat' and The Damned's 'New Rose'. I wasn't really giving it the time or the respect that's needed to master it, and definitely wasn't good enough to be up there with them playing Gary's precious songs.

Night after night I watched them play. My mouth drooled and my fingers twitched and I wished hard that something dreadful would happen to one of them so that I would have to take his place. I felt like the substitute who would never get a game.

After every show, I would carry the equipment out of the pub and into John's dad's old van as the boys stood at the bar slapping each other on the back. I knew I wasn't a roadie, I knew there was more in store for me than that, but I had to start somewhere.

I would go home, climb into bed, close my eyes, and put myself into the band. In the morning I would make the journey back to work and back to playing the idiot.

It was Steve Norman's eighteenth birthday bash at his mum and dad's place, a flat on the second floor of an old tenement building just off Holborn's Kingsway. I was leaning up against the living-room door talking to a young guy called Steve Dagger, breathing in every time someone came past with more drinks or a plate of sausage rolls. We were both the worse for wear after drinking too much of the lethal home-brewed cider that Steve Norman and his dad had mixed together only the week before.

Steve Dagger was two years older than my brother and the other guys and used to go to the same school in Islington called 'Dame Alice Owens'. I had seen him around at Gary's gigs, but we had never said more than the odd 'hello' to each other. I was always too busy carrying the band's instruments in before the shows started and then carrying them out when they were finished. Steve had not long been designated the band's manager, a position he thrived on. He couldn't play an instrument and, unlike me, didn't want to get up on stage, so this suited him down to the ground.

He smiled as he spoke and drank his cider. He fluffed up the back of his wedge haircut with his free hand and seemed to launch into story after story with considerable ease, raising his voice just enough to be heard over the Tamala Motown records coming from Steve's dad's stereo.

The cider had taken hold of us both by the time he said the words I so desperately wanted to hear.

'You know what?' Steve drank his last drop of cider. It was thick and brown and clung to the edges of his glass as it went down. 'You should be on *Top of the Pops*.'

'What?'

'You should be on *Top of the Pops*.'

'Yeah, that would be nice . . . but how?' I laughed, as I always did when I got embarrassed or slightly nervous.

'Why don't you learn to play bass guitar?'

'What for?'

'To play in the band with your brother.'

I was speechless. I looked deep into his eyes to see if he meant what he was saying. I had this horrible fear that I might have misunderstood him.

'We're going to drop Richard Miller and put you in, but there's a show in three weeks, so you'll have to learn fast.'

I didn't ask why or what for, I was speechless. This man in front of me was changing my life and I knew it. This was the gateway to my dreams. To become a rock star. To become famous, to experience a life I knew the lucky few abused, and more than anything to plant the seeds of that special stuff called charisma. The fire that was now burning in my stomach had been fanned even further by standing at the back of a packed Charlton Athletic football ground watching The Who and the Sensational Alex Harvey Band in 1974, to watching Mick Jagger climb over a giant opening Lotus flower at the Earls Court shows in 1976. I was on my way, or at least in my head I was, for that night I could hear people calling out my name at Wembley Arena. What a buzz – that feeling has never left me. Steve's encouragement to this day is just as adrenaline pumping, and always will be.

I did it! I learnt to play those songs off by heart, not wandering from a single note. Staring down at that gigantic fret board without blinking, the strap on my shoulder cutting its first marks into my white skin. It felt amazing to be in that position . . . a gift from God!

That first show at a small college party is one of my happiest memories. The bass guitar felt heavy and cumbersome around my neck, the fret board a mile wide, and my hands dripped with sweat, but I can't tell you how much I wanted to be in that position. I wasn't the lead singer, but it would certainly do. The Gentry's next few shows came and went without much hassle. We had good songs and we played them well, with a good unique feel, but we needed that key, that golden key. The one that would let us into that golden world.

My Salad Days

'The Blitz' happened every Tuesday night at a wine bar in London's Covent Garden. It was by far the trendiest club to rise out of the famous market back streets since the Sixties. Its entrance was in Great Queen Street, just across the road from Holborn tube station. The bar itself was long and narrow and perpetually filled with smoke from the dance-floor smoke machine that smouldered away in a dark corner like some uninvited guest. The walls of the wine bar were decorated with your standard painted mirrors and bar-room photographs of life in Covent Garden in the late nineteenth century.

For six nights a week The Blitz was your run-of-the-mill West End watering hole for office workers and late-night shoppers who fancied a vodka and coke before making the journey home on the tube. On the seventh night of the week, Steve Strange and Rusty Egan created what was essentially a club within a club, a world within a world; they took over The Blitz and turned it into the club we came to know as home. It was the place we could wear what we wanted, say what we felt and above all be ourselves. Clothes were important to us, they were our own personal statements. They might sometimes have been slightly off the wall, but we were individuals and we wanted to show it.

But it wasn't the décor, it was the people who came to this weekly gathering that gave it its life force. Pretty young things in extravagant clothes and strange hairdo's mingled with kids from the local St Martin's College of Art, all wanting that little bit more out of life than was on offer. Steve Strange, the boy from the Welsh valleys, with his huge black quiff and full pan-stick make-up, adding to the smoke with his king-size Rothmans, was on the door, only allowing in the weird and very colourful. George O'Dowd, who was later to become Boy George, worked in the cloakroom under the stairs, and took your Melissa Caplan jackets. Rusty Egan, the drummer from The Rich Kids, mixed Kraftwork and Roxy Music on his record deck as he hit his own electronic drums over the top of the music. It was such a trendy place to hang out . . . if you could get in.

The characters there were all as sharp as the names given to them. There was Electric Barry, who was always buzzing in his brightly coloured outfits and long drooping earrings that swung out of his bleached quiff. He was never short of a story and always spoke at a hundred miles an hour. I could always see the spit solidify in the corners of his mouth and his bright pink lipstick crack as the evenings wore on. There was Barry the Rat, whose white namesake ran around his shoulders and nestled in his bright red mohair jumper as he leaned against the centre of the long wooden bar; his Seditionaries black studded boot rested on the brass foot-rail as he waited for someone to buy him another drink. There was Steve Weird, who was Steve Strange's clone, a complete double – the hair, the make-up, the cigarette held up high between his nicotine-stained second and third fingers. There was the monocled Chris Sullivan in his tweed plus-fours and gentlemen's cap. Olli Mac-Donald, the hairdresser from Smile, in his tartan zoot suits and with his knee-length fob chains, his ginger hair and pock-marked skin, became an important landmark in the club if you wanted to escape for a while and talk about football. There was Steve Marshall, a giant of a man who was just 'up for the crack'; Steven Jones, the milliner, whose hats now fetch a fortune; Midge Ure, the rock star, who later went on to record with Visage with Steve and Rusty and to co-write the Band Aid record with Bob Geldof; Steven Lynard, the clothes designer; David Johnson the writer, a few years older than the rest of the crowd, who always made out he was just writing a story on the cult for some new magazine, but in reality was just as much a part of it as the rest of us.

London's *Evening Standard* called the club's young clientele the 'New Romantics'. The papers like to give a tag to every new pop culture that springs to life. Pretty soon the name stuck and the boys from The Blitz, the New Romantics, were to become the height of Eighties chic, whose strange clothes and fashion details were to set trends that filtered down into the high street and became giant business for Top Shop and Miss Selfridge up and down the country.

It had been a long night of drinking, everyone was taking handfuls of blues (speed) to keep up with the pace and to last the distance. Chris Sullivan, who was wearing a full SS uniform, had started a fight with the local hooligan, who had somehow managed to talk his way into the club that particular night. The fight was over in a matter of seconds, Chris winning it with a swift butt to the bridge of the nose, but the hooligan swore to come back 'mob-handed'.

'I'll get you, you wanker,' he said. Or something very similar to that!

The night went on as normal, with people knocking back cheap wine, grinding their teeth, telling each other their life stories in a matter of minutes. The clock moved on to the dreaded three a.m. when the club closed and the night was over. All there was to look forward to was another week at work, another week covered in printing ink, another week of those pathetic apprentice practical jokes and being treated like an overgrown kid.

I was just on the way out of the club, past the reception desk and out of the swing doors. There was the usual game with my chameleon host – that night wearing a pair of jet-black contact lenses that covered the whole of his lecherous eyes.

'Good night, Mart.'

'Good night then, Steve.'

'Are you sure you don't want to come home with me, Mart?'

'No, I'm sure, Steve! . . . Good night.'

Steve always knew I was straight but he loved the game, and in a weird way so did I. It was the first time that another man had openly found me attractive, and it was flattering.

'What a shame . . . I'll see you next week,' Steve said.

Just then the windows in the door smashed and huge pieces of glass came flying past my face. It was the hooligan's promised revenge. The New Romantics leaving the club stepped back as the mob stormed in. Then, to everyone's complete surprise, the trendies in their frilly shirts, Robin Hood outfits and hair-sprayed bouffants fought back. It was one of the strangest fights I've ever seen. It was like a Christmas pantomime – I really wouldn't have been surprised if the pantomime horse had thrown a hoof or two. The fight went on until the New Romantics got the better of their opponents and managed to send them packing with their tails well and truly between their legs.

Steve Strange became one of my best friends and offered the band a one-off gig at the club. Also, with a little help from Bob Elms, a young journalist at The Blitz, who wore his hair in a GI flat-top with a single five-inch spike that ran down the centre of his forehead, we had decided on our new name, it was to be 'Spandau Ballet'. Trendy enough for the designers and hairdressers not to be frightened away, but heavy enough in case we ever made it to Wembley. 'Ladies and Gentlemen, please welcome the greatest rock and roll band in the world . . . Spandau Ballet' – I could hear that quite clearly in my head. Bob Elms had only just returned from a trip to Berlin and had seen the name scrawled on a toilet wall in a nightclub. The name must have belonged to another band at some point, but now it belonged to us – *we* were Spandau Ballet, and that was that.

The name caused several problems when we first started off. In some places we were dubbed Nazis and anti-semitic; in others, people actually bought tickets to come to watch a new German dance troop. These people stood out a mile from the rest of the audience, and watching their faces from up on stage when we launched into the opening songs was hilarious.

The following Tuesday night, we played at The Blitz. Every new pop culture has to have its band to nail their colours to. The Mods had The Who, the Punks had the Sex Pistols, and now the New Romantics had Spandau Ballet.

To keep up this trendy image, we only ever played out-of-the-way places, not the usual pubs and clubs on the London rock circuit. We played at private parties, London cinemas and on a battleship that is moored on the Thames called HMS *Belfast*.

The *Belfast* isn't a big ship, there's hardly room to swing a cat, let alone a guitar. We were just finishing tuning our guitars and about to go into the opening number – the humidity on board the ship was incredible and was stretching the guitar strings in front of our eyes – when I looked up and noticed a guy dressed from head to toe as a Christmas tree. He was making his way to the front of the stage. Some people, it seemed, could never find the defining line between trendy and stupid. I could see him talking to people as he made his way carefully through the crowd, trying his best not to get his tinsel in a tangle. By the time he got to the small stage that had been set up at one end, the band was between the opening numbers. The stage was so low that my head was in a gap between the hot and cold water pipes that ran overhead. I heard him shout up to me. His voice wasn't thin or effeminate, which to be honest was what I expected, but deep and honest – he was a South London boy. He had obviously put a lot of thought into his outfit and was proud of the way he looked that evening. I tried to give him some respect and not to laugh as he spoke to me.

'Oi . . . Guvnor.'

'Hi, you OK?' I asked him. 'Look, I'm a bit busy at the moment.'

I could hear Gary tuning his guitar strings – that were stretching once again in the unbelievable heat – ready to go into the next song.

'Yeah, but I need an electric socket.'

John Keeble started to count in the band from behind his small drum kit. I leaned forward, pulling my head out from between the pipes so that the Christmas tree could hear me better.

'Over there! Can you see where some of the equipment is plugged in?'

He smiled at me. His gold front tooth shone under the yellow spotlights.

'Ta mate!'

We went into the next number with an opening electric crash that forced your eardrums to close and made your head buzz. He made his way back through the crowd to the electric socket. Then, as if right on cue, at the end of the last number of the night, he plugged himself in and sparkled proudly until the ship's Captain had him unplugged, calling him a fire risk. I thought that was quite polite, considering.

At the end of 1978 my job in the print shop was just about keeping me in enough money to get me to The Blitz every Tuesday night. The time had come to make a few drastic decisions to help my dreams of being a rock star along. I needed to commit myself to the band full time. After several incredible reviews in the music press and a couple of huge articles in *The Melody Maker* and *NME*, Spandau were being touted as one of the year's hot new bands. If I was ever going to make that jump from amateur to professional, now was the time. I spoke to my dad, who had originally got me the apprenticeship in the print shop. I told him that I had to leave the job so that I could concentrate on the band. Can you imagine what he must have thought? To leave a job like that! Most kids from my area would have given anything to have that job, and here I was walking away from it. But my dad and my mum both believed in me, and my dad sat down at the kitchen table, pushed aside the remains of our Saturday afternoon lunch, and wrote the manager of the printing company a letter that I will always be thankful for.

Dear George,

I want to ask you if Martin can leave his apprenticeship position in your print shop. I know the hours of training and hard work you have put into Martin over the last year, but I feel I have to give him his chance in life.

Martin wants to leave to become a pop star.

Thanks for understanding,

Frank Kemp.

I could see in my dad's face that he was as nervous as I was. Over the last year, there was nothing I had wanted more than to leave that print shop, but now I was being given the opportunity and nearly at the point of no return I was having second thoughts. What if the band fell away into obscurity? What if we signed a deal and never sold a record? What would I do? I knew if I stayed at my print job for another three years I would pass my apprenticeship and be able to get work in other print firms relatively easily. It crossed my mind that perhaps I was making a huge mistake . . . Should I be settling down to work like most of my friends? What gave me the right to think that we could follow in the path of the Rolling Stones and the Beatles? What gave me the right to think that I could roll the dice and expect it to come up with a number seven?

My stomach started to twist and my hands started to sweat and my mouth started to grin in a nervous, uncontrollable way as I looked at my dad signing his name to the letter. My dad looked up at me and smiled as he spoke.

'Well, boy, at least you can say you have given it a try.'

He was right, we had to try, it was no good living the rest of our lives with a feeling of 'what might have been'. I thought to myself, I wondered if my dad had secretly hoped for this moment when he went out to buy Gary his first guitar, or when he made him a dulcimer out of old wood. I wondered if he had made a wish in the same way that I make wishes for my children, and he saw this moment as the start of it coming true. Whatever, I think my dad knew he had lit the fires inside Gary and me, and he knew he couldn't put them out the moment they started to burn on their own.

My dad was exactly right. At least we will always be able to say that we gave it a try, gave it our best shot. I hope I can believe in my children as much as that when the time comes.

That Monday morning I walked into work with my letter burning a hole in my back pocket. I went straight to the kitchen and made the fifteen cups of tea and took them out to the guys on the shop floor. I looked over at the door of the manager's office, which had been left wide open. I could see George at his desk reading the morning paper. Shit, I was nervous, but it had to be done. I walked over to the office, past Larry who was busy locking together a page of type. He gave me a strange smile, as if he knew what I was about to do. I knocked on the open door. George looked up from the racing page of his newspaper, his eyes magnified behind his enormous reading glasses.

'Yes, my old son . . . What can I do for you?'

I blew out my cheeks and felt my voice crack as I started to speak.

'Er, I want to give you this.'

I put the letter on the table next to his cup of coffee and watched as he picked it up. He pushed his glasses further back on his face and started to read. He didn't even blink. He just took the letter, folded it up and put it into his top pocket. He then made me shovel up bags of used metal type fonts until the end of the day.

Larry and the guys on the floor wished me all the best, and as a memento I was presented with the map of my spotty teenage face. It left a clean hole on the wall next to the kitchen.

For the last time I walked up the stairs leading to the outside world. My body tingled as I drank in the fresh air and my hair felt as if it was standing up on end. I felt a heavy responsibility in the soles of my trainers as I walked home that day. I knew that I owed my mum and dad for their incredible support, and I didn't want to let them down on this one. I didn't want to have them embarrassed and to be laughed at and be spoken about as if they were crazy. I wanted to pay them back in the only way that mattered . . . with success.

I had made my escape . . . but now to get to safety.

'Do you fancy two weeks in St Tropez?'

'You're kidding . . . right?'

I was sitting on the floor in the corner of my living-room, talking on the phone to Steve Dagger. My mum was ironing at the other end of the room, hiding behind a giant pile of freshly folded clothes and trying to make out she couldn't hear the conversation.

Steve explained. 'They want us to go down to the South of France and play in this club called "The Papagayo".'

'Shit . . .' I said excitedly. I looked over at my mum, I had never sworn in front of her, or my dad come to that. My dad had always said that bad language was to be kept out of the house. I had never heard him swear in front of my mum, or even in front of Gary and me. I tried to catch her face in between the stacks of washing to see if she had overheard me.

'Two weeks?' I said.

I had only ever been to Benidorm, and my excitement was obvious.

Steve carried on. 'This French promoter has asked us to go down there. He's going to put us up in an apartment next door to the club. There's not much money in it but . . .'

'When do we go?'

'At the weekend.'

'Shit . . .' oh no, I did it again! She must have heard me that time.

'Okay then, Mart, I'll call you when I get some more information. Bye!'

I stood up and smiled at my mum, who was just starting to fold away the ironing board.

'Mum . . . I'm going to St Tropez.'

'Not right now you're not . . . Your dinner will be ready in ten minutes.'

It was the summer of '79. Margaret Thatcher had just been elected Prime Minister for the first time, and the Conservatives were back in power. Lord Mountbatten was killed by a dreadful IRA bomb, and I was seventeen . . . with a bullet.

St Tropez was bursting at the seams as our hired Ford Transit van made its way down the tiny pink streets that led to the waterfront and to our promised apartments. Every inch of space in the van had been taken up with our equipment, lights, eight stinking, sweating bodies and suitcases filled with shorts, stage clothes and frilly shirts. It had been a hard trip down the motorway and everyone was glad to have arrived. The tyre that had burst while we were doing ninety miles an hour, giving us all the fright of our lives as the driver fought desperately to keep the van upright, had been forgotten. The aches and pains that had blighted everyone on the journey in the cramped conditions now seemed little to moan about.

In addition to the five of us, Steve Dagger and the equipment, which already filled the small van to bursting point, we decided at the last moment to take along two friends: Simon Withers, who was to be our lighting man, and Graham Smith, who was there to take some photographs and capture the whole episode for posterity.

Our parents had loaded us up with boxes of food, enough to last us for the two weeks we were going to be there. I think when we emptied them all out that afternoon there was something like one hundred and seven bags of Bachelor's savoury rice.

The first thing we did when we arrived was to go and see the club that was to be our gig for the next two weeks. It was upmarket and nothing like I had imagined it was going to be. There was a low ceiling that was covered in small coloured disco lights, a small stage at one end that had just about enough room on it to hold the disc jockey's turntables, and a small wooden dance floor in the centre of the room, surrounded by tables and chairs. This wasn't quite Wembley Arena, but then there are no beaches in Wembley.

Our days were spent on the beaches, tanning up before every gig. Steve Norman and I would lie there on that sand until our skin was overflowing with melanin and we were burnt to the point of intense pain. These were the days before suntans equalled cancer and a brown body was frowned upon. Fair enough, we knew that sunbathing could bring on early ageing, but at seventeen . . . who cares?

Simon Withers, a New Romantic through and through, refused to take off his black jump suit, woolly hat and leather gloves and decided not to join in with the sunbathing. He stayed a noticeable 'milk-bottle white' for the whole trip and was proud of it.

The apartment was tiny, its white walls and red tiled floor tried desperately to give off a holiday ambience, but the bare light bulbs and blocked toilet soon put an end to that. There were only four small beds, and seeing that most of the women that went to the club were actually transvestites, the prospect of finding a friendly bosom to lie on was remote. A rota system was devised.

Pretty soon the living conditions became gross, just as you would expect from eight boys living alone, and before long we ran out of food, money and dignity. The only thing we had in the refrigerator was a bottle of poppers that on the hot windless afternoons could be smelt along the whole of the bay.

The gigs themselves were nothing to write home about but, without us knowing, they prepared us musically for the coming onslaught. St Tropez became the perfect rehearsal room for the journey that lay ahead. There were no distractions, no part-time jobs, no families to worry about, just the band. For the first time we could all give it one hundred per cent concentration. It was the South of France that turned us from boys to men, from amateurs to professionals, and turned our ambitions into a reality.

Back in England there was to be a documentary series on television called *Twentieth Century Box*, presented by Janet Street-Porter. They wanted to give the band and the New Romantics a half-hour slot which was to go out on a Sunday afternoon before *The Persuaders*. The programme was going to follow the band as we prepared for one of our shows in the Scala cinema in London. It was the biggest advert any young band could ever want: millions of people were told that we were the hottest, most exciting new musical property around.

As soon as the programme aired, the record companies were

fighting to get us to sign their contracts. We had calls from Island Records, CBS, Polygram – everybody wanted to talk the band into signing with their labels. It was as if the heavens had opened up and it was raining record deals . . . and we were soaking wet.

Nine months later, after an agonizing wait and in my case a bad dose of hepatitis, brought on by the living conditions in St Tropez, we signed a deal with Chrysalis Records and the journey to glory had begun.

Spandau Ballet

' "To Cut a Long Story Short" has raced up the national charts to number twenty-seven.'

Those were the words that came from Peter Powell over the Sunday afternoon airwaves and into our council house. The old lady with the pretty white hair who lived in the flat below us had died that day, a couple of hours before the chart show had come on, and the paramedics had just arrived to carry her out. The noise coming from our house was incredible. We were jumping and dancing around, making her ceiling come to life even if we couldn't do the same for her. The paramedics must have thought that she had dome something to upset us. All those daydreams, all those wishes were starting to come true. It was our first record release, and it had gone into the charts. My dad opened a bottle of home-made parsnip wine and my mum went into the kitchen to make a cup of tea, as she always did when she was nervous. This was the moment that we had gambled on, and our number had just come up.

There was also a much deeper, incredibly satisfying feeling that came with that record going into the charts. It was being told that we were making music that other people liked. Oh sure, people had told us how good we sounded at gigs and how much they liked the songs, but this time, over twenty thousand people had already bought the record and had taken it away to play in their homes. We were more than just a trendy band wearing funny clothes . . . we were also musicians.

Our house during that first year of success was filled with excitement and my parents loved every minute of it, watching their only two sons climb the ladder of every schoolboy's dream. Everything was new and everything was exciting. Young girls had started to hang around outside the front door waiting to get autographs and pictures, and my dad would wave to them from the top-floor window, slightly hidden by the net curtains, pretending to be me and laughing to himself as they screamed at him.

Sunday afternoons were spent sitting around the radio listening to the charts. Waiting to find out if Duran Duran or Depeche Mode had made it to higher positions. Listening out for the new Adam and the Ants release while my mum brought in the cockles and winkles with sliced bread and butter on a tray.

Top of the Pops on a Thursday evening was almost a religious experience. Mum made sure that dinner had been cooked, eaten and washed up by seven-thirty and dad sat in front of the TV finding fault with anything and everything that was on that week, nothing was as good as us . . . nothing as good as Spandau Ballet.

With the fun came the work . . . *Cosmopolitan* magazine wanted to run a special feature on the Paris fashion shows. They asked Paula Yates to take Steve Strange and me to have a few pictures taken alongside the Eiffel Tower for the front of the magazine.

We landed at Charles de Gaulle airport on a cold October morning. Steve was wearing some kind of trendy Robin Hood style jump suit, green hat, little feather, the lot . . . plus his usual white pan Christian Dior make-up. I had decided to wear what I liked to think of as a monk's habit. In reality, and in the cold world of the Parisian rain, it was simply a brown dress. When we arrived, we carried our bags to the waiting limousine that took us off to the best hotel in town on the Place de la Concorde. While Robin Hood got a cup of coffee and smoked another cigarette, the mad monk checked in.

'Do you have two rooms in the name of Mr Strange?'

He looked at me with those huge cynical Parisian eyes as he checked the bookings.

'One room.'

'One room? . . . No, two!'

'One room, sir . . . It's the Presidential Suite on the fourth floor.'

'One room . . . with twin beds?' I asked.

'No, sir . . . One very large king-size bed.'

I looked over at Robin Hood, who by now had found some tree to hide up . . . I should have seen this coming.

'Sir, it is the only room in Paris available . . . It is the Presidential Suite . . . Do you want it or not?'

I took the huge gold key and shoved it into my deerskin belt. I didn't plan on spending much time in bed anyway. I wanted to get out and sample the night-life that I had heard so much about.

We had arranged to meet Paula for dinner at the Privilège restaurant, one of the hippest in town, so we could add a few words to the phallic photo that was to grace the front cover. When we met, she had on this incredible all-in-one gold lamé Anthony Price gown that wrapped around her tiny body from her neck down. The three of us that evening drank and ate ourselves into a complete stupor, while the fashion models in town danced on the crowded dance-floor as the local paparazzi tried to get pictures of anyone wearing anything eye-catching.

Soon, though, it was time to leave and to make our exit up the huge swirling ornate metal staircase that climbed two floors to the exit. In my monk's dress and completely drunken state, I had decided that it would be fitting and photo worthy if I carried Paula up the stairs in my arms.

As I carried her, the lights from the disco and the Nikon cameras flashed in my eyes, almost blinding me. I reached the top of the stairs but, without knowing, I had the end of Paula's all-in-one dress wrapped around the heel of my boot. She fell back, unwrapping herself from head to foot like some golden spinning dervish. Just then, Robin Hood came bounding up the stairs two at a time to save Paula's embarrassment and prevent the photograph that would have haunted us for the rest of our lives.

Four o'clock in the morning . . .
   'Mart . . . ?'
   'MART . . . ?'
   'Go to sleep, Steve.'
   'Well . . . I just thought I'd ask.'
   'Go to sleep!'

The next morning was spent trying to negotiate a room for the second night. But, as we were told, Paris was completely full of fashion weekenders. Paula had come over to our room for that continental breakfast of croissant, jam and Steve's second-hand Parisian smoke, and was helping with the negotiations, but nothing seemed to budge the helpful Parisian on the desk with the huge bulbous eyes. We had decided to lock ourselves into the room and just squat . . . A Frenchman on the other end of a telephone called to say that the President himself was waiting to use the room as he had a TV show to do in the afternoon, and we had to vacate immediately! What President? I didn't know what France's President even looked like! I certainly wasn't going to give up my room for him that easily.

However, 'To Cut a Long Story Short' hadn't even reached the French top thirty, and Steve Strange was just a very strange person, so our VIP status was always a bit tenuous. It was no surprise when the President took priority over us when it came to handing out rooms.

After an hour of this toing and froing, phone calls and people banging on the door, another room was found. Within an instant an army of maids and bellboys led us from the room carrying our small bags and dirty linen past the waiting President. We all looked in amazement when we saw that it was President Nixon standing by the wall to let us go past. He was covered in his thick French TV make-up. I looked back at Steve, and just for a moment Steve didn't look that out of place.

America. The land of dreams, cartoons, junk food, Elvis and rock and roll itself. This was the place that any self-respecting, ambitious rock star wants to be, wants to conquer. It's like the holy grail of rock, when you drink from its golden cup you become immortalized, written about alongside Chuck Berry, Elvis and Bill 'Rock Around the Clock' Haley. This was the place that to me only existed in the back of my DC comics, where I wanted to send away and buy those X-ray specs and little magic monkeys that swim around in a tank wearing little crowns on the back of their heads.

Every band wants to drive down Sunset Boulevard and see their pictures towering above them, and we were no exception. The American dream bit Spandau Ballet and me very early on. Meanwhile 'The Freeze', our second UK single, had just reached number seventeen in the Radio One chart, which was as far as it was destined to go.

Things were a little worrying, seeing that 'To Cut a Long Story Short' had made it to number five, selling a massive 450,000 copies. Now, with the second single from our first album, *Journeys to Glory*, only just making it inside the top twenty, there was cause for concern. It's no secret just how fickle the record-buying public can be, and today's star can be tomorrow's janitor. It's definitely not the most secure job in the world. All those people who congratulated you the week before are waiting for the moment when they can revel in your failure. There's no other job in the world with the same kind of stress.

The minor slump was quickly forgotten when the news came that there was going to be a show in New York. I couldn't believe it. New York City! It wasn't quite Madison Square Gardens, though. We were booked to play a gay nightclub that was said to be the trendiest place on Manhattan Island. Well, it was a start, and it was in keeping with the idea of trying to play slightly off-the-wall places, rather than the standard rock venues that every other band turns up in. I mean, if it worked at home, there should be no reason why it couldn't work here as well.

By the time we went on stage, it was two in the morning, and the room was packed full of three thousand sweating, disco-bopping young gay men, who were more disappointed that Gloria Gaynor had just disappeared from the giant sound system than excited by the prospect of listening to our new brand of rock music. But in a flash we were on stage, and after those few awkward moments of introduction the lights went up and we were in the middle of 'To Cut a Long Story Short'.

The crowd definitely warmed to us as soon as they saw what we were wearing. Gary in a Robin Hood outfit, Tony in flowing scarves and myself in the infamous mad monk's dress – we looked more like the answer to the Village People than to the disparity of rock and roll.

A small part of the crowd started to push forward. I thought for a moment that things might be looking up, that the audience might actually be starting to enjoy this. Again they surged forward, a mass of drooping moustaches and checked shirts pushing to the front of the stage. I made eye contact with a big black guy who had his right ear pierced in several places, the mass of gold earrings sparkling under the stage lights as he jumped up and down. He smiled at me and winked as he blew me a kiss. Well at least I was being appreciated by someone! My nerves started to disappear a little as I looked over at John behind his ever growing drum kit. He was enjoying every thump of his big bass drum and gave me his usual cocky smile.

It was only when I turned back to the crowd that I realized that the surge towards the stage was because my mad monk's dress had got caught in my guitar strap and was riding well above my crotch. I had thousands of young gay men cheering at my protruding bollocks.

In the end, the show wasn't all that bad – at least we had left our first mark on this land of dreams. And this was New York, and the night was still very, very young.

There was a party a few blocks away. We all jumped in to the waiting limousine and excitedly drove the short distance through the towering jungle, tingling with anticipation of a night out in New York City. The party was in someone's trendy loft conversion in Greenwich Village, all glass brick, bare walls and oversized photography books. A friend of a friend.

By the time we got there the party was already in full swing. Kid Creole and the Coconuts, never my favourite, were on the turntable, and some of the trendy young New Yorkers were scattered around the room.

'Congratulations,' someone said.

'Congratulations.'

'Congratulations.'

'Beautiful show, darling.'

'Thank you.'

'Thank you.'

'Thank you.'

'A glass of champagne?'

'Yes, thank you!'

I drank the glass of champagne down in one . . . I was buzzing.

'Canapés?'

'What?'

'Food?'

'No thanks, just another drink!'

'Did I tell you, your band was brilliant?'

'Yes, you did.'

'Has anyone ever told you that you should be a model . . .'

'No, but thanks.'

'Do you want a line of coke?'

'No thanks, I'm fine.'

'Congratulations.'

'Have you been to New York before?'

'No,' I said. 'First time.'

'Wonderful . . . I'm totally in love with your band.'

Now, I was never one to be shy of a compliment, but this was what living must be about. I took the champagne and moved into the open room. The apartment wasn't as large as I had first thought and there weren't as many people there as it had seemed when we arrived, but still, it was a party being thrown for us. I moved over to the corner and posed for a while with Steve, who was wearing his usual, cute, nervous smile.

Just then, someone right at the back of the room lit a cigarette. It grabbed my attention because the glow coming from the end of it was huge, larger than I had ever seen before. Then a young girl who was sitting on a sunken velvet sofa lit another. This time the glow from the end of the cigarette was of almost biblical proportions, asteroid-like, as tiny bits of sulphur spluttered from its end.

I looked at Steve, whose smile was now stretching from ear to ear, not a nerve in sight. I tried to look deeper to see if his brain was going through the same metamorphosis as mine. I couldn't tell . . . but he looked happy. Suddenly Kid Creole and the Coconuts had become music sent from the gods, and my feet started to tap uncontrollably.

I turned quickly to see if I could find Gary. I was worried by now, even though I felt fantastic. I needed to find my brother, to let him know what was happening to me, but as I turned, the whole room seemed to leave behind it a vapour trail about two foot long, filling the walls with a white fairy dust.

I knew what had happened. For the first time in my life someone had spiked my drink . . . and, shit, I was flying. With the adrenaline of the show pushing whatever drug it was through my young veins I felt amazing . . . Amazing, but a little bit sick.

I thought that I had better get myself to the toilet just in case the worse happened. I didn't want to embarrass myself now, not right at this point in time. I started to walk the short distance from the safety of my corner to the bathroom door. As I walked across the wooden floor I realized I was hitting my head on the ceiling, or at least I thought I was. I felt like I was floating, two or three feet from the ground. The bathroom door opened just in time, but my next problem was how was I going to get my head, which was now pushing up against the ceiling, under the door frame.

Suddenly someone held my hand and dragged me into the loo, bringing me out of my incredible trip and back into reality. It was a face I knew, one of the road crew.

'Someone's spiked your drink.'

'I know that. What was it?'

I was dreading the word heroin, it has always frightened the life out of me. Even in my wildest moments I have never understood why anyone would want to go near that drug. I have always believed that heroin was made for losers. An easy excuse as to why you failed in life, something to blame your failure on. One step away from suicide. It wasn't for me.

'MDMA.'

'What's that?'

'A new drug, a bit like LSD.'

'Shit.'

'Yeah. Look, take this, it'll bring you down, stop it from working.'

I didn't know if I wanted it to stop working, I felt incredible, but I couldn't walk around ducking under the light fittings all night. I looked down, and on top of the toilet seat was a long white line of cocaine.

'Go on, it'll bring you down.'

Christ, here I was in an apartment in New York, high on LSD and now I'm just about to take my first line of coke. I felt like John Belushi. Sure, I had taken the odd blue in The Blitz like every other New Romantic, but this, this was out of control.

I took a long sniff . . . and suddenly my feet were on the floor. He was right – I was back in real time. I caught a look at myself in the dimly-lit bathroom mirror. My eyes were black. My pupils were so large that I almost didn't recognize myself, and the inside of my nose was on fire.

'Do you feel a bit better?'

'Erm. Yeah, I think so . . . Thanks.'

'No problem, I'll see you outside. Don't be long, we're going to Bonds to see Blondie.'

'I'll be right out.'

Bonds was a huge venue in the centre of Manhattan, almost like the Lyceum but dressed in New York early Eighties disco style, with strobe lights and glass floors that were lit from underneath.

I was feeling fine by the time we got there, a little speedy from the cocaine, but more like my old self. As I walked in through the main entrance, I could already hear Debbie Harry in the throws of 'Rip Her to Shreds'.

Someone called over: 'Great show tonight.'

'Thank you.'

Then someone else: 'Great show man!'

'Thank you.'

'Thank you.'

'Thank you.'

All of a sudden my adrenaline was pumping, my heart was racing and my hands were starting to pour with sweat. I looked ahead of me. There was a huge twisting staircase that climbed two stainless steel floors to where the music was coming from. I looked at the other guys, who were now for some reason starting to move an awful lot more slowly than they were.

I started to walk up the stairs, but as I did I could hear a tiny Casio synth version of the 'Star-Spangled Banner'. The LSD was back in my system, firing on all four cylinders . . . but, like before, I felt amazing . . . I was in the middle of a rock'n'roll world, where I'd always wanted to be.

At that moment, though, getting to the top of the flight of stairs was my immediate ambition, and something that proved to be harder than I had first thought. Every time my foot landed on the next step up, it triggered the next note to the American national anthem, and in my present state I thought that this was far more entertaining than struggling to get to the top to watch a gig, no matter how much I fancied the singer.

I must have been there for most of the evening. The other guys left me listening to the tinkles as my foot touched the soft perspex stairs as I walked continuously up and down trying to work out if I could play 'Twinkle, Twinkle, Little Star' on the giant Casio synth.

All of a sudden there was a huge red face staring at me, only inches away.

'You need some more?'

It was the roadie.

'No, no, no . . . I'm fine, really.'

By this time I was ready for my hotel bed. He put me in the limo and kindly sent me home.

The next morning, with a raging hangover, I met the guys downstairs in the hotel lobby before we went to do a press reception on Lexington Avenue. This was the last thing we had to do before catching our flight back home. The huge white limousine picked us up and drove us across town. We were all chalk white and no one spoke a word. We were all suffering in our own private worlds. The alcohol fumes from our breath were so strong that if someone had struck a match the car would have exploded. It dropped us outside a small restaurant where the US press awaited us. After the medicinal hair of the dog from the bar inside the limo, we all made our way inside the restaurant and sat behind a long table in our kilts, thigh-length boots and red eyes. We tried to explain how Spandau were the future of rock and roll. We believed it, and we wanted everyone else to.

It was only just after I had returned from New York that my second LSD experience seemed to jump right out at me. There was a party in London, given by an old school friend of mine. He was looking after a huge house in Knightsbridge and the owner had gone away for the weekend. He'd already smashed up the guy's BMW, so holding the party without him knowing didn't seem quite that extravagant under the circumstances; besides, he thought there would only be about ten people there.

A party seemed like a good idea to me at the time. 'The Freeze', our second single, had worryingly sunk before it made it into the Radio One top ten, and our third single, 'Musclebound', had been released quickly following its demise so that the band didn't lose its initial momentum. It's well known that the most dangerous time for any band is between those early singles. The enthusiasm for a new group can die just as fast as it was born.

When I got to the dark green front door, there was already a queue stretching across the small front garden and to the house next door.

'Martin . . . come in.'

He saw me, thank God! I've never been one for queuing to get into anything. I'd rather walk away and go somewhere else than stand in line.

The minute I walked through the door my friend handed me a glass of wine and shoved his dirty great fist into my mouth, pushing a horrid tasting grey tablet down the back of my throat. I guessed what it was, but with my New York experience still fresh in my mind I felt I could handle this . . . being a man of experience!

The tablet tasted disgusting as it started to dissolve under my tongue. I lifted the wine glass and washed the thing down into the bottom of my stomach and quickly into my bloodstream.

'Shit. What was that?'

'Mescaline.'

My knowledge of drugs wasn't huge, but I had heard something about this one. It was the drug that turns everything into rubber. The Beatles reputedly recorded *Rubber Soul* while high on the stuff.

'It's a big house . . . different things going on in different rooms. Check out the bumble-bee room, that's worth a look.'

'What do you mean?'

'Never mind, just go in and mingle, there's loads of people you know in there.'

I knew I had about ten minutes to do whatever I could, and to say hello to whoever I knew at the party before my whole world started to change shape. Besides, after the New York experience, I was quietly looking forward to the trip.

I moved into the crowded living-room. I could tell straight away that nearly everyone in the house had been greeted with the same dirty fist in the mouth trick. Their eyes were black. Their pupils were so dilated that there was no colour left in their eyes at all.

Moments later my mouth started to dry, I was getting nervous now, and I could feel my heart start to pump a little faster. I finished off my glass of wine and started to look around for someone I knew.

Just then a girl walked past, someone I recognized from The Blitz. Her blonde hair teased up into a giant mountain of lacquer and clips, and an oversized black taffeta ball gown hanging from her broad, manly shoulders.

'Hi, how are you, darling?'

She kissed me on each cheek. God, her perfume was strong! It felt as though it had stung my nose, grabbed my tongue and twisted it into a ball.

'Fiiiiiine, thaaaaaaaaanks.'

I tried again. Something was happening to an internal connection. I wasn't quite sure what, but things were definitely happening.

'Fiiiiiiiiiiiiiiine, thaaaaaaaaaaaaaaaaaaanks.'

It was too late to try and make any sense out of the situation. The whole of my bottom jaw had turned to rubber, it felt as though it was hitting the kitchen floor. I couldn't do anything but smile, a smile that felt as if it was stretching from one ear to the other.

Just then somebody across the room tried to pick up a bottle from the makeshift bar.

'Excuse me.'

I couldn't believe what I was seeing – his arm stretched out about two feet longer than it should have done, like some cheap plastic toy. The mescaline had definitely kicked in!

Maybe the kitchen wasn't the right place for me. I tried my legs. I thought, if I could get out of there, things might settle down a bit. There was too much going on. Too much information for my senses to take in.

There was a strange sensation running through my body. My

mind was racing with the strangest of thoughts, trying to keep pace with my adrenaline. I wasn't scared or frightened at all, but simply fascinated by the way my brain was perceiving the most ordinary of information and turning it into the most colourful of pictures.

My God, somebody just walked by me smoking a cigarette, and the cloud of smoke looked just like a cloud of glitter that had been thrown up into the air and was catching the light, sparkling as the tiny particles started to separate and fall to the ground.

I moved out of the kitchen, and for a moment things settled down. The heavy bass coming from the giant speakers in the living-room felt good as it jiggled around my internal organs, but it was also jiggling around my bladder. I needed to find the toilet.

I walked up the long flight of stairs, past several victims with their black eyes and cat-like smiles. I found the first landing. My senses were alive and I felt good, but sweat was pouring from my hands.

It doesn't matter how out of it you are at any party around the world, you can always find the toilet: it's the room you can't get into, the room with the queue.

I couldn't wait in line there, and anyway someone had just come out of the room next door and my ears had just picked up the strangest sound coming from the open door . . . a sound that seemed to reverberate around my head . . . a buzzing sound.

I walked over before the door closed again and put my head around the corner. The room was lit only by the moonlight coming through the net curtains that hung from the huge windows, sending beautiful patterns dancing over the white walls. The room had no furniture in it, but about twenty people standing with their backs to the walls . . . all buzzing like little summer bumble-bees around an open rose.

I knew this was weird, even in my state, but it had to be tried, there had to be something in it to attract so many people. I stood with my back to the wall like the others and began to buzz . . . and buzz I did. I must have been there for at least an hour.

I was eventually saved from eternal buzzing by my bladder, which was still waiting to be emptied. I opened my eyes, thought about walking, and made it to the door. I was out. I was free, and this time the toilet next door was too.

I closed the door behind me and sat down on the bowl. Then the strangest thing happened. I started to pick my nose, but as I picked I closed my eyes. Then before I knew it I was inside my nostril, digging out these glittering bogies from the side walls with a huge pick-axe. I honestly thought I was mining for diamonds in there. It seemed like I was chipping away at those things for days before someone knocked on the toilet door and brought me back into reality once again.

This time, though, reality was harder. My hands had stopped sweating, my heart had stopped racing and the tiles beneath my feet weren't fluffy and soft, but hard and cold.

At every party there's the right time to leave, and this was mine. The mescaline had started to stop, I needed to make a run for home while the going was good. I came out of the toilet and made my way down the stairs, past the victims and past the people who were waiting to get into the loo but just couldn't put their brain into action and work out how to knock on the door, then down into the front passage and the scene of the original crime.

Good, it was empty, I didn't have to say any goodbyes to anyone. It felt like the scene from *Midnight Express* when Billy opens the final door and walks away to freedom. I could practically hear the Georgio Moroder soundtrack.

It was summer, one of those hot sticky nights that we all hate in August but long for in December, and the warm fresh air hit me in the face as I opened the door. I was lucky I hadn't brought a coat – I would have forgotten it if I had. I felt good as I walked home through those Kensington streets. The drug had worn off and the experience was behind me, an experience I shall never forget, but an experience I never want to go through again.

As I walked, I thought about all the hallucinations and how your brain, the thing you rely on to make sense out of this world, can play those tricks on you, and how stupid it was to ask it to play those tricks in the first place.

I turned the corner into Kensington High Street, I could see a black cab coming, with its bright yellow 'for hire' sign glowing in the side window. I stuck out my arm and flagged it down. I could almost feel the warmth and safety of my duvet.

The cab stopped and the driver rolled down his window.

'Where to, son?'

'Iiiiiiiiiiiiiiiisliiingtooooooon.'

My rubber jaw hit the floor and bounced right back up and slapped me in the face.

'What?'

I looked up. The sky had edges to it, as if I was standing inside a giant cube. Oh no . . . not now!

I clasped my hands on either side of my face, trying to hold it together for one last giant effort.

'Iiiiiiiiiiiiiiiisliiingtoooooonnn . . . please.'

Staying in the best hotels around the world becomes a way of life in a rock band. By the age of twenty-two, and with thousands of 'touring' miles tucked under my belt, I could have written my own 'Kemp's travel guide', with tips on hotels – whether they allow all-night parties, for example, or whether room service will refuse to bring you that extra beer at eight o'clock in the morning. It's also good to know if the mini-bars are well stocked with your favourite vodka. It has to be clear vodka, so that before you leave in the morning you can refill the empty bottles with tap water to avoid the charge as you check out . . . Things you need to know, things that keep you sane.

After you finish playing to ten thousand screaming people in the local arena, all projecting their love and enthusiasm straight down the barrel of your brain, it's hard to go back to your hotel room and relax with a cup of hot chocolate and watch Bobby Batista on CNN.

The hotel became our world, where we would drink and party like vampire rock stars sucking in adulation and flattery from anyone who was willing to hand it out. In Spandau Ballet's 'money-earning years' we would book a suite at the end of the corridor purely for that purpose. A party room? Really a room to shake down people for even more praise, even more of that precious life force that we all so desperately needed before the sun rose and we had to make it into our beds to get some sleep.

The sauna was a major requirement in hotels, it seemed to cure everything, from hangovers and cold sores to homesickness. Germany was always good for them, and with a bit of luck you might even end up sitting next to a naked *Fräulein*, as they were usually mixed.

I had one of my most memorable saunas while we were staying in a hotel in Munich to promote our fourth single, 'Chant Number One', taken from our second album, *Diamond*. The album itself had only just been finished and received an awful welcome from the record company when they heard it for the first time. 'It's different,' they said politely as they walked away from a playback in London's Oxford Street. To be fair to them it *was* different; it wasn't the pop album they wanted and certainly wasn't going to sell by the millions like the one our closest rivals Duran Duran had just released entitled *Rio*, which was a superb pop album. Our fall in the marketplace was written on the wall.

But we were growing up, and our tastes were changing. Gone were the New Romantic frilly shirts and tartan shawls, and in were the zoot suits and fob chains. A band has to move on to stay alive. It has to grow and develop as a natural organism. If it stops for a moment it can become stagnant and die. The only sure-fire hit on *Diamond* was 'Chant Number One', so Chrysalis Records made sure we promoted the hell out of it.

It was nine a.m. and the Munich Hilton was quiet. Steve Norman and I decided to take a sauna and shake off those early morning blues, before going downstairs to pay the dreaded extras bill that we had accumulated from drinking the whole of the well-stocked mini-bar the previous night.

At that hour of the morning the sauna was empty apart from Steve and me. It was a huge room with plastic creepers that trailed from the wooden ceiling and a giant plastic fern in the corner that was ready to slice off any free-swinging part of our anatomy.

After staying in the steam room until our skins had turned purple and our blood pressure had reached dizzying heights, Steve suggested that we went into the 'cooling down room' that was just outside the sauna. I was already cooked, so it sounded like a great idea to me!

Along the back wall of the 'cooling down room' ran a ten-foot box that was filled with soft rounded stones.

'I've seen this before, Mart. It's fantastic. It's just what we need.'

'What is it?'

'It's a box for massaging your feet. You walk up and down it and rub your feet into the soft stone. It's good for your circulation. Y'know, like a massage.'

'Fantastic! They think of everything, these Germans.'

I always trusted Steve out in Germany, as he seemed to be just that little bit wiser than me, just that one step ahead, knowing the language from out of his dog-eared phrase book that he always carried around.

We dropped our towels and climbed in. Steve was right – it was nice. It did seem to massage the feet like some form of Californian reflexology. We pushed our feet around as we walked up and down, digging them deep into the stones. Just then, the swing doors at the end of the corridor opened and a huge, matronly woman came bursting in. Her eyes were bulging out of her head like some Aryan anaconda.

'What in heaven's name are you doing? Are you English completely mad?'

Steve and I looked at one another. We knew something was up, but what?

'I will call security . . . you rock people are all the same . . . we had Soft Cell in here last week and they were the same . . . crazy!'

'Hang on, luv, calm down,' I said, as she obviously understood English.

And then she said it.

'You stupid people are in my plant pot!'

Steve and I weren't just in the plant pot, we were actually outside the sauna and in the corridor by the main staircase, walking up and down in the thing completely naked.

I've always thought that, in that brief moment, the two nationalities were completely summed up. The English, for not understanding how to use the sauna, and the German, for failing to find the whole situation absolutely hilarious.

Most of my life in the band seemed to take place in corridors. Waiting in corridors. In airport and hotel corridors, in TV and radio station corridors, and in the corridors that ran inside the venues themselves like giant rabbit warrens. Sometimes we would wait in those backstage corridors for hours waiting for the venue to fill up, waiting to go on stage.

By far the worst corridor nightmare happened in a gig in Belgium. It was a venue called Le Cirque Royal. It was rather like a down-market Albert Hall, built in a complete circle, with the stage at one side and a giant wooden dance-floor that creaked and groaned under the weight of two thousand jumping Belgians.

It was 1984. Tommy Cooper had just died, having collapsed on stage from a massive heart attack. Torville and Dean had just danced the 'Bolero' for the first time on an ice rink in Sarajevo to win the Olympic gold medal, and Spandau had just reached number ten in the charts with 'Lifeline', the first track off our new album called *True*.

Now Belgium was never one of my favourite places on the European itinerary. It was used more as a stepping stone to get to somewhere we really wanted to go, and as a place where we could pick up a bit of money on the way. This particular night, the place was full to the rafters. Young smoking Belgians were tucked into every crevice, standing on every chair and on anyone who had fallen down in the intense heat . . . It was hot. It felt more like Hong Kong than Belgium, and the humidity was playing havoc with my carefully sculptured Eighties hairstyle.

The show was just coming to an end, and the mixture of Elnet hair-spray and sweat was burning my eyes as we hit those last few dramatic power chords. I squinted out at the audience. They had got what they came for and were already starting to clap for more, as Lionel, my trusted roadie, took the weight of my bass off my shoulders.

I left the stage. The crowd was deafening. Lionel gave me a towel and told me that we were going back on for the encore in two minutes.

Alan Keys, 'The Travelling Iron', who was our wardrobe man, our confidant and at times our mother, took my sweating shirt and handed me a fresh one. Alan had worked with us since the earliest days and knew his job inside out.

Just then the Belgian promoter handed me a huge joint. It was the size of a log, like something you would expect to see in Jamaica. I don't smoke, in fact I've never smoked my whole life, but at this moment, with my adrenaline flowing through my veins at the speed of light, I took the marijuana joint between my fingers and for some unexplained reason took the biggest drag. The smoke went deep down into my lungs and poisoned the network of membranes inside of them. My head started to spin and my peripheral vision seemed to close in on me. I could hear Alan's voice saying, 'Come on, it's time to go back on stage.'

I couldn't speak. It was all I could do to stop from throwing up there and then. I felt decidedly un-rock'n'roll as I clung to the wall. I started to hear the crowd stamp their feet on the wooden floor. It echoed around my head and then around the dressing-room that was quickly emptying out as Gary was rounding up the troops; sending everyone back into the darkness and back on stage. I knew I had to quickly gather my thoughts and my senses to be able to follow the others and to perform in front of the two thousand frenzied Europeans.

And then in what felt like a split second, I had closed my eyes to take a deep breath and then opened them again only to find that I was the only one left in the room. Suddenly, I could hear the audience start to scream and the darkness that once surrounded the doorway was now flashing in different colours from the on-stage lighting that had come back to life.

'Thank you . . . Do you want more?'

I could hear Gary talking to the audience. Oh my God, they were out there without me! And here I was, not even able to walk. I was going to have to make an effort soon before it was too late.

I pulled myself upright and sent messages down towards my wooden legs, asking them to move towards the door. I knew that once I was out there, if Lionel put my bass around my neck, the months of rehearsals would pay off and my instincts would get me through the encore. My legs started to move, and to my surprise I managed to get myself to the door and into the corridor outside.

The corridor seemed longer than I remembered it, but I could hear the band starting to tune up, ready to go into the first song. Then I heard Gary's voice again.

'Where's Martin? . . . Typical.'

Shit . . . I started to run, I felt as if I was running into the Time Tunnel. I ran faster and faster down the dark corridor that was definitely starting to get smaller.

'Where the fuck is he? He must be taking a piss.'

They think I'm in the toilet . . . Good! I looked back towards the dressing-room and back into the darkness. I had no real idea of just how far I had come. All I knew was that Gary was starting to sound an awful long way off.

I passed through a pair of swing doors, and the darkened narrow corridor widened into a huge red velvet foyer. I knew I was nowhere near the stage and was starting to get an overwhelming impression that I was lost. To my left there was another set of swing doors, with two huge round glass windows in each one. I could hear Gary playing for time, introducing the band. I looked through. I was at the other end of the auditorium, looking over the heads of the audience. I could see my brother and the other guys on stage, who by now had to be wondering where the hell I was. It was like a bad dream. It was like one of those dreams where you're asked to perform and you don't know the words or you've forgotten your part, except this was for real.

'On keyboards . . . Toby Chapman.'

Gary introduced Toby, the keyboard genius who worked with us for years. The crowd clapped their hands above their heads. For a moment I couldn't see the stage at all. My heart was racing but my head was actually starting to come back together, as the dope was wearing off. I could think a little bit clearer.

'At this part of the show usually I introduce my brother . . . but tonight, you'll have to wait.'

Toby hit the opening chords to 'True'. They were going to play the song without me, after all it was Toby's bass keyboard on the record anyway, he knew the bass part backwards. The song had only just been released in England but the radio play was already phenomenal. It had the buzz of a number one record and we were waiting for it with open arms.

'Martin, where the fuck have you been?'

It was Alan Keys . . . His friendly voice was the most pleasing sound I had ever heard.

'Where am I?'

He knew straight away what had happened, he was standing next to me when I sucked on that enormous joint.

'Follow me,' Alan said.

I followed Alan back down the corridor, back into the darkness and back towards the flashing coloured lights. At the end of the corridor were the minders, frantically running up and down, asking one another if they had seen me.

'I found him!' Alan shouted out excitedly.

They turned around, all looking at me in complete disbelief. I felt Alan gently push me in the back and the next thing I heard was the deafening roar of the crowd.

'And at last . . . my brother on bass guitar.'

Lionel put my bass over my shoulders and I turned around to face the audience, this time from the right side of the auditorium.

Gary opened his eyes wide and glared at me. I couldn't work out if he was swearing at me under his breath or asking me if I was all right.

And then, two songs later, the gig was over and I was back in the changing room, taking off the stage clothes and opening the usual bottle of champagne. I looked over at the door as the Belgian promoter came walking in. His face framed by his huge handlebar moustache and yet another giant spliff!

'True' was that number one record that we had all been waiting for. That we had all worked so hard to achieve and that we had all dreamed of so many times . . . night and day!

The morning we were given the news we were in a Nottingham hotel, recovering from our Jack and Coke hangovers. We heard the day before that the record had sold over sixty thousand copies in one day and that our closest rival had sold only a third of that . . . The party had already started.

The week's chart positions were always phoned through to our rooms by Steve Dagger at about eight a.m. on a Monday morning if they were good, and at about ten a.m. if they were bad. This particular morning the phone went at seven forty-five. It had to be good news, it had to be number one!

'Martin . . . we've done it! "True" is number one . . . and with the amount it's selling it looks like it could stay there for weeks.'

I couldn't speak. Even though I expected the news, it was still a shock to hear it officially from Steve.

'YES!' I finally shouted out at the top of my lungs, and put the phone down. I wanted to see Gary and hug him. An image of him sitting on his bed in Rotherfield Street with his first guitar rushed through my head. How must he feel? I wanted to see him.

I rushed out of my room and came face to face with Keeble being pushed up and down the corridor in a hijacked room service trolley, with a bottle of champagne held up to his mouth and its contents frothing over on to his leather jeans. Further down the corridor, Tony and Steve were just coming out of their rooms in their boxer shorts and t-shirts and with smiles on their faces that I didn't recognize, that I had never seen before. This was a good morning to be alive . . . Then, just as I was about to go and join them in pushing John on a lap of honour around the hotel corridors, Gary grabbed me from behind.

'We've done it, Mart . . . We've fucking done it.'

It was a dream come true, and we all had to pinch ourselves more than once to make sure it was real. Before we climbed back on to the tour bus and set off for the next gig, we sat in the restaurant and cried behind our scrambled eggs, sunglasses and bucks fizz. We were just so happy.

After that record life wasn't the same for any of us. It was hard to walk the streets without being mobbed. The band became so popular that it was like being one of the Beatles. Hundreds of young kids would sit all night outside our hotels hoping to get an autograph or a photo. They would pop up in the strangest of places with cameras. One girl came through the shower room window that was four storeys up in the Liverpool Empire just as I was drying off. Luckily she never got her picture.

They would literally be everywhere, throwing themselves at us. We would escape from gigs in the back of ambulances and police cars, set up decoy manoeuvres that would make the army proud, and from time to time be caught and torn to shreds. It was fun, but it took its toll. When you start off in a band you dream of being that popular, and when it happens you hide behind a pair of dark sunglasses.

I remember in particular a gig in Manchester. The crowd there had always been loud, even in the early days. That night it was stinking hot and the audience were going completely wild. The girls in the front rows were dropping like flies, fainting as they screamed out our names in turn. It was almost painful to watch as I teased them and wiggled my ass behind my bass guitar. The bouncers in the venue were pulling the girls out and taking them backstage, where a St John's paramedic would try to resuscitate them. This night, there were just too many, over three hundred kids lay flat out backstage, it looked like the famous civil war scene from *Gone with the Wind*.

When the show was over and we went back to our dressing-room, we were walking over body after body. We decided to make a quick getaway before they started to come to. We started to change out of our soaking wet stage clothes in the corner of the room when, just at the wrong moment, they started to come around. Each one in turn gave out an ear-splitting scream on seeing us half dressed or completely naked and fainted for a second time, falling back to the floor or into the arms of the paramedic.

We were enjoying our success, we had worked hard for it and at last we were starting to earn some money. It wasn't a fortune, as we were still only really selling records in England – the rest of Europe was only starting to catch on, and the concerts cost as much to put on as we could earn – but it was still more money than I had ever seen.

It was time to leave the family home, to move on from the house in Islington where my bedroom walls were still covered with my childhood memories and adult wishes. I had finally saved enough of those first rock and roll wages to buy my own flat. I bought a place on Highbury Fields, right opposite the park. It was a little to the north of Islington, but that's how life works around there: it seems that the better you do, the further north you go. From Islington to Highbury to Highgate to Hampstead. Well, this was my first stop on the A to Z.

The flat was small but nice. It was right next door to an old café that would come in handy on those mornings when you needed that calorie intake to settle the morning hangovers, and was right opposite the local swimming pool.

My brother already had a flat a little further up the park, and a friend of mine, a girl singer called Sade, had just moved into a house at the end of the road. It was becoming North London's answer to Bel-Air. We even had the Japanese tour buses passing through, filled with kids trying to spot the stars.

Things were changing for my mum and dad at home as fast as they were for us. The floral wallpaper on the walls of their council house was now covered in gold and silver records and coach loads of kids camped outside the huge Georgian front door.

My dad had the job of driving my car and Gary's to his work on alternate days in order to keep them running while we were away. We both had Porsche 911s. Gary had a red one and I had a blue one, bought with the first few royalties that made it into our young hands. My dad has often spoken about the kick he got out of that, parking next to the manager of my old firm – the one he wrote to, asking if I could leave the printing apprenticeship to become a pop star!

Just after I had bought the flat, I decided to go and see my mum and dad and stay over for the night. It was late when I got there, so I went straight to bed. My old bed was comfortable, my body clung to the contours that had been pushed into it over the previous twelve years, and my room was still my room. The same posters clung to the walls, the furniture stood in exactly the same dents in the patterned carpet, nothing had been changed. It was like a beautiful time capsule that made me feel warm and safe and made me smile as I smelt the familiar air. In a matter of moments I was asleep. Then came my dream.

I was back in the living-room on the top floor of the house. There was no floral wallpaper on the walls or gold records fixed to the cork tiles. It was all just black. Everything was black apart from the brown leatherette chair that my dad was sitting in. My mum was bending down next to him, holding his hand and wiping some sweat away from his deathly white face. He was having trouble breathing and was saying goodbye to my mum as his life seemed to be slipping away.

Even though the vision was shocking, I found that I could completely hold myself together, ringing for the ambulance, looking after my mum and talking calmly to my dad. To this day it is one of the most vivid dreams I have ever experienced.

The dream must have only lasted moments before my mum came into my room to wake me up.

'Martin – quickly, come upstairs – it's your dad!'

'What? What is it?'

'Just get up and come upstairs.'

I jumped out of bed and ran up the two flights of stairs to the living-room. There was my dad, sitting in exactly the position as he was in my dream. He was in the middle of a huge heart attack. Five of the arteries leading to his heart had blocked from years of abuse and over work, too many hours of overtime trying to bring home those extra few pounds to give us a better life, to give Gary and me that extra Christmas present and to make my mum proud of him.

Somehow my dream had given me the strength to take care of the situation calmly, without panic. It felt as though I was doing things for the second time around, that I had already been through it, through the stress and pain. The dream was obviously given to me to help save my dad in the coming hours.

He was rushed to St Bartholomew's Hospital, where they performed life-saving open-heart surgery on him. I'm glad to say that the old thing is still pumping as I write.

The decision to move out of my parents' home was made easy for me now that I had fallen madly in love with a cute little blonde girl named Shirlie. We obviously needed more to our relationship than the odd hotel.

I met Shirlie at the opening night of a musical called *Yakety Yak*, it was the summer of '81. There were the usual bunch of free ticket flyers and Spandau Ballet, who went anywhere when somebody mentioned that there might be free wine. There was also a new band called Wham that I had seen on *Top of the Pops* the week before performing 'Wham Rap'. I hadn't taken much notice of the song, but I did remember the girl in the white dress with the split up the side. I thought she was the sexiest thing I had ever laid my eyes on, a cross between Marilyn Monroe and Doris Day.

During the interval, as I went to get that free glass of wine that I had been promised, someone tapped me on the shoulder. I turned around and there she was, the girl from the television. I had definitely not had my full quota to drink at that time – the usual champagne bravado was missing – but I mumbled my way through until they rang the bell for the second half of the show. There's a feeling that runs through your body when you come face to face with your destiny, a feeling that hits you between the eyes and thumps on your chest. I believe that some things are laid out in front of you the moment you are born, and this for me was one of those moments.

After the show there was a party in a little wine bar called Cheers in Islington. I saw Shirlie at the bar as I walked in, and I could feel that strange magnetic pull in between my shoulder-blades pulling us together. I tried to avert my gaze, but again the force was too strong. I had to be careful here, because I knew that Shirlie was seeing one of the guys in Wham who was standing only a couple of feet away from her at the time, but still that magnet drew us together. We didn't say much to each other that night, but we looked. At the end of the night, somehow I managed to pass her my phone number, never expecting her to call . . . She called me two days later.

I took her to a Mexican restaurant in Covent Garden. I thought there might be enough distractions there, so that we would have other things to talk about apart from each other. The usual goings on in a Tex' Mex' on a Friday night – people spilling beer on one another, fights on the tables and groups of boys taking it in turn to go outside and throw up before going back in for another pitcher of beer and margarita.

The music was loud, and the atmosphere was as hot as the Jalapeno peppers that people were chewing on, and my stomach was making weird rolling sounds that I could hear echoing up through my denim shirt. I was so nervous, I couldn't eat a thing. I just sat back and watched as Shirlie tucked into the plate of Nachos and refried beans with cheese. I found myself wondering how on earth she could be so thin if she ate like that. I was mesmerized by her energy and her incredible sense of humour. She was so relaxed, and I fell in love even before she ordered her dessert.

The feeling that I had that evening was so intense and so fulfilling that a warm flow of adrenaline passed through my body. There was an electricity between Shirlie and me that I had never experienced before with anyone else. Someone or something was telling me that I had just met my soul-mate, the person with whom I would share my secrets and my failures, who would hold me when I cry, laugh with me when things are funny and care for me when I'm sick. This was the girl who would share my life in every way possible.

I've always believed that you don't choose your soul-mate, but that you are attracted together like two halves of a magnet. The unmistakable force pulling you together is unstoppable.

Rock'n'Roll

The band, Steve Dagger and John Martin, our long-time tour manager, were unusually quiet in the back of a limousine. There was no Bon Jovi blasting out of the stereo, no crude piss-taking of John's shiny bald scalp or the fact that he hadn't achieved 'the ride' over the previous six weeks of touring. The atmosphere was reserved, even sombre, and the only sounds were that of Keeble tapping his monogrammed drum sticks on the leather bench seat in front of him and the quiet rumble of the five-litre engine turning over beneath us. Gary was sitting next to me, his book on the history of the Rolling Stones cradled in his brown leather trousers, and looking out of the darkened windows at the passing traffic on the North Circular Road. Tony, as always, was sitting up front next to the driver so that he could smoke, with the glass partition closed behind him so that we didn't all have to suffer the effects of nicotine. Steve Norman was on the end of the bench seat – always an uncomfortable position, no matter how big the limo, with someone's knees digging into your back, and not enough room for your own. The sun had set over North London about an hour ago, leaving a beautiful cold, clear winter's night and a sky that was filled with stars.

We were stuck in traffic leading to Wembley Arena, and the route to the venue was jam packed, as it always is when a big group is about to appear. Tonight, though, was different: the big band was us. We were about to play the first of six nights at the mythical arena.

Wembley Arena . . . It was the moment we had all dreamed of. When I was a boy I remember hearing that Led Zeppelin were doing two nights there and thinking to myself just how enormous a band has to be to be able to fill the arena twice. Not in my wildest dreams did I ever imagine that we would be doing it six times, or even once come to that. It was to be the jewel in the crown of a very successful British tour. Since starting out on the road six months earlier, we had seen 'True' go to number one, sending ticket sales through the roof. We had progressed from the 2,000-seater theatres in Scarborough and Liverpool to the 10,000-seater arenas in Birmingham and London practically overnight.

The limo made its way slowly up the dual carriageway until we turned into Wembley Way and through the huge wire gates that made the backstage car-park secure. Outside the gates was a thick crowd of young girls holding out pens and small pieces of paper, waiting to get autographs from us. They smashed their fists on the roof of the car and left lipstick marks on the windows as we drove through. I never minded signing autographs, it was always the kiss I had to try my hardest to avoid. Sometimes it was just unavoidable and a great big dirty tongue was thrust down your unsuspecting throat.

I recognized most of the kids outside the wire gates, many of whom I had come to know over the tour. The same faces would be waiting outside every venue, to see you in, see you out, see you back to your hotel, and wave at you through the hotel window as you ate your breakfast. But the same girls that you could talk to quite sensibly in a one-to-one situation would go stark raving bonkers when they were thrust together into a crowd. They would transform from a sensible, responsible human being into a screaming, uncontrollable fan. Usually it would take six of them, sometimes even as few as five, to set the madness in motion. Steve Dagger always called it the crowd factor. A strange, bewildering phenomena that had been passed down from the Beatles. It was as if the energy coming from each individual sparked an unstoppable chain reaction, and that little secretary you were speaking to outside your hotel as you signed her autograph would transform into a raging, violent vampire who wanted to grab hold of you and suck out your blood, pull out your hair or just take home a piece of skin under her fingernails for a souvenir.

Today, we didn't have time to sign any autographs. The traffic had delayed us and we had to go straight into the arena to get ready for the show, and anyway the crowd factor was just too big, we would have been torn to pieces.

An enormous scream went up as the car door opened and I got out of the limo. John, Gary, Tony and Steve followed right behind me. You couldn't help smiling at moments like this, no matter how cool you were trying to be behind your Ray Bans. Being greeted like this sent a shiver up your spine and lit up your ego like a fairground ride.

'I'm afraid we have to go inside, boys,' John Martin said with his head-down, ready-for-action mumble. 'Curtain's up in thirty minutes.'

John led us across the car-park and through the double security doors. As I walked in I could hear the crowd buzzing as they moved around the hall finding their seats. At Wembley there's only a thick black drape that separates the backstage area from the main arena, and the atmosphere seeps through the cloth and into your dressing-rooms like ink on blotting paper.

We walked into the dressing-rooms, Alan Keys had hung all our stage clothes up on one of those movable metal rails that you find in shops. I was going to wear my bright red military jacket, blue silk shirt with my collection of cheap bead necklaces from Miss Self-ridge around my neck and my trusted leather jeans.

On the other side of the room was the 'rider', laid out on a white table cloth as if for some teenage party. The rider is some-thing that is written into your contract. It always consisted of Jack Daniels, beers, water, champagne, lemon tea and honey for Tony, a selection of cheese and biscuits, a few sandwiches and nuts and crisps in giant bowls. The rider was the same at every gig, no matter what country you were in. Sometimes in Eastern Europe they struggled to find certain brand names but always replaced the missing items with local substitutes. To be honest, as long as the JD was there we couldn't give a toss. I opened a can of Coke and sat down on the sofa. I couldn't drink alcohol before a gig. I had too much to remember, I needed every brain cell in my cranium alive and kicking. I felt strangely tired, drained from the adrenaline that had been moving around my body most of the day.

John Martin put his head around the door.

'Quick as you can, guys.'

'How many people out there, John?' Steve Norman said as he was pulling on his brown suede ankle boots.

'Packed fuckin' solid – nine thousand!'

Gary and I smiled at each other. This was an ambition that had been part of our lives for so long, and here we were about to live out the dream. I couldn't believe this was for real, that this was really happening.

Tony was standing in front of the mirror going through a range of weird vocal exercises as I walked into the en-suite loo. My nerves were at bursting point and my bowels were too. I had always suffered from this reaction even at the smaller shows when we started out – the sniff of a crowd and my bowels exploded.

'How many out there?' Tony squeezed out between his second and third octave.

I shouted out through the toilet doors, my trousers around my ankles, 'Nine thousand. John said it was packed, sold every seat in the house. He said we have to hurry up – they're ready for us.'

I could hear Tony giving his quiff one last spray. His voice came back to normal.

'Tonight, mate, they can fuckin' wait for us.'

He was right, tonight was our night, why did we want to hurry these moments along.

'All our parents are out there, Mart. They're all sitting up on the right. I saw your mum and dad when I peeked out front.'

'Ooo . . . That's better,' I said.

'What?'

'Nothing.'

I flushed the toilet walked outside and breathed in a cloud of sticky hair-spray.

'Fuck me, I don't know what room smells worse,' I spluttered.

Just then the walls started to rumble, and I could hear the opening chords of Marvin Gaye's 'I Heard it Through the Grapevine' coming out of the house speakers. It was the last song before we went on. Tony and I walked out of the toilet and back into the dressing-room. My roadie was waiting with my bass, ready to strap it around my neck and wish me luck for the last time. Gary, Steve and John were ready, Tony was right behind me, taking one last drag on a fag.

John Martin was in the doorway again, this time with a smile on his face, calling out 'Let's do it!'

We all shook hands with each other before being led the short distance to Wembley's giant stage.

The stage curtains were down when we climbed the small set of stairs on to the wooden boards. It was pitch black apart from the tiny red lights on the amplifiers and the roadies' torches cutting through the dry ice, and it looked just as if we had taken a wrong turning and landed on a different planet. The crowd's whistles were muffled behind the thick fire curtain, I tried to call over to Steve to share the moment, but he couldn't hear me, he was in his own world, going through his sax solos in his head one last time. I made sure my bass was in tune as more smoke started to fill the hidden stage.

Just then a voice came over the house speakers that was so loud it shook the ground beneath me. They were the words that I had lain in bed dreaming of night after night with my eyes closed, wishing that one day I would hear them for real.

'Ladies and Gentlemen . . . Spandau Ballet.'

The fire curtain dropped from its hinges high above us and several huge blinding white aircraft lights shone out from the back of the stage. I could see the whole of the arena as we hit those opening chords. It was massive, it was everything I had dreamed it would be. Nine thousand people up on their feet, screaming at us . . . What a buzz!

A wave of emotion ran through my veins that was so powerful it made me feel sick, almost giddy. I recognized the feeling of excitement – I had felt that a million times before on stage – but the anxiety that was also there was something new. A terrible thought hit me – was I at the top of my ladder? was this it? how was I going to find experiences to equal this moment? would everything seem small and worthless after tonight? I had lived for this dream for so long, and now it was a reality.

The party that night was in the Holiday Inn at Swiss Cottage. My stomach was filled with champagne, my pockets were filled with cocaine and my head filled with applause . . . This was rock'n'roll . . . and I loved it.

'Congratulations.'

'Well done.'

'You were fantastic tonight.'

'The sound was great . . . we could hear every note.'

'My God you were incredible.'

'Congratulations.'

The superlatives were unstoppable and food for our ever growing egos. It was like walking on the moon, with no gravity to keep our feet on the ground. We were starting to float high above the real world, looking down from a position of privilege that we didn't quite understand, but were only too willing to accept. It was a wonderful time, by now the whole planet was listening to Spandau Ballet records and opening up its arms to welcome us into it's arenas, and being polite working class boys from North London, we weren't about to refuse the invitations.

On our way out to Australia we met a young British Airways hostess, who came to one of the first after-show parties during our stay in Sydney on that leg of the tour. She decided to drink most of the champagne that was behind the bar that night. In fact she drank so much that within an hour of getting to the hotel suite she had collapsed and fallen against the wall. One of the minders kindly picked her up and put her to bed in one of the empty hotel rooms opposite.

Exactly twenty-four hours later she came around, wandering out of her room and into the following night's post-gig party. She was still wearing her drink-stained uniform and laddered tights from the night before, and her hair had come loose from its British Airways plastic clip. She was completely unrecognizable from the pleasant air hostess who had served us our first-class cheeseboard and stood for our crude North London sense of humour with a cheerful elegance.

I went over to say hi as she made her way to the middle of the room to start that stockinged shuffle that most women do when they've had a few drinks too many.

As she spoke I could smell a mixture of duty-free perfume and what could only be the bottom of her stomach.

'Great show tonight.'

'Tonight?'

'Yeah, at the Arena.'

I tried to jog along with her. I was never one for dancing but I could see she wasn't going to stop.

'You came to the show tonight?'

'Yeah, Tony and Steve invited me, y'know, on the way over.'

She flashed the laminated backstage pass at me and then carried on putting down a layer of positive ions across the nylon carpet.

'Yeah . . . Tony's voice was fantastic tonight.'

Y'know, that's the thing about playing bass guitar, no one ever says you played great tonight, or your guitar sounded good out there.

'You mean last night.'

'No . . . I mean tonight.'

My nan, 1965. She always said my blue eyes made me look German, I just clicked my heels and smiled at her.

962 Caswell Bay, South Wales. My First trip o the coast.

My great grandfather. Are brain tumours hereditary? I had to find out where mine had come from, I couldn't handle not knowing.

1965. Gary shows who's in charge of our relationship at a very early age.

1968. After school my mum held my hand and took me to Anna Scher's Children's Theatre for the first time. My shy grin gradually turned into a huge smile.

FA Cup Final day 1977. Arsenal vs. Ipswich. Our palace in Elmore Street. An inside loo and no more trips to the public bath house.

1978. 'You should be a pop star' Steve Dagger said as he finished his pint of home brew. Two weeks later I lined up for this photo with my new band!

At home before the 'battle of the "Blitz"'. The New Romantics vs. The Hooligans.

1979. Signing the record deal. On tour weeks later our first record had gone into the top five and life would never be the same again. (Photo: Graham Smith)

1980. Recording 'Journeys to Glory'. I was more interested in my high score than my base lines. (Photo: Graham Smith)

1981. A trip to New York altered my state of mind. (Photo: Graham Smith)

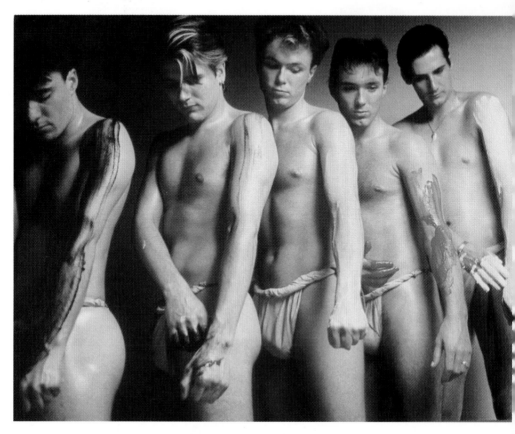

1982. The 'Paint Me Down' video was banned from top of the pops ... thank God! Was it art or just a mistake? (Photo: Eric Watson)

1983. Could Gary and I play *The Krays*? The front cover of the NME that started the original idea and got the ball rolling. (Photo: Pennie Smith)

1985. The whole world was listening to Spandau Ballet records and we toured the globe in true rock and roll style. (Photo: Mike Prior)

1985. Live Aid. I couldn't wait to get out into the sunshine and play our three songs in front of the world, but it was all over too soon! (Photo: Redferns / K. Thandi)

Suddenly her face started to change colour as a green wash spread upwards. I repeated myself.

'You mean last night.'

The poor thing had just realized that she had missed a complete twenty-four hours and wandered back into the same party, in the same room with the same people standing in the same places. It was like a scene from *The Prisoner*.

It was the winter of 1984. We were out in Germany recording yet another TV appearance for yet another single. We were appearing in the middle of some naff game show that was the Bavarian equivalent of Ted Rogers' *Three-Two-One* show that used to ruin a decent Saturday evening back in England. The carrot at the end of the stick on these trips wasn't the fact that it would help promote the record and make us more money, but the huge record company dinners that used to follow. The best restaurants, the finest wines, a record company exec with an expense account that had no limit. His only job was to take us out and satisfy our every whim, and of course get us completely pissed.

The cameras had stopped rolling and the girls dressed in Bacofoil had left the stage as we made our way between the six-foot furry snake and the polystyrene Bengal tiger back to our dressing-room. We were only in there a moment when Steve Dagger came in.

'Good one, chaps.' He was trying his hardest to keep a straight face as he played with the back of his blonde hair.

'Where are we going tonight, then?' I said.

John joined in. 'Yeah there's supposed to be a good club in town, I wouldn't mind some of that after dinner.' He was in the mood for a drink, I could tell.

Dagger looked down at the green carpet tiles before he spoke. 'Well, listen, you might want to get an early night in tonight.'

The room went quiet. It was obvious that someone must have died. An early night was something that had never been spoken about. It sounded like Steve had decided to speak in a strange alien language for a few moments.

Gary broke the ice. 'What . . . I mean, why?'

The disappointment on John's face was already registering. He wasn't the best at hiding his emotions.

Steve carried on. 'I've just had a call from Bob Geldof, he has put together a charity record for the people in Ethiopia. He wants us to be on it.'

'What, just us?' I said. I was as fed up as the others. I couldn't believe that we had travelled all that way to Germany and weren't going to knock back their incredibly strong schnapps.

Steve could tell he had to press the point. 'No, listen, there's going to be about ten bands – Boy George, Duran, Status Quo.'

Tony chipped in. 'No, listen, they're really nice geezers.' Tony said that about everyone and their aunties, but on this occasion he was right.

Dagger carried on. 'I think we should do it, I've booked the Lear jet for seven thirty to get us back to Heathrow.'

'What – in the morning?' Steve Norman said in a state of shock.

The band spoke in unison: 'Ooh, fucking hell.'

'I know . . . but listen, I've spoken to the Duranies' manager and he said that they have to get a scheduled flight home.'

The room spoke as one again: 'Hooraaaaay . . . Wankers.'

'Their manager has organized a make-up artist to be at the airport for when we arrive. Well, it's for Nick Rhodes really, but he said we can use her because both the planes are going to land at the same time. We're organizing security between us. There's going to be hundreds of screaming kids at the airport when they find out that Spandau Ballet and Duran Duran are coming home to do the track – could be riots!' I felt my adrenaline rush through my body at the thought.

We landed at Heathrow in our Lear jet at ten thirty and were met by the head of the airport security and several police officers. They took us to a small back room, where Nick was in the middle of having his face put on.

Alf Weaver, who was head of our personal security, was there as well. He was a kind of cross between Frank Sinatra and Dickie

Henderson. He always held the band's itinerary rolled up in his right hand as if it was his microphone, as if he was just about ready to walk on stage at the Royal Albert Hall. The parents loved him. He was never flustered, was polite to everyone and knew his job backwards.

'Hello, boys. Good trip?'

Tony cleared his throat. ''Ere Alf, are the Quo doing this "Band Aid" thing as well?'

'Yeah . . . so I heard, Tone.'

'Good. Nice bunch of blokes they are.'

Alf spoke up above the roar of another plane leaving the airport. 'Right, when we get outside the limos are going to be right opposite the main glass doors. The most we can do is to ask all of you to keep your heads down and get into them as quick as you can.'

'How many kids are out there?' I said.

Alf turned to the young policeman who was standing right behind him. 'How many do you think?'

'I don't know, I haven't been out there all morning, but there's gotta be a few hundred judging by the amount of extra security that's been drafted in.'

My adrenaline surged once again. The ends of my fingers felt as if they were starting to swell with anticipation.

Duran were being gathered together at the other side of the room for what looked like a similar briefing. I wondered to myself just how many kids were outside. Black-and-white scenes of the Beatles arriving at the airport with thousands of screaming girls on the overlooking rooftops crossed my mind. Steve Dagger was talking to the Duranies' manager when word came through that we had to go.

'Go go go!' said Alf.

'Go go go!' said the famous Cook twins, who were minders for the other camp at the time.

I put my head down and went went went . . . There wasn't one kid in the airport, only about fifty policemen, ten private security guards and the airport security men. Just then I heard a voice.

'Martin . . . Martin, can I have your autograph.' I looked up. It was Doris and Ingrid, two devoted German fans. Doris held out a picture and a gold ink pen. Before I could speak to them, five policemen were on them like a shot. How embarrassing – our self-importance was out of control. We were whisked into the waiting limos and away from the empty airport. I looked out of the back window, Doris and Ingrid stood in the middle of the massive security force waving goodbye. Some of the policemen were waving goodbye, but not with the same hand gestures as the two devoted Germans.

Sting had arrived before us in his Golf GTI, Paul Weller had caught the bus there, and Boy George had come in a minicab. We had turned up in one of those great big stinking black limos that the Queen goes to film premieres in . . . Who did we think we were! I have to be honest – at this point it was more a case of us not wanting to be left out of what was obviously going to be a giant record, than about making money for the African famine victims. I for one didn't have a clue where Ethiopia was . . . but I knew this was going to be good.

Inside, the cappuccino machine was working overtime, and the stainless steel toaster had stuck in the on position as the best of British rock tried helplessly to pull the electric plug from the socket. Phil Collins sat reading the paper while Kenny Jones slept on the leather armchair next to him. Paul Weller kept himself hidden behind his long brown fringe, as he read through the lyrics of 'Feed the World'. Bono smoked another short cheroot in the dark corner just by the loos.

Bands had never been asked to mix together as friends or to work together in a studio before. This was the first time anything like this had been done. It took several hours of power play and strategic teasing before the tensions died down and Boy George had forgotten what Simon LeBon had called him in last week's *Record Mirror*. This was new ground for everyone.

One of the several television camera crews that were inside the foyer came up and spoke to Steve Norman.

'Steve, have you got anything you would like to say to the poor people in Ethiopia?'

Steve didn't have to think about that. 'Yeah, I'd just like to say sorry we couldn't tour down there this year but we'll try and fit it in next year.'

That was us. Steve's statement showed just how removed you can become being in a band. We had completely left reality behind, but who could blame us!

'Feed the World' took the day to record, and by five o'clock everyone there was singing along to the chorus in the main studio. We had all made new friends that day and an awful amount of money for a very worthy cause. The rest is history.

Another gathering of bands was for Prince Charles's Princes Trust charity. We had donated the proceeds of a gig to the Prince's charity, as had many other bands over the previous year. Prince Charles and Princess Diana had organized a small informal gathering at Air Studios in London's Oxford Street to say thank you. It was always an incredible buzz mixing with royalty, although it was amazing just how fast you found yourself running out of things to say and just how easily your mouth would dry up.

Charles was always polite. He always made sure that he knew something about your work or about your background, but you could feel that he wanted to move on, that he had more important things to do.

Diana was different. She was not only beautiful, but made you feel as though she was one of you, that she could have been one of your backing singers. She was interested in everything everyone said, and had the odd joke to gently take the mickey. She could have been one of the girls down your local pub as well as being a princess – she was wonderful.

The party was to start at eight, and as with every royal occasion things were supposed to go like clockwork. Everything was to be timed to the second, from the arrival to how long you spent talking to the royal couple. It was like a military exercise, and we were expected to fall into line. Unfortunately, rock and roll was never built on military timing, or map-reading, come to that.

Oxford Street was packed with late-night shoppers. Alf Weaver sat in the front of the limo, his smile reflected in the windscreen and visible through the glass partition that separated the driver from the passengers. We were all cooped up in the back seats. Those cars were big, but it was still a push to get all of us, Steve Dagger, a minder and the driver into one.

Steve Dagger was getting nervous as we approached the studio. A huge crowd had gathered around the glass doors and there were television cameras and press photographers everywhere.

'OK, Alf,' Steve said. 'You won't be able to come in with us tonight, the royal security team is only letting in the six of us so you'll have to wait in the car. We'll see you when the party's over.' Alf went everywhere with us, he was practically part of the band. I could see Alf trying to smile.

''Ang on, we're nearly there,' I said. 'Jesus, there's a lot of people there to see us.'

Gary looked at me and spoke through his clenched teeth.

'They've come to see Diana and Charles, you prat!'

It was like a movie premiere, the whole place was lit up with television camera lights. A rush of adrenaline surged through my body and into the others as it always did at times like this.

Just then the car came to a stop and Alf jumped out to open the back doors.

'Come on, boys, let's go,' he said.

The crowd went wild, it felt incredible to be appreciated in such a way – we were only going to a party, even if we were playing second fiddle to Charles and Diana.

We got out of the limo and stopped for a few minutes to sign autographs and to stand together for the photographers in our tried and tested group shot pose. Steve Dagger came from behind.

'We have to go in. They're waiting for us.'

We had milked the applause long enough as it was, and made our way into the studio doorway.

Crack . . . I smacked my face on the door handle.

Bang . . . Gary's head smashed into the back of mine.

John had tripped over the back of Tony's dangerously long legs, and Steve, who was still blowing kisses to his fans, walked head first into the pile-up. The five of us were in a heap.

The crowd's cheers and excitement started to change into whistles and laughter. I looked up, I banged on the glass doors, I couldn't see through the glass, they had a kind of green reflective film on the other side that only allowed me to see into my own eyes, the doors were locked. I knew the security was going to be tight and we were a couple of minutes late, but this was ridiculous. I heard Tony shouting from the back, 'Ring on the doorbell.'

I was starting to feel stupid, we were looking more like the Goons than a rock band.

'Martin, for fuck's sake, knock on the door,' Gary said. Why was I at the front, I thought to myself. I hated responsibility.

Once again I smashed my fist on the glass door. I tried shouting through the crack, 'Hello, we're here . . . Excuse me, Spandau Ballet are here.'

There was no response at all from behind the doors. By now the crowd had seen enough, and even they were starting to feel embarrassed for us. They started to shout out in unison, and suddenly I started to make sense of what they were saying.

'You're in the wrong doorway!'

I looked up and came out of the blind panic that had disorientated me. They were right, we were standing in the doorway to the shoe shop next door. The crowd and the photographers were in fits watching us make our way out of Ravel and back into the street to get to the studio next door.

This time we were in the right place and the glass doors were swung open by a man in an official-looking uniform. His gold tooth matched his epaulets and his grey moustache was stained brown from nicotine and whiskey.

'Evening, lads. You want the second floor.'

Even he laughed as we got into the lift.

The party was already under way when we got in there, and Charles and Diana were working the studio room with expertise. Their armed guards were carefully making sure that no one got too close and that everyone in the room was watchable. Prince Charles was talking to Phil Collins and Diana was in the process of moving on from Dire Straits to Pete Townsend. Steve Norman and I grabbed a glass of champagne as the waiter passed, his silver tray toppled to one side as we caught him unawares. I was aware that Steve was still feeling embarrassed by the earlier episode when a voice whispered in our ears.

'Diana will be over in a moment, chaps.' It was Alf.

'How the fuck did you get in here? I thought this place was supposed to be as tight as a drum.'

Alf smiled. His nickname was 'Slippery'. It stuck with him all the time he worked with us.

At the end of 1985 we were getting ready to go out on tour once again. We had been in rehearsals in the Nomis studios in Shepherds Bush for over five weeks, and everyone was itching to get out and try the new show on the waiting audiences that had bought their tickets several weeks in advance. I could remember only too well that feeling of holding a ticket to a concert in your hands and looking at the date, wishing the days away. It gave me a nice warm feeling to know that the upcoming shows were already half sold out. Even at our most successful we always worried about empty seats.

Our last tour had been amazing, with nearly every ticket sold, but the down side is that touring with a rock band is incredibly expensive. Every band will tell you that sometimes the money that you make on the merchandising subsidizes the whole tour. It's heartbreaking when you've spent all that time away from home and then realize that there is no pot of gold at the end of it to share among you.

Spandau were no different from any young band. The money we made in the theatres was just enough to keep the band on the road and to pay for the nightly parties. The expenses are incredible. The hotels, the travel, the crew of eighty men, who all need to be fed three meals a day unless they have given their fifty pounds a day allowance to the local drug dealer and have lost their appetites. There's also the minders, the wardrobe people, the lighting crew, the sound crew – every spare penny just seems to get soaked up. Every time you turn around you are spending the profits.

Steve Dagger and John Martin, the tour manager, walked into the rehearsal room just as we were finishing the last song. They sat down at the back of the room and winced as their eardrums adjusted to the sheer volume that the stacks of speakers and Marshall amps were pushing out. When we finished the song with that thunderous clichéd crash that leaves the inside of your brain wishing you worked in a library, John Martin stood up and said 'Hi'. He had a bit of a cold, and held his paper hankie around his mouth as he spoke.

'Hi, guys. That sounds good.'

Tony looked concerned. 'Have you got a cold then, John?'

Steve Norman was taking his saxophone off and was putting the delicate instrument on to its stand. 'Has he got a cold! Hadley, what are you? On my life . . . look at the state of him.'

Tony moved back and held his hand over his mouth as he spoke. 'You better stay away from me, John – that's the last thing I need.'

JM coughed and cleared his throat. 'I know . . . I will . . . but Steve and I have something important to talk about and I thought I should be here to discuss it with you.'

Gary had finally finished giving Lionel his last-minute instructions as to how and when he wanted his guitars tuned up through the set and at what point he wanted to change from his electric to acoustic.

JM had grabbed everyone's attention, even Keeble's, who was already swigging on a bottle of Carlsberg behind his kit.

'What is it? What's wrong?' Gary said, I could hear some anxiety in his voice. Once again he spoke for all of us. He looked at Dagger, who was sitting on the sofa and hadn't said a word yet.

'Steve . . . what is it?'

Steve pulled himself out of the sunken sofa. He looked as if he had had a heavy night the night before. I had seen that look on Steve's face many times over the years. Steve walked to the middle of the room and sat back down on a speaker cabinet before he said what he had come to say.

'Well . . . it's about the tour.'

We all looked at one another, quietly held our breath and waited for the bad news. Maybe the ticket sales weren't as good as we thought – anything and everything was going through our heads. John Martin started to explain through the paper hankie held in his rolled-up fist. Tony moved deeper into the back corner of the room away from any free falling germs. I was always happy not to have to worry about catching a cold – it didn't make any difference to me – but for Tony, and for all singers, it's a nightmare. Catching a cold can lead to cancelled concerts. I didn't envy that kind of responsibility, that kind of burden.

'We have to cut back,' John said. 'We need to save money . . . If you want to earn some proper money out of this tour then we have to find some corners that we can cut.'

We all breathed a sigh of relief and agreed completely with what JM was saying. It made complete sense. We did need to cut some corners, no one fancied working for nothing.

JM coughed again and carried on. 'Excuse me. Well, Steve and I have been through all of the accounts from the last tour and tried to dig out any stuff in there that we thought might be a waste of money.'

We all listened and waited to find out exactly what Steve and John had regarded as a waste of money. Their needs were slightly different from ours. We were the ones at the front of the arrow when it came to touring. Was it going to be the first-class travel, the five minders on call twenty-four hours a day, or even the party suite that we hired in every hotel we stayed in with a bar full of champagne.

'Boys . . . *the rider*. You remember what the rider is: the teenage party that greets you in the corner of every dressing-room. We think we should cut back on some of the rider, the amount of stuff that's thrown away after you leave the venues is criminal.'

John looked around the room and waited for some kind of response before he went on. 'So . . . what do you think? Do you want to do this?'

The room answered as one voice: 'Yeah . . . a good idea, John.'

John smiled and opened a black file that he had put down on the side and pulled out some handwritten documents. He wiped his head with his decimated tissue, he was obviously sweating, the room was warm but not enough to have that sort of effect. Steve Norman looked at him and sensibly said, 'John why don't you take that jumper off? You might feel a bit better.'

He was wearing a thick black turtleneck fisherman's jumper.

'No . . . I'll be fine. It's best if I sweat this thing out.'

I could see Tony shrinking even further into the sound-proofed corner. John Martin glanced down at his sheets of paper and started to go through the list of things on the rider to see if there was anything on there that we could wipe off.

'OK then. Let's start at the top . . . and obviously the most expensive . . . the drinks. There's the case of champagne, the case of beers, the case of water, the case of cokes, the case of lemonade, the bottles of tequila, vodka and Jack Daniels, and the carton of orange juice.'

Again the room spoke again as one. 'Wow . . . that's a waste . . . you can see where the money goes when you're not looking.'

Steve Norman spoke up from under his freshly bleached fringe. 'Yeah, I've never had a drop of orange juice in my life. I've never seen any of us drink the stuff, no one drinks vodka and orange. Have you ever had tequila and orange? Yuk!'

Gary joined in the debate. 'Yeah, but all that drink is good to have for when people come backstage after the gigs . . . Some of them like orange juice.'

John Martin butted in: 'Hang on guys, why don't I put orange juice down as a standby? What do you think, Mr Keeble?'

Keeble waved his beer up in the air from behind his kit. 'I don't fucking care!'

'Right then . . . he doesn't care.' JM's feelings were slightly buckled, but he went on all the same.

'Let's move on to the food . . . There's the plates of sandwiches, biscuits, olives, crisps, nuts and Hoola hoops . . . none of this stuff gets touched, it just gets slung into the bin after you guys leave to get back on the tour bus.'

Gary got up off his chair and started to pace around the rehearsal room in between the microphones and sound equipment.

'Look . . . when people come back stage after a show, they expect a few things to nibble on, that's just how things are.'

John Martin had an answer that he had obviously prepared earlier. 'But Gary, most of these people get invited to the after show party as well, back at the hotel, where there's even more food and drink laid on. Look, we have to cut back somewhere.' John blew out his cheeks and sniffed before he spoke. 'Let's carry on with this, shall we? The last thing is the cheese board.'

The whole room was in agreement about this one. John had at last found a link between us and himself. Tony spoke up from his corner. 'Yeah, that cheese board just sits there stinking . . . Count me in, I'm all for getting rid of that.'

John smiled and put a tick down by the side of the cheese board. At last he was getting somewhere.

'Mr Keeble, can I take it that you'll be going along with that decision?'

'I don't fucking care, John.'

'Mr Norman?'

'Absolutely . . . I never eat that stuff, it smells like someone's been sick in the corner and hasn't wiped it up.'

'So I'll take that as three.' John ticked his sheet and looked at Gary, waiting for a nod of approval.

'Yeah . . . cheese board is history.'

John tried to justify the meeting. 'Look it may seem like nothing, but that cheese costs us twenty pounds a show, that's one hundred and forty pounds a week, that's over five hundred pounds a month on something that is being thrown in the bin.'

I had been quiet through the whole discussion, I hated meetings after rehearsals, I just wanted to get home. Making your way through that Shepherds Bush traffic at six o'clock on your way back to North London can be a nightmare. JM looked at me, the sweat was pouring off his bald head and running behind his ears. He looked like he needed to go home and get into a bed with a Lemsip and a copy of *Playboy*.

'Mart . . . what do you think?'

I shrugged my shoulders. 'OK.'

Steve Dagger stood up and stretched his arms above his head and yawned as he brought the meeting to a close. 'Come on then, John, leave it at that. I got the taxi to wait for us . . . let's go.'

John and Steve grabbed their coats and slung them over their shoulders and started making their way to the sound-proofed swing doors. John turned around and looked at the room. He looked terrible.

'See you then, boys.'

Just then, it hit me: what about that cheese roll that I sometimes make myself after the gigs and take back to my hotel room? I used to enjoy that before I got into the shower to get ready for the party.

Steve Dagger and John Martin were just walking out of the room when I called them back.

'John. Come back a sec.'

He poked his dripping head around the thick black door.

'What's that, Mart?'

'Look, that cheese board . . . I like a bit of cheese after a gig.' John was stunned. 'Keep it on,' I said.

Steve tried not to laugh, but the situation was ridiculous. We were going out on this massive tour that was going to cost the earth, and the only thing we had successfully agreed to cut back on was a carton of orange juice . . .

Diary of a 'Tax Exile'

Shirlie and I were skiing in Austria. We were high up the mountains of St Antoine when a blanket of fog dropped from out of nowhere. We could hardly see each other, let alone the trail we were meant to be on. The fog was thick, cold and damp and brought with it an eerie silence that wrapped itself around our shivering bodies. I knew that the trail led to the left because I had done the run many times on my own, so I blindly led the way. We had to move; if we had stayed still we would have frozen. We skied on for about five minutes, every inch seeming like a mile. Shirlie hung on to my pole (don't laugh) and we moved gradually across the snow.

Then, just as quickly as it had come down, the fog lifted. We were completely lost.

'Which way?' Shirlie said.

I didn't want to worry her with a minor problem like this.

'Oh, it's just over the ridge.'

'Over there? Are you sure?'

I tried to look confident. The mountain range around us looked wonderful as it started to catch a shaft of sunlight on its jagged edges rising out of the low clouds.

'Yeah, follow me.'

As I led off, I could feel that the snow was fresh and powdery under my skies, so it was obvious that no one had been on this slope for a while. Supposedly knowing where I was going, I led the way over the ridge. I went over the edge, what looked to me to be a gentle slope turned into a sheer drop. My skis sprang loose from their fixings and I fell vertically for about fifty yards down the mountain. I smashed into a small bush, which broke my fall, and clung to it for dear life. The first thing I thought of was: my God, Shirlie! I tried to shout up to her to stop her from coming down over the ridge, but with my face mask on and her hat pulled down over her ears, there was no chance. Just then I heard the sound of her skis cutting through the soft snow on top. And then nothing. I could hear Shirlie falling. As I looked up she was falling straight towards me. I knew the bush I was hanging on to spread out below me, so I moved over to one side and let her get caught up in it the same way I had. Surprisingly, both of us were unhurt, but we were frightened.

'Are you all right?'

'No.'

I could see Shirlie was full of anger.

'Are you OK?'

'You idiot.'

Shirlie had one of her poles in her left hand, while the other was hanging on to the bush. She started trying to hit my hanging legs with her pole.

'You idiot.'

'Christ, give me a break.'

'I thought you knew the way.'

'Look, let's think about this sensibly.'

But for the next couple of minutes she carried on trying to hit my legs.

'You bastard.'

I think I got the point.

When she had calmed down we decided that we would have to slide the rest of the way down. Luckily the bush we were hanging on to wasn't the only one. There were a few more spaced out below us. We slid from bush to bush until we reached the bottom of the mountain.

Eventually we got back to our lodge and made it to the bar. The butterflies and shaking limbs started to subside, and the more we told our story, the higher the mountain became . . .

Absence makes the heart grow stronger. It must do. Shirlie and I spent most of the Eighties in different corners of the globe, only ever talking to each other on backstage telephones or in the early hours of the morning from our hotel rooms, if we could work out the differences between our time zones.

She would be touring with Wham and I would be touring with Spandau Ballet. At the time it was hard, but both of us knew in the back of our minds that it wouldn't last for ever. Both of us knew that we were getting the chance to live out these incredible adventures that most kids would sell their souls for at the drop of a hat (it was hard!), but the real test of our relationship had only just begun.

We had just come back from Austria, where we had thoroughly spoiled ourselves. It was a gentle way to break in the idea of being away from home for eighteen months as a tax exile. A prospect I wasn't looking forward to! A tax exile year is where you can only stay in the country for a maximum of sixty days. It's hard, but the rewards are great. You end up with a completely tax-free year. In a business where you can't guarantee constant success you have to make the most of your money when it's coming in. So many bands over the years have worked their fingers to the bone, only to come out at the end of it with a head full of incredible memories and nothing in the old bank book. This was our chance to put a few quid by . . . a pension fund. The *True* album had been a hit all around the world and was still in the charts in several countries. The follow-up album, *Parade*, had done just as well, with three hit singles being taken from it: 'Highly Strung', 'Only When You Leave' and 'I'll Fly for You'. These were lucrative times for the band and we had to make the most of them while they lasted. I have never been one to save money, but the tax year made sense even to me.

The hardest part of course is being locked out of Britain. We chose the closest place to England we could find, essentially so that we could get home on those precious sixty days as quickly as possible. In retrospect I think it would have been easier if we had broken our ties with the country completely and gone to some far-off exotic land. It was hard being that close to home but so far away.

The tax exile year was meant to coincide with a world tour that was scheduled to last for the best part of the year, but during one of the first shows, in Los Angeles, Steve Norman slid across the stage in a dramatic scene-stealing saxophone solo and tore the ligaments supporting his knee. That was that, and we were destined to see out our sentence in Dublin. Not that it's a bad place; in fact it's one of the most beautiful places I've ever seen, and the people are some of the friendliest in the world. It was just that it wasn't home, and it was too far away from Shirlie.

We decided to spend the opening few months in Dublin constructively and prepare the songs for the next album, *Through the Barricades*. We needed to find a suitable rehearsal studio and somewhere to live.

In those days Spandau Ballet took minders wherever we went, and Dublin was to be no exception. A new guy called Rick had just joined us the week before, so we were going to take him with us. We had had a succession of minders. It's rather like finding a nanny for your child – the bright ones are hard to find. Anyway, Rick was a body-building maniac who ate more food than the whole of the band put together. The bills coming from his room service were astronomical. He wasn't very tall but he was wide, with a small moustache that clung to the underside of his regimental broken nose.

There were some good minders who worked for us over the years. There was Alf Weaver, who still works in the trade today. Big Russell, an ex-butcher whose curly red hair was a major attraction in the backwaters of Japan. There were the Cook twins and Robbo, whose good looks kept us on our feet. Sometimes even the fans were mistaken as to who were the stars and who were the minders.

At one point we had five minders working for us all at once, all ready and prepared in case one of us wanted a night out at the local club. They would take their duties in turn because for some of us a night out would turn into a two-day binge. I can remember being on stage in Barcelona without having had a wink of sleep for three days. The minders had to be fitter than us. At least we were enjoying the night out; they had to stand around – and weren't allowed to drink any alcohol.

There was a minder we left behind in a hospital in Hungary because the lifestyle was simply too much. His name was Mauri, and he was a lovely guy, but pushing on in years. He once stayed in my room sitting next to my bed after an all-night binge. I had taken it that step too far as usual, and when I went downstairs to meet the others for a seven a.m. departure, I threw up in the lift. If I had tried to make it home that day I would have been busted at customs for carrying too much alcohol. Anyway, he stayed with me while the other guys left me behind and went to catch their plane.

One of the best minders we ever had was a black guy called Quentin. He was intelligent as well as being forceful when he had to be. He understood that the job isn't just about being SAS trained in the art of collecting teeth as battle souvenirs. Most of the time the minders have to deal with young screaming girls who are beside themselves with emotion. They have to be diplomatic, polite and sensitive. After all, they represent us as people. If they were ever rude to these kids, it would come back at us and they would walk away thinking we were a bunch of pigs and didn't care about our fans.

This tax exile year is an interesting year to look at, because if old Dr C was right and my tumour had nestled in my head for the past ten years without being detected, then this was about the time that the little fellow might have decided to pop up.

During that year I kept a diary. It became a friend to confide in, someone outside of the band, outside of my relationship, someone I could talk to, laugh with and moan at. Someone I could trust, that I knew wouldn't run to the Sunday papers with a tell-tale exclusive, and someone who didn't want anything in return like a photo or an autograph. My diary kept me company when I was left alone with my thoughts and while I was locked out of the country I called home. So on a cold wet morning in May, I got into my white Porsche with my new friend in my bag and drove to Holyhead to catch the ferry to Dublin.

SATURDAY 17th MAY

We've been here a week now. I think I have finally found a place to live, but still no rehearsal room for the band, and we are all desperate to get started on some work, if for no other reason than to break this unbelievable boredom and to keep us out of the local pub. We have been holed up in Jurys hotel, trying to sneak between conventions to get to the restaurants. I took a wrong turn yesterday and ended up signing autographs for about half an hour . . . I know full well that they will throw them away by the time they get on to the brandies. It's not a bad hotel, but certainly not the best Dublin has to offer. It has a wonderful fish restaurant at the back, but the smell of cheap aftershave and la-di-das coming from the business reps is enough to put anyone off.

I've just taken Shirlie back to the airport and, you've guessed it, I'm missing her already. She has a way of keeping me happy and feeling fulfilled that I struggle to find anywhere else. Anyway, I will see her on Tuesday. Sometimes I wish she wasn't so ambitious and would stay here in Dublin with me.

SUNDAY 18th MAY

Everton 1 Man Utd 0.

I used to love FA cup final day when I was a kid. I used to watch every minute of the day's television. The 'It's a Knockout Special', 'meet the players' wives', the team profiles, the lot! It was the biggest day on my tiny calendar, far bigger than my birthday and, if it was an Arsenal match, bigger than Christmas. We would decorate the front of the house with red-and-white banners and streamers and hold a small street party in the middle of the road. God, that seems a long time ago now!

I saw a quiz show on TV last night. The host asked the questions, 'What was Hitler's first name?' The contestant slammed his hand down hard on the buzzer and a premature smile of success pulled at his lips.

'Yes. . what's the answer?' said the host.

'Heil,' said the contestant.

Oh well . . . What with that and the weather, there was no mistaking where we were.

TUESDAY 21st MAY

After a bad hangover had finally left the inside of my head, I was once again faced with boredom. The new bodyguard seems OK . . . but you can never tell. It's hard to trust someone you don't know. He has a friendly look in his eye but a wonky moustache . . . Who knows?

Going home tomorrow for a photo session and a radio interview. I can't wait. Shirlie says it's not raining at home. I can't believe that, a land that doesn't perpetually rain!

WEDNESDAY 22nd MAY

Up 5:35

Depart Dublin 7:36

Home 10:32

Studio 11:07

Home 5:32

Radio 7:31

Every minute counts these days. I feel like a giant clock is ticking away inside my head. I seem to be timing everything I do. I nearly bought a stop-watch, I must be going mad!

THURSDAY 23rd MAY

Going back to Dublin today. Shirlie wasn't well . . . PMTs . . . but we still had fun. She always makes me laugh, her impressions of different celebs are just fantastic. I don't have to record EastEnders these days, I get a whole theatrical rendition . . .

FRIDAY 24th MAY

Moved into my tiny two-bedroom flat. It's on the second floor of a small apartment block. It seems to have good security and there's a great tennis court behind the car-park that might come in handy. It has a real fire in the living-room that might be cosy on those cold days. Everything here in Dublin is green. Even the carpet, the bed sheets and the fucking curtains in the apartment are dark green. I've just bought a box of 'Shake and vac'. This place has a funny smell that I can't get rid of. It smells like my nan's old flat. I have to go out and hire a television and video!

Steve Dagger rang today. We were offered a tour, supporting the Power Station on an American tour. It's a band put together by John Taylor and Andy Taylor, with Robert Palmer on vocals . . . I for one don't fancy supporting anyone, especially Duranies. We have come too far to start supporting people. We should have done that years ago, when getting on a bus for ten hours with a bottle of Jack and a couple of porn movies seemed like fun.

PS Just finished unpacking when a gust of wind came down the chimney and covered everything in soot . . . Fuck it! Went to the pub.

SUNDAY 26th MAY

Shirlie arrives at one. God I feel like Papillon here, waiting for my visitors . . . I think I'll take her for a curry tonight, not very romantic but it has something of a homely vibe to it. I better change out of my arrowhead suit and put on a bit of a smile.

Tried speaking to Rick . . . I couldn't find a thing in common . . . There's not much going on upstairs . . . Know what I mean?

MONDAY 27th MAY

I desperately want to marry Shirlie. I have thought about it for some time now and being away from her has made my mind up. I hope she wants to marry me? . . .but it's such a huge step to take. What are my mum and dad going to say? what are the band going to say when I tell them? . . .why do I care what anyone thinks? If I want to marry her I should ask her.

WEDNESDAY 29th MAY

Liverpool vs Juventus.
Shirlie went home . . . I went to bed thinking of those involved in the

horrific football disaster at the Heysel stadium in Belgium. I have never seen anything so horrific. This has to be soccer's darkest day! Margaret Thatcher said that those responsible had brought 'shame and dishonour' to the community of football. For once she is right . . .

All this after the terrible Bradford fire last month – what's happening?

THURSDAY 30th MAY

Went to lunch with Gary, Tony, Steve and John and . . . Rick!

We all sat down and watched Rick eat a huge lunch, though to be fair we had quite a laugh. At the end, after Rick's third portion of apple pie and custard, I called for the bill. I couldn't sit around and watch him eat any more.

When the waitress came over in her green uniform I told her to put it on my room. Rick leaned in close, and a piece of apple pie hit me in the ear as he whispered to me: 'Let me put it on my room . . . It's free!'

I couldn't believe he hadn't realized that we were paying his bills.

FRIDAY 31st MAY

The last day of May.

A lazy day. The tour with the Power Station isn't going to happen, thank fuck . . . What am I going to do with myself? When I was a kid and I used to hear of bands doing a tax year, I used to think of it being this glamorous world of casinos, yachts and Rolls Royces. Well, here I am finding out first hand that it is not like that . . . or maybe we just haven't sold enough records.

We have no chance of selling records at the moment, we have come to blows with the record company. It started about six months ago and has now built into a huge row and looks like we are heading to court. Spandau Ballet vs Chrysalis records . . . Oh shit!

The problem is getting to all of us and affecting the mood of the band. All we want to do is what bands do – make records! Everyone will be happier when this is solved. It all started because we felt that they weren't doing a good enough job for us. We couldn't understand why Duran Duran were selling more records than us . . . why more kids wanted to see them than us . . . Our records are just as good. Now we have asked to *move to another label and they have refused (what a shock), thus we have stalemate situation . . . If you ask me it's all a load of bollocks . . . We're gonna fall flat on our faces.*

Gary has written some great songs, but Chrysalis have put an injunction on the band, stopping us from recording. The stupid thing is that this has come after 'True,' 'Gold' and 'Only When You Leave' all went into the top thirty in the USA. I can't help thinking that we are cutting our own throats. We can't achieve anything locked up in this miserable place, and by the time we release our next record the name Spandau Ballet won't mean a thing . . . especially in the States.

PS I must try harder to write something. I know I can, but how do you do it when you're depressed? Maybe I'll go upstairs and talk to Tony . . . if he's in!

Tony had the flat above me. Somehow he coped with the loneliness a lot better than I did. He made friends with the locals a lot more easily, and after only the first couple of weeks he had a real little social scene happening. I've never been like that. It's always taken me a long time to get to know new friends and to let them into my protective bubble. Tony is one of your all-time nice guys. I don't think I ever heard him say a word against anyone in the whole time we spent together. He would drink more than anyone and nine times out of ten he would collapse and have to be carried off to bed.

Once, in Rome, after a huge stadium show with an audience of twenty thousand people, Tony and I and two of our minders tried to get to the bar of a packed disco we had been invited to. The crowded dance-floor swept to one side and everyone stopped dancing and turned to watch us make our way through the club. The DJ came over the speakers, his frenzied Italian tones scorching our ears. There were times when it could have been nice to go somewhere unnoticed, especially now as we were both pissed out of our brains and were just about remaining upright. The champagne in the dressing-room had flowed rather freely that night and was whizzing around our bloodstreams. We were so drunk that the idea of getting one of the minders to go and get the drinks didn't even cross our minds.

'Here they are . . . Spandau Ballet,' the DJ shouted.

Every eye in the building was now watching us. We were nearly at the bar when I noticed Tony was starting to wobble a little. He was practically there, practically at the bar, when out of the blue he fell to the floor like a giant bag of parsnips. The crowd let out a huge synchronized 'OOOOOH! . . .and then silence, nothing. Even the music had stopped. Everyone in the building watched in anticipation as Tony clambered back to his feet, using the bar as support. It took a moment, but none the less he made it. You could have heard a pin drop as Tony made his ascent. When he got to the top, he looked straight at the beautiful Italian waitress with her classic Roman lines and deep brown eyes. Tony spoke in his best cockney accent. 'Two pints of lager please, love . . . [burp] . . .and a Sambucca.'

Another time, at an airport somewhere in Europe, we were coming out of the gate when we noticed that Peter Gabriel was standing at the far end of the building. Tony walked straight up to him and congratulated him on his fantastic new record . . . 'Bilko'. Of course the track was a political song that had a lot of meaning for Peter Gabriel. It was called 'Biko' and was about the anti-apartheid crusader Steven Biko – not, as Tony had thought, Sergeant Bilko.

By far my fondest memory of Tony is a conversation I heard in a rehearsal room one day, over in Shepherds Bush. My brother had just come back from an art exhibition somewhere in the West End. He had obviously enjoyed the work, as he was raving about it. If Gary ever sees anything good – an exhibition, a show, a movie – he wants everyone to see it, no matter how uninterested they are!

'Was it that good, then?' Tony said.

'Yeah, fantastic. You should go if you get a chance to, you'd love it!'

'No . . . it's not really my thing.'

'You'd love it if you went.'

'How much were they then?'

'What do you mean?'

'The pictures. How much?'

Gary smiled as he replied, 'Well, they're all different prices.'

Tony looked at Gary and drew a small box in the air with his fingers.

'All right then, how much was one about this big?'

THURSDAY 1st JUNE

We went to see Springsteen at Slane castle. The most exciting part was the helicopter ride back and forth. I am itching to play again, it seems like ages since we were on tour. Watching that band on stage made my fingers pop. It reminded me of watching Jailhouse Rock *when I was a kid and wanting to get up and sing for the first time.*

I go home tomorrow. It will be nice to sleep in my bed again.

TUESDAY 4th JUNE

Caught the 19:50 back to prison . . . When the fuck will we be able to record this record? The strain is telling on everyone. For the first time ever we seem to be losing that bond we have always had.

PS Rick has been sent home . . . C'est la vie.

WEDNESDAY 8th JUNE

My car alarm went off last night, and now I have a broken window on the Porsche to deal with. I left the car at the garage and went shopping with Shirlie. I bought an engagement ring and gave it to her outside the shop . . . Ahhh! . . . She said yes.

I'm nervous about telling the rest of the boys and Gary . . . I have never loved her as much as I do now.

THURSDAY 9th JUNE

I can't write today. I'm on my own again. Shirlie had to go home.

FRIDAY 10th JUNE

Today I feel rich with Life. Last night's depression has done me good, it's funny how sometimes you need a good cry to make things better. I'm such a wimp. The Sun *says I'm going to star in a movie based on the lives of the Kray Twins with Gary. That's news to me, although I wouldn't mind doing a bit of acting again. Mind you, I wouldn't mind doing anything at the moment. But the Krays . . . What a coincidence, as I am reading* The profession of Violence *at the moment. Can you imagine . . . That would be so cool! . . . Fingers crossed.*

Shirlie and I are going to Ibiza tomorrow for a holiday with Steve Norman, Gail, his girlfriend, and Kenny Everett the disc jockey. It will be nice to get out of this hole for a while. When we come back, the Live Aid gig will be upon us, so that might give me something to boost my idle adrenaline.

Over the years Ibiza has given me some of the finest fun I have ever had. That deadly cocktail of sun, sea and sangria seemed to be my perfect solution to living in a city. I first found the island in 1978, when I and eight of my friends all bought ourselves a ticket to the island, hoping that we could find some kind of basic accommodation when we arrived. It certainly was basic, in fact there were only two beds in the apartment. We took it in turns to use the beds, and the others would have to huddle up on the floor if they couldn't find a space next to a charitable woman.

The island is split into two distinct halves. San Antonio, where the package holiday-makers fight in the local English pubs over who knocked their beer into their bird's egg and chips. Then there's the other side of the island, where pints of beer turn into pints of champagne and egg and chips reappear as caviar and pommes frites. They're like two different worlds joined by a strip of road that runs for about twenty miles across the centre of the island. My first trip to Ibiza with my friends was obviously to San Antonio. It was only when I went back with Spandau Ballet five years later that I sampled the exotic side of this nirvana.

The band were booked to play a show at the Koo club, which is simply, even today, one of the biggest clubs in the world. It's stunning, with a giant swimming pool in its centre and lit by several aircraft searchlights at night. Any hardened clubbers could be forgiven for thinking they had found the magical land of Narnia. My memory of the gig itself is slightly blurred from the effect of drinking too many Coco Locos before we went on, but as I sobered myself up afterwards, and found my way out of the dressing-room area, I couldn't believe what I was seeing. A bull appeared from one of the side doors. Now this wasn't some cute baby bull, it was a fully grown black bull with fully grown horns and saliva dripping from its gaping mouth. The bull ran around the club trying to butt anything that got in its way. People jumped into the pool to escape. At first, I have to say, I found the whole thing hilarious, that is until the bull stopped playing the field and started to make a bee-line for me. Christ, what was I going to do? Be charged down by the bull and risk the embarrassment of being taken away on a stretcher, or take the route into the pool like everyone else and mess up my carefully crafted hairstyle? Now that might seem like an easy option to most people, but to me . . . I knew that I would have to stand and have my picture taken with people for the rest of the night, and this was the Eighties, the decade of hair-spray. What was I going to do? There was no option, I was going to have to face the bull. As it stood and tried to stare at me in the eyes, I looked around for something to climb up on to. There was only a low chair that was built into the bottom of the bar, with satin pillows scattered on it, but that would have put me at an even more compromising level – I mean I'd rather take the blow in the stomach than between my legs. As I turned back to the bull I realized that everyone around me had now left – it was just me and him. It must have been the red Robin Hood costume I was wearing that was driving him wild and making me his target . . . Now this wasn't the way things were supposed to happen, I thought, as the headlines in the following day's *Sun* flashed in front of my eyes . . . 'Martin Kemp, killed by bull while trying to save his bouffant'.

Just then the Bull started to scuff the floor with his right hoof, and I realized my moment of truth was about to come. The bull started to make his move for me. Then, from out of nowhere, I found the power in my legs to lift myself up and grab one of the metal supports of a small tent-like marquee that covered the drinking area, and in true Errol Flynn fashion I swung myself across to the other side of the bar. The bull crashed into the wall below me before being grabbed by its handlers and slung into the swimming pool to cool down. What could I say? This was Ibiza, this was the Eighties, and this was rock and roll.

One of my funniest memories of Steve is the night Gary was playing at a charity concert that Pete Townsend had organized at the Dominion Theatre on Tottenham Court Road. The bill was varied and amusing, with comedians mixing with musicians to give a fun show. Gary was on towards the end, singing 'Through the Barricades' on an acoustic guitar. Even though I might be a wee bit biased, he was fantastic – his voice was made for that song, which was always my favourite Spandau number. It made a change to hear Gary sing it softly, rather than Tony belting it out in front of the full rock band.

After Gary had finished and stood for his deserved applause, Chris Quentin, the *Coronation Street* star, took the stage. He came bouncing on like a circus performer, doing several back flips and somersaults, all very over the top and completely out of keeping with the mood that Gary had just set. Chris was singing 'Get Back', the Beatles hit. Quite how he found the breath to sing and do back flips at the same time I don't know. Then in the middle of the song Chris turned to the audience.

'Now I know that we have Spandau Ballet in the audience tonight . . . I know they're here somewhere . . . Maybe the guy on the spotlight up there can help me find them!'

All four of us sank in our chairs. It was like that awful moment when a comedian catches you walking out to the loo in the middle of his set and decides to pick on you for the rest of the night.

'I know you're here somewhere . . . I need you to help me with this song.'

Then, as we ducked down in our seats and the spotlights buzzed our hair-spray, the nightmare got worse. Out of the corner of my eye I could see Chris starting to get down off the stage, and soon he was climbing over seats coming towards us.

'Get back, Get back to where you once belonged . . . There they are, come on Spandau, sing along.'

The lights stopped circling and homed in on Steve. The dyed blond streak in the front of his hair shone out like a fluorescent beacon. Chris climbed over more chairs, pushing people out of the way, until he landed in the empty seat next to Steve, that was saved for when Gary returned.

'Get back, Get back . . . Come on, Steve,' Chris shouted down the microphone. He shoved the mike under Steve's nose. Now I knew Steve well enough to know when he was upset, embarrassed or pissed off, and at this particular moment he was all three.

'Get back to where you once belonged.' Again Chris shoved the mike towards Steve, and again Steve pulled away. I was just thanking my lucky stars that it wasn't me sitting on the end of the row.

'Come on, Steve, you must know this one?' This time Chris almost shoved the mike down the back of Steve's throat, and this time Steve took it. Steve's words echoed out of the giant speakers and around the auditorium.

'FUCK OFF . . . OFF . . . Off . . . off . . . off . . . off . . . off . . . off . . .'

Chris took the mike back and made his way back to the stage with his tail between his legs.

Steve was never one to be pushed into a corner. On the surface he came across as happy-go-lucky, always ready to make others laugh, but underneath he was shy, compassionate and nervous.

Steve's also a fantastic musician, he could bend his ear to play any instrument he wanted, and all to the standard of a first-class session musician. He has just started on his first solo record, and I'm sure it will surprise everyone. Steve was captured by the wonderful island of Ibiza and a beautiful Spanish girl called Menchu and has set up home there with her and their two children. I love Steve, I miss him like crazy.

SATURDAY 7th JULY

I slept at Shirlie's house last night. Her bed seems to be made from cotton wool after that tough old thing in Dublin. As I came up the motorway in a minicab, the back wheel fell off. The driver said it was sabotage – a rival minicab company. Anyway I was up at six to get back to my flat, and then out by eight to catch the helicopter to Wembley Stadium for the Live Aid concert, where seventy thousand people would be crammed on to the sacred turf to watch this huge piece of rock and roll history happen before their eyes.

It looks like Chrysalis have finally given up in the legal battle and soon we will be able to find ourselves a record company and record some of the new songs . . . and all that extra cash from the settlement in the tax year won't go amiss.

We arrived at Wembley, which was buzzing with excitement. Everyone from the cleaners to the stars was hyped up and ready to rock. There were several small portable cabins backstage that were being used as make-shift dressing-rooms, and a small piece of astro-turf had been laid down between them, with a bar at the far end giving away free water and Coca-Cola. I stood for a while and spoke to Rick from Status Quo . . . he was flying with adrenaline and had a permanent smile spread across his pink face.

11.00 am Charles and Diana walk down the long line of stars including us, shaking hands with everyone.

12.00 Ladies and Gentlemen, it's Saturday the thirteenth of July at Wembley Stadium and it's . . . Live Aid.

The announcement sent shivers down everyone's back, including my own.

12.05 pm Status Quo opened with 'Rocking All Over the World'. It was the perfect song to start the show and the perfect band to get everyone in the mood for the rest of the day. I watched the first half of the song on the backstage monitor that was hanging above the astro-turf area, and for the second half I walked out to watch from the side of the stage. It was amazing, I have never experienced that kind of anticipation before. I couldn't wait to get out there in the sunshine with the boys and play our three songs.

1.47 pm It was our turn. Three songs. 'Only When You Leave', 'We are Virgin' and, of course, 'True'.

My blood ran through my veins at the speed of light. I had forgotten what it felt like to be so happy inside the band. We had played at Wembley Arena before, but never the Stadium. Seventy thousand people cheered and clapped along as we went through the set. The three songs seemed to go past in a flash, in a matter of seconds. It was simply surreal how fast our fifteen minutes passed by.

2.00 pm My part in this occasion was over, all that was left was for me to sit back and enjoy the rest of the show until the final 'Do they know it's Christmas?' where everyone would come back on stage and wave goodbye.

3.00 pm Tucked up in bed with Shirlie, watching the show on our little TV, eating crisps and drinking Coke . . . This is living.

9.00 pm Drive back to Wembley. Do a few interviews and photo sessions and open a bottle of Jack . . . I'm so tired, I don't think there's anything that would perk me up. Then before I knew it I was pushed on stage to sing the final farewell with a generation of rock stars.

10.00 pm A party at Legends. No one had any energy. Everybody was exhausted. We left after ten minutes.

THURSDAY 18th JUNE

Back in Dublin . . . Rehearsals don't start until next Thursday. How can I see out another four months? Had to sell my car as it kept being broken into over here . . . who cares! By all accounts it's an Irish pastime to steal cars with English number plates. The time is starting to go faster now. This morning I couldn't believe my eyes – I looked over the balcony and I was sure I saw Tony and Steve smoking pipes . . . I must be mistaken.

THURSDAY 18th JULY

Woke up and read for a while . . . The Profession of Violence. *it's hard for me to read about it now without putting my face in the movie, after the pieces in the* Sun *and the* News of the Screws. *It's a nice daydream.*

I phoned my parents, which upset me. I worry about them so much. I think I'm turning into a manic depressive. I can't stay happy for more than a couple of minutes. My problem is that I have nothing to fill up my down time apart from waiting. I don't draw, I don't paint, in fact I do fuck all except complain about how lonely I am. I need a hobby . . . Collecting beer mats sounds good!

SATURDAY 20th JULY

Well, six months of the sentence gone. Strain has appeared on the faces of everyone . . . Gary must be under pressure, he's the only one who takes the responsibility of writing songs. Why that is is a mystery, everyone is capable . . . but sometimes it's just simpler to take that back seat, and the idea of the others judging my attempt is just too daunting. I would hate them to turn around and tell me that my effort is crap, or, even worse than that, for them not to say anything but to give me the silent treatment and move on to something else. I know that I'm not a fantastic musician, I never wanted to be. But then, to be fair, I have never worked at it. What a lazy sod I am, I have all this time on my hands and I am still sitting around dreaming and not making the most of all this free time. I know that other people would be putting it to use, learning something . . . or teaching themselves something useful. The most I do is get over a hangover by cooking up a fried breakfast and watching the afternoon re-runs of Eastenders *. . . What a slob.*

I almost have a fear that if I try too hard to get anything, things will stop happening for me. I have always found that good things only fall into my lap when I'm not worrying about it. If I stress out about anything . . . they don't happen . . . Either way, I'm still a fat-ass slob – I must try and write something and stop making excuses.

SATURDAY 27th JULY

Hire a guitar to write songs . . . Play 'Blue Suede Shoes' one thousand times . . . Fuck it!

A guy called the office. He wants to write me into the Roy of the Rovers *comic, playing with the Melchester Rovers team alongside Roy for a season . . . fantastic, I might finally make it as a professional footballer – a dream come true!*

Being written into the Melchester Rovers side for that season was so much fun. It got me out of the four walls of my green flat and on to the football pitch once a week. It was pure escapism, and I loved it.

I used to get my copy of *Roy of the Rovers* delivered every Saturday in the same way my *Beezer* would drop through my letter-box twenty years earlier. My dad saved every copy and bound them up in plastic bags ready to give to my children. That season Melchester Rovers won everything and made it to the FA cup final. It had always been my dream to play at Wembley on that day. I couldn't do it in real life, but at least I could get there in the comic and read about it as if it had really happened.

The morning Melchester Rovers were due to play in the cup final came around. I was like a little kid. I was up at seven having my breakfast in the kitchen, waiting for the metal flap on the front door to swing open and a tiny hand to push through my copy of the comic. Something was wrong – it was the first time that the paper-boy had failed to turn up. I should have taken that as some kind of omen, maybe the newsagent had seen something in there that he wanted me not to see; maybe I had been put on the subs bench; or maybe I was just being paranoid and, given the sort of form I had been in over the last few weeks, I would score the winning goal, or at least make a winning contribution before holding aloft that silver cup with blue and yellow streamers flying from the handles.

I walked around the corner to the local paper shop to get the comic. The moment I came out of the shop I was flicking through the soft pages, looking for my caricature with the funny haircut. I couldn't believe it, I was so shocked when I opened the centre pages and read that I had been dropped because Spandau Ballet had a gig somewhere in Europe. Just my luck. I felt like leaving the band. The escapism had gone to my head. I was depressed enough already without this happening.

'Can I have your autograph, Mr Kemp?' A young kid was staring up at me, I wasn't sure if I could see tears behind his soft blue eyes.

'Sure,' I replied.

'It was a great goal you scored last week, a real belter.'

'Thanks.'

'You really let the side down, though.'

'What?'

'We would have done the double if it wasn't for you.'

'Wait a minute. I . . .'

'How could you do that to us?'

'But I . . .'

'Where's your loyalty?'

And with that the small boy raced away on his rusted bicycle. I thought about handing in my resignation to Roy . . . I can't handle this. There was now a whole country of kids that thought I had let them down.

The last time I appeared in the comic was when Roy had persuaded the band to do a charity concert on the Melchester Rovers pitch . . . Live Aid the sequel.

It was fun while it lasted.

SUNDAY 22nd JULY

We went horse racing at Phoenix Park. It was fantastic to get out and mix with some different people.

I lost thirty quid. We met a man who was talking to us about buying our own horse. A top trainer by all accounts . . . or so he said.

Pepsi and Shirlie have decided to try and work together as a partnership . . . 'Pepsi and Shirlie'. They have some great people working with them on the songs. I hope it happens for both of them. It's hardly fulfilling, dancing to young guns every night, and they both have great voices that they both want to use. I certainly know how frustrating it is not to be able to achieve your full potential. The only thing is that it will keep us apart even more . . . you can't win.

I'm quite sure it never stops raining here!

MONDAY 29th JULY

Well, today sees the start of rehearsals for the new album, even though we haven't got a record company yet. Shirlie left this morning at nine, but it's not so bad now I've got some work to do. It's the start of a new year for Spandau Ballet. We have to break the US properly this time . . . Still raining.

Gary is leading the charge to buy this horse . . . It's difficult, you don't want to be the one left out if it's a winner. I can't believe John wants to go along with the idea. He used to work in a bank, surely he must have O'level maths – the odds against winning are ridiculous.

John always lived to be the king of rock. He wanted to drink more, party more and put his small frame through as much punishment as possible. His dark Porsche sunglasses never came off the bridge of his nose from the moment we set foot on that tour bus to the moment we got off again six weeks later. He was a drummer and lived a drummer's lifestyle. When we were on stage he always looked trapped to me, as if he wanted to pick up his kit and carry it down to the front, knocking Tony out of the way, to become the centre of attention. John was the instigator behind many a wild night out. If he ordered a bottle of Jack Daniels he would throw away the top so that he had to drink the whole thing that night. If you were at a party and had reached that point of no return, when you knew that you would be going home to a spinning room and talking to God on the great white telephone, you could always guarantee that John would be there with you.

We were in Japan, I had come out of an all-night club as the giant red sun was rising in the East and the army of Tai Chi disciples were going through their morning paces in the local park. I had fallen over on the curb outside the main door and in my drunken state had decided that it would be far easier just to stay there, than try to get back to the hotel. After a few minutes, I turned around and saw that John was on the other side of the road in the same state, if not slightly worse. We both carried each other to the local cab rank and went on to the next club.

John will always play drums. 'I hit things with sticks for a living' was his favourite phrase, and I'm sure he'll be using that for the rest of his life.

THURSDAY 1st AUGUST

Rehearsals are now going well. A new song called 'A Man in Chains' is coming on. Kenny Everett came over and Steve cooked a wonderful curry. Afterwards we went to the Pink Elephant and hung out with Def Leppard who are in the middle of their second tax year . . . They must be mad!

PS I'm worried about my brother. He seems to be under a lot of strain. He carries a lot of responsibility on his shoulders. He keeps the band in hit songs.

SUNDAY 4th AUGUST

My headaches . . . let me rephrase that . . . my hangovers are getting worse. I'm sure I never used to have such severe banging . . . Went to the pub for a drink – that always does the trick.

MONDAY 5th AUGUST

Well here I sit all alone.
Shirlie's gone away back home.
So much time to sit and ponder.
On the day I can finally wonder.

PS Mum and dad are coming over at the weekend.

TUESDAY 6th AUGUST

We start a new song in rehearsals today . . . I hate it. I get so uptight because I haven't got any confidence in my bass playing . . . basically, I'm crap.

Anyway we started on a song called 'Swept' . . . maybe a new 'True', who knows – we could do with it.

I think I'm gonna buy mum and dad a house. Dad can't cope with those stairs and Islington isn't the same place any more. They need to get out of there. I've spoken to Gary about it and I think we are going to go halves . . .

TUESDAY 13th AUGUST

What a miserable day. Wake up at 8.30 and read more about Ron and Reg.

Mum and Dad were here. We had a great time staying in some old castles. They really enjoyed it.

Rehearsals are drawing me out . . . Gary is so dogmatic sometimes, and I'm worried about the approach to the new songs . . . They're just not commercial enough.

Diet starts today. I'm so fat, but I eat through boredom. Making a curry takes up at least a couple of hours . . . and then eating it another twenty minutes.

WEDNESDAY 4th AUGUST

Rain, rain, rain – no wonder it's so fucking green here.

MONDAY 16th AUGUST

Back in my own bed with Shirl . . . look for a new house . . . Haven't got time to write much because I want to make the most of my time at home. Writing in this diary is something I do when there is nothing else to do.

PS My diet must be working, I've lost five pounds.

THURSDAY 19th AUGUST

I took Shirlie to the airport. She has gone on tour with Wham for three weeks to America. I miss her already. As you see I haven't written anything about the Chrysalis problem because it is just too depressing.

PS 9.30 pm Back in the green hole.

FRIDAY 20th AUGUST

Pissed out of my brains in the Pink Elephant last night – boy, it felt good.

Sometimes I need to blow off steam . . . hung over before I even made it to my bed . . . I took a sleeping tab . . . Fab!

They are becoming a real habit, I think I should throw the rest of them into the bin. They make me sleep like a baby and forget about how much I miss home, but I feel like a plank of wood the day after. It's the most I can do to get up and get dressed and keep my eyes open.

SATURDAY 21st AUGUST

A week off from rehearsals . . . What am I going to do? Gary showed me the best song he has ever written . . . 'Through the Barricades'. It's a ballad written about Northern Ireland. It's the most touching song I have ever heard him sing.

I always feel like saying 'Why don't we put a synth bass on that one?' Just to lose the responsibility of having to come up with bass lines, and besides, 'True' had a synth bass and that didn't do too bad, but then I have always regretted not playing on that one . . . Who wouldn't?

I hope Tony can sing the song as well as Gary did when he showed it to me. I always feel that Tony loses some of the emotion when he belts out the song at his ear-splitting volume . . . I don't know why he uses a fuckin' microphone sometimes.

TUESDAY 24th AUGUST

A good day at Phoenix Park races. Won £200. Went for a celebration drink. Mixing Guinness and champagne is great. Two hundred quid doesn't go far in 1985! It's not what it used to be . . . Bah, humbug.

WEDNESDAY 25 AUGUST

Up at nine with a stinking hangover . . . Bang, bang, bang . . . Might go and look at a few horses to buy.

Spoke to Shirl on the phone . . . Wham are huge in the States (Hoorah for them!) and this court case is killing us out there. Even if we win the case we will lose the following we had, especially in the States.

Fuck my diet . . . 'Fight for Ourselves' is a great song. Rehearsals start on Monday.

SUNDAY 29th AUGUST

Took a sleeping pill again last night. I did throw the last packet away but I found another one tucked in my wash bag . . . Oh well. It was wonderful, my dreams were so vivid. I had to get up on stage with Eric Clapton and play bass, but when I got up there I didn't know the song. The audience were waiting for me to practise it in one corner, but I couldn't learn it to save my life. I have that dream so often, but it's not always with Eric.

I had a great day until my phone was cut off and a debt-collector knocked on my door because I haven't paid for the video machine either.

I went mad – I didn't care much about the machine, but not being able to phone Shirl is driving me insane.

Tonight we watched Spinal Tap *with Def Leppard. I don't think they got the joke.*

I would love to act again, it must be fun. The Spinal Tap *people looked like they were having such a laugh. I know that I could, I spent long enough practising when I was a kid. I bet it's like riding a bike – once you learn you never forget!*

TUESDAY 31st AUGUST

Flew into Bristol, then drove down to Devon. Parachute training all day. I got a huge headache from the stress of it all. It's costing me a fortune in tablets. I wish I wasn't doing this.

WEDNESDAY 1st SEPTEMBER

My jump was planned for exactly 20.00 hrs as one of the highlights of a charity fair. By the time they came to take us up in the plane it was too fucking dark. Never rely on the army for planning – my mum could have told you it was going to be dark at that time.

THURSDAY 2nd SEPTEMBER

Flew back to Dublin completely dejected. Got home and found that my flat had been broken into. What do you expect when it's in the paper that you won't be at home this weekend. They took the lot. Money, clothes and photographs.

128

PS Good job the debt collector had already taken the video machine.

SUNDAY 5th SEPTEMBER

I got the flat fixed up with some new locks and a huge alarm. I don't fancy them coming back . . . It's the first time I have ever been burgled and it's a horrible feeling. It makes me want to get out of this place even more . . . I hate it here!

Steve Dagger came out with Gary Langam to listen to the band in rehearsals. We went out for a Chinese after. Tony must have ordered the whole menu and drunk nearly all the wine in their cellars. We had to carry him out of there. I miss Shirlie so much it hurts.

WEDNESDAY 8th SEPTEMBER

A cab driver has just driven over here with my loaded wallet. I can't imagine that happening in England. He said he found it in the back of his car. . . What a geezer!

A great new song called 'Fight for Ourselves' . . . Why can't I write that? It's hardly a 'Bridge Over Troubled Water'.

FRIDAY 10th SEPTEMBER

Shirlie comes home from the US. I have been up since ten trying to tidy the mess. I even shaved for the first time in four weeks . . . it took half an hour to get it off. I should have left the beard on, I now just have a face of cuts and scrapes to show her. I might take her away for a couple of days . . . on our own.

SUNDAY 12th SEPTEMBER

Off to Paris for a couple of days with Normsky and Gail and Shirlie . . . Oo là là.

Not quite on our own, but I love Steve and Gail, they're good fun!

SATURDAY 18th SEPTEMBER

Paris was great. Still no sign of that elusive record deal. We're going to Munich to record 'Fight for Ourselves' next week. Looks like we'll pay for it ourselves as well. I can't help thinking that this argument with Chrysalis is costing us our careers.

SUNDAY 19th SEPTEMBER

Shirlie goes home today. Back on my diet. Her 'Pepsi and Shirlie' tracks are great, they must get some sort of record deal soon. They're just recording some demos at the moment. It would be fantastic if they could get a hit record out of it! I know it's frustrating for her just dancing behind George and Andrew. She has a great voice.

MONDAY 20th SEPTEMBER

Off with Gary and John to look at some horses. They all look the same to me, especially after five pints of Guinness. We met a trainer, and I think I showed myself up!

'Look at its lovely mane.'

'Main what?'

'No, no, no – I mean it's beautiful mane.'

'I heard you . . . Main what?'

I think Gary felt as embarrassed as me, and he moved the conversation along.

'How much then?'

WEDNESDAY 22nd OCTOBER

Nearly a month has gone by since I last wrote in this diary. Rock Hudson died, Orson Welles died, Yul Brynner died, and we finally recorded the track in Munich. A nightclub called P1 took most of our money behind the bar. Jack Daniels is expensive in that place, and John throwing away the top every time we buy a bottle meant my hangovers were huge.

Came home, and my heating and water had been switched off . . . I bet this kind of thing didn't happen to Elvis.

Shirlie's working hard recording her demos.

We are so close to going home for good now that I feel like it's the last ten minutes of a football match that's dragging on and on, waiting for the ref to blow his whistle.

SATURDAY 25th OCTOBER

Well, six weeks left in Dublin. Scored for Melchester Rovers today. What a great way to start the day . . . I knew I could play a bit, but I'm surprising even myself. There's going to be a Spandau greatest hits album coming out . . . It looks like even the record company are fed up with the stand-off . . . They can see that if they don't release it now we could be over by the time this court case is finished . . . Steve Dagger is trying to stop them from releasing it . . . Fuck knows why!

We bought a horse and have called it Tamarama. Gary named it – there's a surprise. We couldn't even think of that between us, let alone write some songs to go on to the record. It cost us £25,000 . . . Am I mad? Shirlie thinks so, and for once I think she might be right.

'What are you going to do with it?' she said.

'Race it.'

'By the look of that you're going to beat it.'

It was worrying, because Shirlie knows a bit about horses.

Tamarama was kept in Ireland for about a year after we had moved back to England. It cost the five of us about £200 a week in fees, which at the time didn't seem to be a lot of money, but over the course of a year it soon mounts up, especially with the vet's bills that started to follow. We never saw that horse once over its first year, although the reports that we were getting back from the trainer were encouraging, that is until it was time for its first race. Then the trainer called with the news that she had an ulcer on her shoulder and couldn't run. And that's as far as she ever went. Finally we sold her for £1,000. If you're ever desperate to get rid of some of your hard-earned money, just buy yourself a racehorse, keep it in a different country where you can't go along and see how it's getting on, then sell it after a year to somebody you have never met!

SUNDAY 26th NOVEMBER

The nights have really drawn in now and it seems to rain more than ever. I'm losing interest in the diary, my true companion. I'm counting

*every day now as the clock ticks away the minutes left in this green
land.*

*The greatest hits album is at number six this week. The record company
problem isn't resolved properly yet by a long chalk. I find it amazing that
Reagan and Gorbachev have just shaken hands at the summit in Geneva,
but we can't shake hands with them in Oxford Street.*

MONDAY 27th NOVEMBER

*We're having a drink in the Colony to say goodbye to everyone in a
couple of weeks. Shirlie thinks she is close on getting a deal for her
records . . . I miss her like crazy, but I know if this comes off I will have
one happy bird!*

MONDAY 3rd DECEMBER

*Another week gone, and the record is up to number three. It's sold a nice
half a million already. It would be nice to have it at number one for
Christmas, and the money is all coming in over the tax year.*

THURSDAY 6th DECEMBER

*I wish I was at home today, it's my Mum's birthday. Last day at
rehearsals . . . glad to see the back of that dump . . . I love Mum and Dad
so much, I wish I could give them more time.*

*I think I've changed so much over this year. I'm not the same happy-go-
lucky guy I was.*

*I had a row with Shirlie on the phone, and then when I called her back
she had gone out. I feel like going crazy. I'm always waiting for the next
day, the next week, the next year . . . When will I learn to appreciate
every day as it comes?*

FRIDAY 7th DECEMBER

I want to go home . . . HELP!

*Tony had a bouncing baby girl called . . . Toni. I was thrilled when he
asked me to be her godfather – what a responsibility – but I wouldn't like
to be in that house when the postman brings the mail for T. Hadley when
she gets a few years older; his boy's name is Tom.*

SUNDAY 9th DECEMBER

I had just got back to the flat after a game of tennis, and switched on the TV – and had the shock of my life when our minder's face filled the screen. I was watching Police Five *and he was being sought for armed robbery. Next time we should use our* instinct!

MONDAY 10th DECEMBER

Four days to go. I've already packed. We are now only going to be at home for a couple of days before we drive down to the South of France to start recording the album in a studio called Miravale. It sounds like fun and, besides, Shirlie is going to come with me. It looks like there is an end to the record company hum ding . . . They might let us go to Sony. Who knows, maybe I was panicking about nothing all that time and should have trusted Steve. I just know that it looks like it's going to be a great Christmas.

TUESDAY 11th DECEMBER

Three days to go.

WEDNESDAY 12th DECEMBER

Two days to go. I have packed and repacked. I have never been so excited to be moving on with my life.

THURSDAY 13th DECEMBER

One day left. I feel so nervous. My stomach has permanent butterflies and I have a giant headache from stress. I think I need to take a sleeping pill to help me to relax.

We stayed home over Christmas, then went down to the South of France. It was beautiful. Why in God's name did we choose to stay in Dublin all that time? It was so lovely looking at a dry, brown, sun-drenched horizon.

Spandau Ballet finally moved to Sony records from Chrysalis, signing the deal in the Georges Cinq Hotel in Paris. The first release from the *Through the Barricades* album was 'Fight for Ourselves'. It might not have been a 'Bridge Over Troubled Water' . . . but it was a hit none the less, and we were back in business.

Fragile China

Going home was something of an anti-climax. No sooner had I walked through the door, carrying my suitcase and waving my souvenir shillelagh above my head, than Shirlie told me that she had to go back on tour with Wham. She was going to China for about ten days, and in that time would get to play two shows to the music-starved kids of the East. In reality it was a brilliant promo idea by Simon Napier Bell, who was managing Wham at the time. No bands from the West had yet ventured to China, and it was guaranteed every centre-page spread around the world, from the broadsheets to the tabloids to the trendy music press magazines. This was going to be a superb PR coup.

It was after the first show that Shirlie noticed one of the boys in the band, Raul the trumpet player, looking at her in a strange way. That's nothing unusual, but the next day, when they were due to fly on to Beijing to play the second show, he had locked himself in his room, telling the other band members that the only person he would talk to was Shirlie. Again this isn't really surprising. Shirlie has that effect on a lot of people. People trust her for good advice.

When she finally got to see Raul, he was standing in the middle of his room in complete darkness, with his hands wrapped in a white towel. He had tried to hurt himself in some way. He was mumbling something to himself, but all the time he just stood statuesquely, looking straight ahead. Now Shirlie is a strong girl, but this was a bit much even for her. She could see that something wasn't right here, and after that one quick look she carried on going.

Being in a rock band on the road can do funny things to people. I can vouch for that first hand, but I have to say this was more than a drink too many.

Shirlie got on the band's bus as usual and carried on to the airport. She noticed that Raul had been left behind, which was something of a relief to Shirlie. The bus made the short journey straight on to the airport tarmac and pulled up alongside the old Chinese aeroplane. Everyone grabbed their hand luggage from the overhead shelf and made their way up the small flight of stairs, into the cabin of the plane.

The plane had a strange thick smell of Chinese mothballs and fried rice, but if you've ever been to those far-off places you'll know that everywhere has that same smell; even the rich government buildings in the centre of town have that smell; it seems to get into every corner of life. The band all took their seats in the plane, which would have looked more at home in an Indiana Jones movie than at an international airport.

Shirlie took her seat next to Pepsi, who was sitting in the coveted window seat. On tour this is always the prime seat, not so much because you can look out of the window and take in the view, but because you can rest your head against the rattling Perspex window and get some sleep, before you're marched off the plane and towards the next sound-check. Behind her were George's Mum and Dad and the band's PR, a wonderful woman named Connie, who over the years has been as kind as anyone could be to Shirlie and me. The seat next to Shirl was left empty, and she was just starting to spread out a little and get the circulation back into her cramped legs, when Raul appeared. He looked ill, his skin was grey and his eyes watered as if he hadn't blinked since the moment he woke up. Shirlie's body stiffened as Raul headed straight for the empty seat next to her and sat down.

As the plane took off over mainland China, Raul pulled out a pair of mirror shades from his bag and began to stare at his distorted reflection in the silver glass. He growled at himself and mumbled strange words.

Shirlie looked over at Pepsi, who was now drifting off into that aeroplane meditation. There's nothing quite like it as your body tunes itself into the rumble of the single jet engine and your mind and the giant machine become one.

'Look at that beautiful field . . . The grass is so green.'

Raul was now starting to talk his nonsense directly at Shirlie. There was no beautiful field, in fact there was no field anywhere to be seen, just grey concrete that spread out as far as the eye could see.

'We could play football on that field.'

He growled again as the plane hit an air pocket and dropped in the grey sky. This time, though, the growl was heavier and more intense. Raul bent down once again to his bag, that was tucked under the seat in front of him, and pulled out a knife. He smiled at Shirlie, who by now had seen enough. She was trying to wave to people behind her, trying to make any sort of gesture that might attract some kind of attention like sticking two fingers up at the cabin behind her, but this was rock and roll, people often joke around on planes. Raul played menacingly with the knife against his leg, smiling all the time as he spoke his inaudible gibberish and growled at himself. Then, almost in a slow motion, as all dramatic moments are, he raised the knife and plunged it into his belly, once, twice, three times. Shirlie sat frozen as this man next to her tried to take his own life. Blood started to seep through his shirt and cover his hands, some off it splashing up on to Shirlie. Pepsi woke up just in time to see it happen and started to scream, she grabbed hold of Shirlie and somehow managed to get her over the back of the seat and on to the laps of George's parents. By this time the whole plane had realized what was happening, and the two minders that Wham had taken with them on the trip had to use some of their SAS training to jump on top of Raul and stop him from doing himself a permanent injury.

Raul started to shout out the most disturbing words, almost as if he had learnt the *Exorcist* movie script off by heart.

'The Devil is on this plane with us, you fuckers.'

'This plane is going down, you mother-fuckers.'

Whatever Raul had intended to do, he was scaring the hell out of everyone.

Just then the Chinese pilot, hearing that there was trouble, thought he was being hijacked and took the action that is obligatory in China in this situation. He took the plane into a steep twenty-thousand-foot dive.

'I told you . . . This plane is going down . . . The devil has us in his hands.'

Everyone on board started to pray as the bags fell from the racks above and the minders struggled to keep hold of Raul, who seemed to have the strength of a hundred men.

'We're all going to die, mother-fuckers.'

Shirlie and the rest of the band could be forgiven if at that moment they actually believed Raul's words and that the devil really was piloting the plane. Somehow the minders kept hold of Raul until the plane started to level out and came into what was essentially a crash landing.

The moment the plane was on the tarmac a doctor appeared and injected Raul with some kind of sedative. Even that didn't slow him down completely. Before he was escorted from the plane, he found enough energy inside himself to turn back to the main cabin and the distraught band members and sing the American National Anthem while giving a military salute.

Raul was taken off to a hospital to have his wounds seen to, and then the Chinese sent him home as quickly as they could. Having Wham in their country was a promotion exercise for them as well as for the band, and the last thing they needed was a story like this.

Poor Shirlie came back from the trip exhausted and literally a complete nervous wreck. She still carries the whole experience with her as if it happened yesterday. Even now we never watch a horror movie or talk about the unexplained before bed. She was scared deeply on that flight over China. I took Shirlie to see several Harley Street doctors to see if they could help her overcome her experiences and get her to relax. Apart from giving her handfuls of sedatives, no one seemed to be able to help. Once I walked into a room and she was wearing this huge brass colander on her tiny head with a million wires coming from it. It looked like a scene straight out of *Ghost Busters*. Eventually one of the doctors said, 'Take her away on holiday . . . just the two of you. It'll do her the world of good.' Sounded fine by me!

I went to the travel agent and picked up one of those touring guides through France. I knew that she wouldn't want to get back on to another aeroplane just yet, and I had just bought a Porsche 911, so the idea of a nice long drive sounded good.

I had mapped out a route that would take us about ten days to get down to the South of France and into the sunshine. Along the way, we would stay at some of France's finest old châteaux, which really are beautiful.

We left London in the pouring rain and the convertible roof had decided to leak on Shirlie's side, but still, we were going on holiday. We finally got down to Dover, onto the hovercraft and across into France. The sun had come out, the roof was off, the Eagles were on the tape deck and we were flying.

It was about five in the afternoon when we got to the first château. It was incredibly beautiful. It looked in every way like a castle from a fairy story, with a moat, a drawbridge and even low, fluffy white clouds hanging around the several pointed turrets just as they were supposed to.

We checked in and went straight up to our room. The room was quite dark, almost medieval, with its four-poster bed, white silk sheets and a huge dark wooden ceiling. From the window we could look out over the drawbridge and across the green fields of France.

That night we climbed in between the silk sheets on the four-poster bed and turned off the lamp on the side table. We were both exhausted from the trip.

'Good night,' I said.

'Er . . . yeah . . . good night.'

Just then the skies opened up above the old building and lightning filled the room.

'What was that?'

'Oh, it's just the rain . . . Try and get some sleep.'

'Yeah . . . er . . . good night.'

CRASH . . . The thunder followed. One of those giant, delayed apocalyptic claps that you never forget.

It's funny, I've always enjoyed electric storms. The energy coming from them seems to work its way into my blood. As a boy I used to itch to stand and watch and wait for the next lightning strike, but my mum would always tells me to come away from the windows.

Shirlie by now had her head completely under the covers.

'That's it.' Shirlie had decided that all of this was far too much for her (in her present state of mind). That the whole castle idea was far too 'Hammer House of Horror', and that staying anywhere other than a Holiday Inn just wouldn't settle her down. She could almost see Dracula himself coming down the steps. I have to say that at that moment, as another lightning bolt lit up the room, I could definitely see her point.

It was spooky, and this trip was supposed to help her to recover from the whole 'Wham in China' affair.

I got on the phone and booked us straight on to the first flight to Florida, to the newest, brightest holiday resort the travel agent could come up with. A tennis camp in Minnesota where the creepiest thing was watching the seventy-year-old women follow around the young tennis coaches with their tongues dragging around on the floor. We got into the car and drove away, I looked in the mirror . . . Another time. We drove back to London with the rain pouring in through the convertible top and got on the first plane out. Shirlie was going through the roughest time, and I could only try to help.

Porsche 911s were my passion in those days. They seemed to

represent everything I was – a fast, flash pop star who was taking from the world any exciting things it had to offer – and for me these cars were one of them. If you have never been lucky enough to drive one, they are the closest thing to driving a motorbike, but you're wrapped in a beautiful safety blanket of German protection.

I strayed away from the 911 twice – once to buy an old E-type 4.2, which was magnificent with its shiny red bodywork and chrome wire wheels, and once to buy a Porsche 944. The E-type was beautiful but spent far too many days in the garage having its pipes replaced and minor problems fixed, which was only to be expected, as it was an old car. The 944 was my biggest disappointment. I bought it at four o'clock one Wednesday afternoon and drove it down to Poole, in Dorset, where my mum and dad were now living. On the way back the next day I stopped and with the help of my new tax free wonga traded it in for the first 911 that I could find . . . This pop star excess thing was definitely getting to me.

The only car Shirlie and I bother with these days is one you can get the kids all into and off to school in each morning without them being late . . . I still have the Porsche sunglasses somewhere!

Shirlie and I were married on a cliff top in St Lucia, overlooking the Caribbean Sea. It was 1988, Russian troops were moving out of Afghanistan, Reagan had made his first trip to Russia, bringing an end to the Cold War, and I had just come back from a tour of the world, bringing to an end the promotion for our fifth album, *Through the Barricades*. It had been harder work than the previous tour and somehow not quite the same laugh. The excitement of early mornings in airports and coach rides through a freezing cold Europe had started to wear thin. The record itself didn't do nearly as good business as its predecessor, *Parade*. The singles that were taken from it were all hits, but none had that same sweeping success that 'True' had back in 1984. It seemed that things were starting to slow down, and that the record-buying public had moved on to fresher and younger faces, although we never spoke openly about it in case the reality was too much for us all to handle. It felt as if our roller-coaster car was waiting for the massive chain underneath to pull us once again to the top of the track. But I was happy just to be home, and all things considered, still in one piece. As soon as I got back from the tour I went to my trusted travel agents and booked our trip to the West Indies.

Unfortunately there was no horse-drawn carriage to take Shirlie to the top of the cliff, but a local gardener offered her a lift in his truck instead. I had to smile at the sight of my beautiful bride climbing down from this old wreck of a truck wearing the shortest of white dresses, trying to hang on to her dignity as she wobbled precariously on her stiletto heels.

It was the first time I had seen Shirlie since the night before, when we sat on the beach beneath the stars, got completely sloshed and ended up having the biggest row.

The ceremony, which was conducted in the deepest West Indian accent, was over in moments. The woman minister in her brightly coloured silk dress and giant spectacles raced through the shortened version of the marriage vows so that we could get out of the sun that was starting to tear up our white skin.

'Do you take this beautiful Shirlie to be your bride?'

I was wearing a shirt and tie for the first time in years and it was choking me in the heat. I loosened my collar.

'I do.'

'And you, Shirlie, will you love and look after Martin all your life?'

'I will.'

'Then you are now Man and Wife.'

All that way up the mountain for that – and now we had to walk back down in the blistering midday sun, because the guy in the old red truck had decided to leave. It wasn't a long way, but for Shirlie, in high heels, it was miles.

The fact that we got married on our own prevented the obligatory family arguments at the wedding reception. My brother had got married the year before, and some of my relatives were still not speaking to each other. There's always someone you forget to invite or someone sitting on the wrong table. This way was easier: no one there . . . no arguments.

We got to the bottom of the hill, both sunburnt, both exhausted, but both happy. And that's the way we still are, eleven years later.

That night we ate at a restaurant that was in the most beautiful of settings. It was perched right on the side of a small pond – it looked like the 'Pirates of the Caribbean' ride at Disneyland. The smiling waitress sat us right on the water's edge. The moon shone down, and the crickets were serenading us with their delicate song. It was so romantic, I filled our glasses with champagne and we clinked them together while we stared into each other's eyes. Everything was perfect, until we noticed a man standing by the bar with his back to us. Shirlie and I looked at each other. We had both seen a giant cockroach crawl up this poor man's jacket and climb into his shirt collar and free-fall down his back. Straight away I felt something crawling up my trouser leg. Another giant black cockroach. We were sitting in the middle of a nest! Hundreds of them crawling around our feet. A black shimmering floor of perpetual movement. Shirlie and I jumped up and moved across the empty restaurant to tell the waitress, who was completely unimpressed by the news and offered us some of her best banana pie as a peace offering. She still smiled that Caribbean 'nothing matters' smile and just showed us to another table further back, away from the edge of the pond. It wasn't a great start to dinner, but this was the Caribbean and you grow to accept little things like that.

A couple of minutes later, as an incredible lobster was being delivered to our table, Shirlie poked me in the arm and pointed out that a family from Manchester had just walked in, the older of the two men asking for the best table in the house, just as I had done only half an hour earlier. The waitress, who was still showing her huge white teeth, led them straight to the table with the cockroach nest.

I have to say, they lasted longer than us. They were well into their starters when they began to scream. The insects had found a new

Mancunian home. They were crawling in and out of this woman's heavily hair-sprayed bouffant. The poor people – the insects were everywhere. The only thing the waitress could find to settle them down in her overly relaxed manner, was to walk up to them while they were in a complete state of panic and offer them that free banana pie. If it hadn't been so hilarious I would have cried for them.

We had been trying to bring a little Kemp into the world for the whole of the previous year without any luck. Shirlie had driven my sperm in little plastic canisters down to the doctor at breakneck speed to have them tested while they were still alive, and hopefully kicking. I couldn't go down there in person, I wasn't that brave. I had tried everything to kick the little chaps into gear – cold baths, weeks without taking the top off a bottle of Jack Daniels, anything that might make the magic work, but there was nothing, no response at all. No matter how hard and how often we tried, it looked as if we were going to have to spend our lives without the sound of our own children.

Now on our wedding night, without any help from the old ice pack or baggy boxer shorts, things clicked and one of my little fellows found its way to the top without Shirlie doing handstands at the end of the matrimonial bed or even the old 'wheelbarrow technique' that Shirlie's mum had kindly suggested. It's incredible how things work out when the moment is right, and when our beautiful daughter Harley Moon was conceived our happiness was complete.

My wedding celebrations went on for days when I got home. I'm surprised that Shirlie didn't ask for a divorce. There's a guy called William Hunt who has been one of my best friends for as long as I can remember. It's one of those relationships where we might not see each other or even talk to each other on the phone for six months, but both of us know that the other one is there. He's one of those lucky people who have the precious gift of being able to cheer others up when they're down, lifting them out of a slump or making them laugh when it seems impossible to do so.

William owns a first-class clothes shop in the heart of London's Covent Garden. His clothes are well made and slightly flamboyant, which could even be the right way to describe him. Sometimes he reminds me of a cross between Jean-Paul Gaultier and Bernard Manning. His Mancunian accent has thinned slightly over the years, but his heart is still as full as it ever was. It was with William that I had some of the funniest times, some of the best parties and some of my most outrageous experiences.

One night we were trying to get to a party in the darkest part of South London. Now, South London was a place that I have never quite felt at home in. I've never quite been able to string together its geography. We had come out of a club in the West End, both of us tripping on a tab of ecstasy that had been given to us moments before we left, but this was a boys' night out and boys will do boys' things.

We managed to stop a minicab. It was one of those minicabs that roam around the West End looking for strays trying to get home. The car was an old navy blue Cortina, at least it looked blue under the dancing electric lights from the Cambridge Theatre behind us. I got to it first and opened up the back door and slid into the fur-lined cocoon. William followed me in. The car had that warm smell of fake nylon fur and air freshener that was trying to hide a faint smell of curry that must have been coming from the driver's breath. As the driver turned around we saw an old Indian guy whose turban seemed to grow out of his face, the end of the material turning into his leathery brown skin and wrapping itself around his tiny skeleton. He spoke in a strong accent.

'Where do you want to go, lads?'

William leaned over my lap, his fourteen stone nearly crushing my balls.

'Do you know the Elephant and Castle?'

'Of course I do.'

William started to rummage through his trouser pocket to find the address. The back seat seemed to be getting smaller with every movement.

'Ah, here it is . . . Do you know it?

'I don't, but we will find it when we get over the river.'

I hate it when cab drivers say that – why can't they just look in the A to Z before they leave? – but I was in no state to argue. The most I could do was to breathe a sigh of relief as William climbed down from my bollocks.

We drove through the autumnal rain and across the Thames, looking out at the young lovers and homeless people taking cover together in the shelter of doorways.

'I know what we need.'

William always seemed to know what we needed to get that extra rush. He started to lean forward to talk to the driver. This time I moved over to the other side of the imitation fur seat, protecting my balls from any further assault.

'Do you have any music in here?' William asked.

'You like music?'

'Yeah! Do you know Spandau Ballet?' William replied.

'No . . . Who's that?'

'You don't know Spandau Ballet?'

'No, but I have an Elvis tape. He was the King . . . still is.'

'Oh yeah, put it on,' I said. I wanted to move the conversation away from Spandau Ballet as quickly as I could, and I've loved Elvis ever since I first saw him in *Jailhouse Rock*, the one where he kisses the girl and she asks him why he did that and he turns to her and says, 'It must have been the beast in me.' I remember watching that one Christmas lunchtime and spending the rest of the day with my shirt collar turned up around my ears.

'Elvis will be great,' I said. 'Have you ever heard "Aloha from Hawaii"?'

The driver turned around excited – he had obviously found a soul mate. 'Hey, I love that.'

We once took the horn soundtrack and sampled it for one of the Spandau Ballet records.

146

The Indian driver took his deep brown eyes off the road for longer than I was really happy with and bent down to load his antiquated eight-track cassette player with the 'King'.

William and I looked at each other with a blank, loving look that would seem ridiculous in Marks and Spencers . . . but here, in this travelling nightclub, with the street lights flashing past and the music distorting out of the tiny speakers mounted in each door, it was entirely appropriate.

The three of us, William, myself and the driver, all started to nod our heads in time to the opening bars.

'Because you're all I have, my boy . . . you are my heart, my soul, my joy . . .'

The music started to seep deep into our souls. Every word hit deep into our brains and had the feeling that the writer must have intended but probably never quite believed was possible.

'Oh yes, you're all I have, my boy . . . you are my heart, my soul, my joy.

I could see William close his eyes and soak up the atmosphere. I watched closely as the lines around his mouth creased upwards and that huge northern smile spread across his face. I knew exactly where he was. Exactly how he was feeling.

Suddenly the music became louder and the distortion level far from acceptable even in our state of mind. I looked over at the driver, who was now singing at the top of his voice, and small beads of sweat were starting to drip from under his turban and down his neck, turning his hair into small black rats' tails.

'One more time, please . . . Oh yes, you're all I have my boy . . . you are my heart, my soul, my joy . . .

William was now wide awake and singing along, his arm around my shoulders . . . I felt like I was back in infant school with my best friend walking around the yard singing 'We want more men'.

We were all singing at the very top of our lungs. The car had become a travelling mass of emotion. Suddenly the driver turned around to look me straight in the eye, and tears were rolling down his brown face. He was trying hard to hold on to any composure he had left. With his cute Indian accent and his voice breaking as he tried to raise it above the music he said, 'I wish my son could see me now.'

Then he turned back to the road, and back to Elvis. 'Oh yes, you're all I have, my boy . . .'

The track finished just as we reached the Elephant and Castle, which was moments away from where we were heading. We stopped the cab as the driver stopped his eight-track machine. William and I climbed out of the back seat and into the cold night air as the driver wound down his window.

'How much is that then?'

I looked at our friend, the third member of our small group, and his eyes were bright red and filled with water, his face still sopping wet with tears.

'How much is that then?' William asked.

The driver cleared his throat and wiped his nose.

'Nothing . . . no charge . . . I forgot I could be that happy . . . I only wish that my son could have seen me.'

And with that our friend drove off into the electric horizon. He leaned out of his window for one last time and called back to us, 'Thanks, boys . . . Thank you very very much.'

It's nice to do some good now and then.

The Krays

By the beginning of 1989 the rumours about Gary and I playing the Kray twins in a film were beginning to sound less fanciful.

The Krays movie had been spoken about for as long as the twins themselves had been behind bars. Everyone from Bob Hoskins, to the McGann brothers, to Roger Daltry had been pencilled in to play one of London's most frequently whispered names. But why in a million years were the producers of this long-awaited film about to trust it to Gary and me? After all, it had been years since either of us had attempted to act. We had been on stage thousands of times over the last ten years with the band, and in front of hundreds of rolling cameras around the world, but this didn't give us the right to march in and claim the parts that any self-respecting actor would give his right arm to take on. Acting is a completely different skill from being a musician, as Sting and Bowie and countless other ambitious rock stars had found out to their dismay.

Gary and I were brothers, but we certainly didn't look like twins. There were so many options available to the producers of the film as regards to casting these golden roles, that even I had to wonder why they were interested in us.

In 1986 we were shooting a series of pop promos for three of the tracks off the *Parade* record: 'Highly Strung', which was to be set in Hong Kong, 'Only When You Leave', which was back in London,

149

and then 'I'll Fly for You', for which we were going to one of the most exciting places in the world, New Orleans. All of these videos had budgets around the £100,000 to £150,000 mark. Our contract ensured that the whole of the video budget was picked up by the record company as promotion, so of course the sky was the limit when it came to ideas. These days, a band is lucky if they get the record company to pay half.

The producers on these shoots were a bunch of young guys called Fugitive. One of them, Dominic Anciano, was good friends with Steve Dagger, and between them they came up with the whole concept of the movie and, more importantly to us, of placing Gary and me in the title roles. These though were very early days. We had nothing, no script, no finance, and the rights to the Krays story were still in the hands of Roger Daltry, but like I said these were very early days and a lot of water was yet to pass under the bridge.

It was out in New Orleans that I came eye to eye with one of nature's living nightmares. We were working inside this amazing putrefied forest. A swampy lake covered in thick green algae clung to the base of hundreds of petrified trees, all with moss hanging from their branches. It was like something out of a *Star Wars* movie. For this particular shot, the director wanted me to lie on a log in the middle of the swamp with the quintessential young video model towering above me. I had no trouble with that, I mean it looked amazing, and with the smoke being blown in and the soundtrack being pumped out of two huge speakers it was almost inviting.

It was only as I lay on the log that I realized just how unsafe it was. The log was ready to roll over at any moment, and on closer inspection the algae that sat on the surface of the lake really stank. The director shouted at the model and myself, 'Are you OK?'

'Let's just do this and get it over, can we?'

'Can you both lie down on the log?'

'I don't think so, I don't think there's room.'

'How about if she kneels?' the director said.

'I don't think so . . . I don't think this log is that safe.'

'OK . . . OK . . . just do what you can. Give me some movement.'

They rolled the track, and it sounded eerie as it echoed around the putrefied forest.

'Action . . .'

The model started to move, trying to make her way down to me, and the fucking log started to sway. It was like being on a lopsided dingy.

It was then that I saw something move – a smaller log floating towards us. It had some algae and moss twisted around its bark, but it was strange how it was the only thing in the lake apart from us that was making ripples on the surface.

'We're going to go for one more,' I heard them shout from the bank as they played the opening chords of 'I'll Fly for You'. Then like a true professional I forgot about what was going on around me and got on with my job.

This time as the model started to make her way down to me I noticed a glint of apprehension on her face. In fact she had frozen in fear. That log that had been floating towards us earlier was now right next to us. I turned my head to the side and there it was – I was eyeball to eyeball with an alligator. The whole swamp was infested with the things. I didn't move as we looked at each other for a few moments, and I felt my heart pound in my ears and my breathing stop. It was a few moments although it seemed like an eternity before the alligator had decided that it had seen enough and went back along its way.

'We want to do one more,' I heard them call through the smoke.

I stood up slowly. 'No. Enough's enough.'

The relief on the girl's face echoed my own, and we were brought back to the shore by the small rowing boat that had dropped us there twenty minutes earlier.

By early 1989 Shirlie had grown into an enormous woman, she was almost unrecognizable in the last days of her pregnancy. She was so huge, I was making plans to look after triplets. She was big, but incredibly beautiful.

Shirlie found the weight hard to cope with, it was bringing her down. She has always had more energy than anyone I have ever known, and to be chained to a sofa was simply killing her. I could feel daggers in my back every time I walked out of the house. I had to keep reassuring her that she would be even more miserable if she wasn't pregnant. Only eight months earlier both of us had been so excited on finding out that we were going to have a baby. I remember coming home and seeing a small test tube on the shelf in the bathroom with a little brown ring in the bottom of it. I treated that test tube as if it was the baby itself. The next day, when I came home from the studio and found that Shirlie had washed the small glass tube out, I was heart-broken. I felt as though she had poured the baby down the sink. We had seen the last scans several weeks before and had stood in tearful wonder, as do every other expecting couple, at the enormity of what we were looking at. Now every day was a slog for her, and for me.

By now Fugitive had acquired the rights to the Krays movie and had a script written by a young writer called Philip Ridley. Everyone was overjoyed at the script, which was fantastic, and everything we wanted. It wasn't a shoot 'em up movie, and it certainly didn't glamorize the twins' violence – which we all knew could have been the one major pitfall. It was the perfect script.

Gary and I felt that we had better do something about working on our acting skills. After all, it had been years since we had even tried to act, and I for one wasn't sure if I still had it in me. We called up Anna Scher, our old coach, and arranged some private lessons with a few other young guys from the school. It was the strangest thing walking back into that place. The school was in a different building now, but the smell, the boxes of wigs and hats and the old upright piano were exactly the same. It was as if we had walked into a time warp.

Once the 'how are you, haven't seen you for years' thing was out of the way with Anna and her husband Charles, it was time to get down to some serious work. Charles had Gary and me going through the same warm-up exercises that we had gone through when we were seven-year-old boys. It was in some ways a very warm experience, to be taken back to the beginning. After all, this was the woman who had originally lit the fire inside Gary and me. We owed her everything, and I would go so far as to say that Spandau Ballet would not have existed without her.

Charles took the lesson on that first day. After the warm-up was over and we had shaken out any nerves that we both had, Charles asked us to sit on the floor crossed-legged and pretend that we were seven years old . . . in fact, Ron and Reg at seven years old. I sat down in front of Gary and looked at him in the eyes, this was some kind of weird therapy. There was something powerful happening in my head and it was scaring me. Improvisation was the main stem of Anna's workshops; I don't think I can remember once working from a script.

As we started to act out playing children, I realized we were just doing what we used to do. We weren't acting, we were just reliving. We were revisiting our past and it was fantastic. All the arguments we had over the years, all the fights we had since the day I was born seemed to fade away into insignificance. I found hard to hold back the tears as I realized just how much he meant to me, just how much we had been through together and just how much still lay in store for both of us over the rest of our lives. It suddenly came to us that Ron and Reg Kray were no different from us as children, so if we used that as our grounding then the task in front of us was a lot less daunting.

In the afternoon Charles had us working on several different aspects of the characters, including their complicated emotions. I was really starting to enjoy myself. I had shaken off any fears I might have had that morning and was now looking forward to any task Charles would throw at me.

For me acting has always been an intuitive thing. It isn't something that I plan my way through, it just happens and pours out of my body as a natural, instinctive process. I think it comes from learning the skill at an early age. The hardest thing when you work from an intuitive angle is that different emotions can really hurt, as you take the character's emotions, filter them through your own, and find yourself knocking the scabs off old wounds that have been covered up for years. It's sometimes an incredibly painful process, but one which has to be done to achieve success.

I walked out of Anna's that first day with mixed feelings of excitement and fulfilment that I hadn't felt for years. All of that time in Dublin, all of that awful frustration seemed so far away. I felt as if it was at the beginning of the yellow brick road and the Munchkins were showing me the way.

I went home for a couple of hours to check on the size of Shirlie and then went back to the studio that afternoon to work on a new song with the rest of the boys. It felt strange after the morning's class with Anna and Charles, almost as if, by straying away for a brief moment from the thing that I'd wished so hard for, I'd committed adultery. We were recording some songs for what was to be our final record, 'Heart like a Sky', and things were moving as slowly as usual. I had already put down the bass guitar tracks a few weeks before, so for me the recording was over. I couldn't wait for the next trip to Anna's.

Ron and Reg were keen boxers when they were growing up, so Gary and I suggested that to play these roles properly we needed to get into a boxing ring and soak up some of that unique atmosphere. Boxers have a way of holding themselves that travels with them outside the ring. It's almost as if their centre of gravity is a lot lower than that of anyone around them. You can spot a boxer from a mile off, in the way he walks, the way he shrugs his shoulders and small mannerisms that become part of a boxer's persona. The Kray twins had all of this and more. It was an integral part of their make-up. There was so much to explore, and this seemed like a good enough place to start.

In the meantime, Fugitive had arranged for us to meet Charlie Kray, the eldest of the brothers. He could among other things give us a first-hand account of his side of the story, as well as some valuable advice on some of Ron and Reg's more unique manner-isms. Charlie had done a twelve-year prison sentence for playing his part in the twins' empire and was enjoying his freedom when we worked together on the movie. I was as stunned as anyone when he was recently put away for another twelve years for drug running. He was a nice guy to me and Gary, and helped us with any questions we had about the twins, the firm and London in general in the early Sixties. He was a valuable source of information, but Gary and I both knew that there were two people that could help us even more, and that we had to meet . . . Ron and Reg.

Fugitive had promised us a meeting with the top men at some point, but when? Reg was locked up on the Isle of Wight, a Category A prisoner who was only allowed one visitor every two weeks, and Ron was locked away in London's Broadmoor hospital.

Meanwhile Charlie had arranged for Gary and me to go over to Whitechapel and meet the twins' Aunt May. She was played in the movie by Charlotte Cornwell. This old woman was a remarkable character, with a zest for life that I hadn't seen for years. On the way over to Aunt May's house, Gary and I were stopped by the police while we sat in the back of a minicab, as the car circled the entrances to several tower blocks. Each of us was wearing a black suit with dark sunglasses and carrying a small bunch of flowers.

One of the policemen put his head in the window. 'Can I help you boys?'

'Yeah, we're looking for Mrs Kray.'

'Who – old May Kray?'

'Yeah, do you know her?'

The two policemen looked at one another and then back at us . . .

'It's the Kray brothers, isn't it?' The policeman shook his head and smiled to himself. ' . . . I mean the Kemp brothers?'

'Yeah, do you know her?'

'Yeah, follow us.'

We followed the small police car until it took us to Aunt May's tower block. She was a wonderful character, a creature from a different era with a fantastic insight into the twins. She opened up her private photo albums and showed us pictures of Ron and Reg from when they were babies, right through to the height of their control over London. There was one thing that most of the pictures from the later years had in common. In most of the group photos there were people missing, each figure cut out of the photograph, leaving a perfect silhouette. May didn't mention the holes in the photographs and quickly moved the subject along when I asked her about them.

'They turned Queen's evidence, luvvie . . . Horrible men.'

Everyone who had turned against the twins at the end had been neatly removed from the photographs with a sharp pair of sewing scissors.

Charlie Kray arrived after about half an hour, and May brewed up more tea in her best china. I made May laugh by telling her how the police had given us an escort to her flat and how she must be famous.

'Oh, they all knew me around here, luv.'

Charlie joined in. 'That's true . . . they all know her.'

May carried on, her eyes sparkling with the memories. 'You should have seen it when the trial was going on . . . I had the old bill 'round here every day.'

'I bet that was a pain in the neck, May?' I said.

'No . . . you're joking, I loved it . . . I was like some kind of movie star . . . Marilyn Monroe. You should have seen me in my furs and skins . . . Most excitement I've ever had, luvvie.'

When I got home that evening Shirlie had left a message on the pad next to the phone. 'I have gone to the doctors, nothing to worry about. Fugitive have a meeting for you tomorrow. PS Dinner was in the oven, but I ate it!' Could this be it? Was this the meeting with Ron and Reg that I was waiting for? I called the office straight away. It wasn't exactly what I wanted, but Gary and I were booked to start boxing training with the one-time welterweight champion of the world, John H. Stracey.

Later that night, with my stomach full of takeaway pizza and my back full of daggers, I went back out. I popped into the studio to see the band for a while, Gary had beaten me there and was sitting in his chair in front of the mixing desk. It was the captain's chair, whoever sat there took on this strange power and became a megalomaniac.

Gary sat there for years. He was in complete control of the band, but then why shouldn't he be? He wrote every song on every record apart from one, a track on the last album called 'Motivator', that Steve Norman wrote. Sometimes you could have been forgiven for thinking that Spandau Ballet was a fascist state and that Gary was the all-powerful leader. It wasn't all his fault. In the early years the rest of the band didn't want to take control, myself include. Then, at the time of the Dublin rehearsals, when we did want more of a say, we just couldn't find it in us. I was depressed, and the others . . . well, they all have their own side of the story. The band was Gary's and it always would be. His songs, his ideas, his momentum. Even if we brought in a producer to even out the balance of power, before long we would still be making Gary's record, sounding Gary's way. He had a knack of controlling everyone in that 'control' room.

I always knew that my input into the band was a much more physical thing. It was based on my looks. I was the pop star portion of the band. From those first early interviews and covers on *The Face* and *Just Seventeen* I knew where my hat would be hung, even though my hook was made of the most flimsy of materials. It always takes more than just one man to form a band. A band is about chemistry, it's a formula, and without all of the pieces in place it just doesn't work, no matter how small some of those pieces might be. We've often seen an enormous band split up, so that the members can go solo, only to discover that without the other parts of the molecular set-up the public just isn't interested. After Spandau split, both Gary and Tony had poor receptions to their solo efforts.

That night in the studio there was a strange atmosphere. The room had a weird electricity, just like moments before an earthquake hits, when a cold chill runs up the back of your spine and makes the hair on your neck stand on end. It was as if the other guys had discovered my affair, had found out that I had been cheating on them. They were quiet, and I could feel that they just didn't want to talk about this huge thing that was happening in my life. I could understand it to a certain extent. Spandau had become terra firma for all of us. Now all of us in the band knew that the foundations we had built up over the last ten years of our lives were moving slightly. It was an uncomfortable feeling even for myself, but it was also something that I couldn't stop, and didn't want to. I needed a way to give my life some substance, a way in which I could experience success and call it my own. After all, in a few years my face wouldn't be that of a pretty teenager any more, and I didn't write songs.

John H met Gary and me at the door of the gym. He had put on a few pounds since I had seen him win his championship belt on TV. It was a fantastic fight at Wembley Arena against José 'Mantequilla' Napoles. The whole of England cried for him that night, as his trainers and friends lifted his super-fit body on to their shoulders in a victory lap of honour. I have always found boxing a thrilling sport to watch. A sport? Well, it seems like a sport when I sit in front of the TV and call for blood, but now, as the thought of getting into the ring hit me full in the face, I wasn't that sure.

Our sports bags were slung over our shoulders, filled with the new red boxing equipment that we had picked up the day before, as we entered the gym. Now I had been in a thousand gyms around the world, but this one definitely smelt different. It had a much thicker atmosphere. It was, after all, a place where you came to hurt and be hurt. Now I wasn't very good at the latter. I had been a pampered pop star for the last decade, so what was I doing putting on a pair of boxing gloves and climbing into a ring with Mr Stracey, even if it was just to spar? I looked at the hundreds of photos that hung around the gymnasium. They all showed moments of triumph and pain, the victor dancing in the blood of his slain opponent. I could feel my head start to thump, as it always did when I was under stress.

After the formalities and niceties that seemed to drag on were over, John's puffy face dropped; his smile and his expression suddenly changed.

'If you two want to get changed, I think you should get in the ring with each other . . . so I can see what you both look like.'

Christ . . . he wanted me to get in there and fight Gary.

The giant hand on the oversized clock made its way around to the top and a small electronic bell rang out. I took a look back at the rest of the gym, everyone had stopped their workouts and had gathered around the ropes. Gary was in the opposite corner. I looked into his eyes that shone out from under his red headgear. I couldn't believe it, he actually looked serious. There was no way I was going to lay into my brother for the enjoyment of the lads that were watching. I looked again at Gary, and I tried to send him thought waves, telling him that I wasn't going to hit him as hard as I could, that if he held his gloves up we could get away with a gentle spar.

I had fought with Gary thousands of times over the years, but there was always some kind of justifiable argument or meaning behind it. When we were on tour and the feelings between the band members were running high, and the tensions needed releasing, Gary and I would always end up in a fight.

Boxing in a ring was a different thing entirely. I was still trying to let Gary see that I was smiling at him. It wasn't the easiest thing to do with my head guard hiding my face, my mouth stuffed up with a plastic gum-shield. Gary's expression was one that I hadn't seen before: a glazed, almost removed look that frightened me. I had the distinct impression that he meant business. I knew Gary too well – he wouldn't want to embarrass himself in front of the crowd that had now gathered around the ring. After the first punch came flying through the air, I knew it was for real. We fought like two hardened warriors fighting for our lives. Right hooks, straight lefts, uppercuts to the chin, left jabs into the body – it was hit or be hit.

When the big hands on the giant clock reached the two-minute mark and the electronic buzzer sounded, Gary and I didn't even hear it, we carried on fighting until John H had to pull us apart. I heard him turn and talk to the crowd, who were quite concerned that this friendly bout was getting out of hand.

'It's OK, they're brothers,' he said, as if that made everything all right. The crowd sighed with relief and watched us fight on through the break.

My shoulders were killing me just from holding up my guard that was starting to drop by the second. Then, before I knew it, I was hit by a blow that must have sent my brain smashing into the side of my skull. My senses left me, my eyes couldn't see the next one coming and I was hit again. I noticed that the first punch hurts, but the second and third are almost nice. It's as if your body has been anaesthetized in anticipation of moments to come.

'OK . . . that's enough,' I heard John call out. And then, just as Gary let his guard down and was about to turn and walk away the victor, I caught him by surprise with a good straight right hand . . . nasty but necessary. After that we only sparred with John. It was an honour to be in there with this former world champ. I made the most of the experience, but left after every session with a stonking great headache.

The most rewarding thing that came out of those sessions was being able to meet some of those great boxing characters. To be able to observe how they held themselves, how they shook hands, said goodbye and showed affection for one another – all of this was valuable to me as I prepared for the role of Reg Kray.

It was funny, but there was never any argument or even the smallest discussion as to which of us was going to play Reg and who was going to play Ron. There was certain aspects of the two characters that we could both align ourselves to, and besides, Gary's eyebrows met in the middle just like Ronnie's.

I was glad that I was not just having to play the schizophrenic gangster. I liked the fact that Reg had a softer side to his personality, as I felt there was more depth to play around with and a chance to construct a deeper character study. We went back to Anna Scher's several more times over the next few months. My confidence was growing as an actor and also as a person. Anna had helped me conquer some of the rigours of puberty as a teenager, and was now giving me a platform to stand on as an adult. We were in the middle of the day's class when Dominic came through the doors and told us that he had arranged for us to meet the man himself . . . Ronnie Kray.

It was a cold overcast day and the wind was whistling along the giant walls of Broadmoor prison. The giant gate towered above us as Gary and I waited our turn to be taken inside, to come face to face with the man they called the Colonel. There wasn't much of a queue waiting to get into the prison that morning, but Broadmoor is a prison hospital and visiting is a lot more relaxed than in other, ordinary prisons.

The small side door swung open and a guard called us through. Gary and I signed our names in the book and walked through another cage-like door into a corridor. The smell of the dinners cooking in the kitchens and the white painted expanse of brick wall reminded me of being back at school, waiting in the corridor to see the headmaster. A few more people came through the mesh wire door and stood beside us. I thought to myself just how lucky I was that this was going to be a one-off visit, and how awful it must be to do it on a regular basis. I felt almost guilty of something – I wasn't quite sure what – in the same way I always do when I walk through customs at the airport.

I looked around. I had met many famous people over the years, had spoken informally with Charles and Diana the time the band played for the Prince's Trust charity, some of my closest friends were the biggest stars in the world, but meeting Ronnie Kray made me nervous. I knew so much about him, about his family and friends and the world that he lived in. I had every detail of his life embedded in my head. I had read *The Profession of Violence* countless times and was now about to meet the man for myself. I was going to play his brother. I wondered whether he would look at me and laugh. I mean I didn't look like Reg, and Gary and I didn't look like twins; I didn't want to disappoint him. This was the story of his life, and no matter what the man had done he deserved to be represented correctly, the same as anyone else.

I looked at Gary. We might not be twins, in fact there are two years separating us, but there had been times when it almost seemed as if we were. I remembered one Christmas many years ago when Gary was lying on the sofa with an incredible back pain. He must have been sixteen, and had just discovered the pleasure of real ale. He was in terrible pain and the following day went to the hospital for an X-ray. The doctor told him that he only had one kidney and the sheer volume of beer he had drunk the night before had given him the pain, a kind of fluid overload. Two years later I had the same pain. When I went for my X-ray, they discovered that on the side where Gary didn't have a kidney, I had two, so I had three in all. It was as if our maker, after realizing he had mis-counted, had stuffed Gary's missing kidney into me, hoping that I would hand it on to him . . . Strange, but true, and that's the closest Gary and I are to being twins. We are very different people in a million ways, right through from our colouring to our very different personalities.

A guard appeared from the opposite end of the corridor and looked at me. 'Who have you come to see?'

I felt strange, I felt as if he thought I might be one of those hundreds of people that had just come to stare and please their morbid fascinations.

'Ronnie Kray,' I said.

'OK, follow me.'

The security guard led us into a huge open room where there were several tables, at which families were spending time with some of the other inmates. It looked like my school dining-room; they even had some of the same grey plastic chairs that used to hurt my back.

Gary and I followed the guard to a table at the back of the room, and there behind it was the man himself. He stood up to meet us, and he was much smaller than I had pictured him. I had read that Ron was only a small man, but this still surprised me. He was also a lot thinner than his pictures. His heavy bloated bulldog look had been exchanged for the frail frame of a man who had spent years on medication, and had been institutionalized and locked up for most of his adult life. Still, in front of me was the man who with his brother Reggie ruled London's underworld during the first part of the Sixties with an iron fist. No one did anything, stole anything, or said a word out of place without consulting them first. It was written in stone that they were the bosses and that was that. The man facing us was a legend who ranked alongside Al Capone and Bugsy Siegel. We smiled . . . He smiled back.

Gary and I shook hands with Ronnie.

'Hello boys . . . sit down.'

Ronnie's white shirt was neatly pressed, and the embroidered R.K. on his breast pocket stood out proudly under the fluorescent light.

I sat down. I was right, the chair dug into my kidneys at exactly the same place it did during my years at grammar school.

I spoke first. 'How are you, Ron?'

'He smiled. 'Gooood, gooood.' Ronnie seemed to have a habit of stretching out his words, making them two or three times as long as they should be.

'Would you like a drink boys? . . . Tea, beer – it's non-alcoholic, but it's quite nice?'

'Tea would be fine, thanks,' we both said in a strange unison.

An orderly in a white coat came over and took the order down on a piece of paper.

'Well, boys,' Ron said, 'they told me you were good looking . . . gooood, gooood.'

'Don't worry about that,' I said, 'once they put the make-up on for the movie, you know, we'll look more like you.'

Shit, did I just insult the man in the first couple of minutes? If I did, it seemed to go over his head. He came in closer and lit his extra-long Rothmans cigarette with a pretty gold lighter.

'So, Charlie told me that you went to see May?'

Gary answered. 'Yeah, she's a lovely woman, Ron. She reminds me of our old nan in a lot of ways.'

'Gooood, Gooood . . . Where are you from then, boys?'

'Essex Road . . . Islington.'

'Oh yes, I know it well.'

'It's changed a bit since you last saw it, Ron, it's far more middle-class,' I said.

'Yessss, goooood.'

Ron's smoke was drifting right into my face and finding its way up my nostrils. I've never smoked in my life, in fact it's always made me feel quite sick.

'Is my smoke worrying you?' Ron said.

'No . . . of course not.'

Ronnie came in even closer, and the smoke from his cigarette drifted out of his mouth and run up his nose in one continuous cycle. This time he lowered his voice to a whisper.

'Don't feel frightened, boys . . . Ask me what you want, I want to help, Charlie has seen the script, he says it's great . . . goood.'

The orderly reappeared carrying a tray with three teas and about ten cans of non-alcoholic beer.

'Twenty pounds, please.'

I looked at Gary – we hadn't ordered that. The orderly quietly explained. 'The beers are for Mr Kray . . . He likes me to put them in his room.'

'No problem . . . of course.'

I took my and Gary's tea and sat down again, while the orderly put Ron's tea in front of him. I looked at Ronnie's hands, which were starting to shake, not badly, but enough to make me wonder just how he would cope with his cup of tea. Gary picked up where we had left off.

'Ron, one question I wanted to ask you, what did you do after you had killed George Cornell?'

I went cold. Sure, Ron had said ask him anything, but, we'd only known the man for a few minutes . . .

'Cornell . . . He was a bad man, he did a lot of wrong to a lot of people . . . He worked for the Richardsons, tortured people, stuff like that . . . know what I mean? Listen, he would have done your

164

mother if he had the chance, he was doing good people . . . I had to stop him.'

I could see that Gary had hit on a nerve. Ron rubbed his hands together nervously as the memory raced through his brain.

'We went back to a boozer we used to go to . . . it was safe, it was closed up for the night . . . We went into the back room and switched on the radio to see if it had come over the news while some of the boys gave me some fresh clothes. Y'know, I had blood on my shirt so I had to get rid of it.'

Ron rubbed his shaking hands together and looked at Gary and me with a removed stare. It was as if he had stopped talking to us, but was telling himself the story.

'And then it came over the radio that they had found Cornell in the Blind Beggar pub. A huge cheer went up and I told everyone to be quiet, I wanted to find out if he was dead.'

'Why? Were you having second thoughts, were you worried he might be?'

'Noooooo, I mean, if he wasn't, I'd have to go back and do him again.'

I could see Ron was getting more and more agitated thinking about the Cornell killing, so I thought I might change the subject.

'Do you get to speak to Reg much these days?'

Ron relaxed and sat back in his chair and lit another Rothmans extra-long.

'Yesss . . . We write to each other every day, and speak on the phone sometimes . . . It's hard, though, because those bastards have got him as a Cat A prisoner, no privileges . . . nothing . . . They still watch him have a shit . . . bastards.'

I turned to have a look around the room.

'What's it like here?'

Before Ron answered, suddenly I realized who was sitting on the table across the room. The Yorkshire Ripper. I recognized him straight away, even though in the flesh, and with a woman on the chair next to him, he looked almost innocent. As Ron spoke I reflected on what a weird situation I was in. Sitting in Broadmoor talking to Ronnie Kray about murder with the Yorkshire Ripper sitting right behind me. This wasn't *Saturday Morning Superstore*.

'It's not bad here. They let you have a TV in your room.'

'Do you think they'll let you see the movie when it's finished?'

'I don't think so . . . If they do they might let me see it on my own.'

The orderly had noticed that Ron's hands were starting to shake quite badly and came over to the table.

'It's time for your medication, Mr Kray.'

'Yessss . . . goooood.'

I could see in his eyes that his concentration was wandering and that it was time to go.

'Yeah, it's time we made a move.'

We hadn't spoken for long, but what we saw was enough. Above all, we felt that Ronnie had sanctioned the movie and was happy to let Gary and me dig deeper into his life. Meeting Ronnie was an experience, but for me it wasn't one I thought would help us in the movie. Ronnie was a different man now. The man we wanted to portray was in his thirties, lived in the Swinging Sixties and was completely invincible. I decided not to meet Reggie. Apart from the fact that his visiting hours were precious, I didn't think it would help me much. After all, I didn't want to mimic his actions like a second-rate Rory Bremner, and he would now be a very different man from the Reggie Kray I had to portray.

We walked out of Broadmoor and I felt the wind whistle around my ears. I thought to myself, 'Why don't they show young kids the inside of a prison?' One walk around a place like that would deter anyone from a life of crime.

By now the movie was nearly on top of us. Everything was in place, including the cast, with the fabulous Billie Whitelaw taking on the role of the twins' doting mother, Violet Kray. The press were gearing up another 'free the Krays' campaign, and there were even questions in the House of Commons as to whether or not the film should be allowed to go ahead. Everything was coming to a climax.

People on the street stopped me to wish me luck or to ask when the movie would be on the screen. Everyone in London it seemed was hyped up about this long-awaited movie, on a subject that seemed to assume almost mythical proportions for Londoners from all walks of life.

London's famous taxi-cab drivers had more advice to give me than anyone else. Every Londoner knows the feeling of watching that driver's window being slid back, and the sound of the radio being switched off before you hear those cabbie tones . . . 'All right mate? . . . Busy? . . . It's dead out here today . . . You'll never guess who I had in here the other day . . . Yeah, I get all sorts in this cab – funny, innit?'

There was one piece of advice I heard from a cab driver that I'll never forget. He was in his early forties and had a strong Bethnal Green accent. I was on my way to a wardrobe fitting at a costumiers called Morris Angel on Shaftesbury Avenue. I hadn't been in there since I was a small boy, when they dressed me for a part in a BBC 'Play for Today', based on the life of Katherine Mansfield. I hated it, being squeezed into a tiny pair of nineteenth-century knicker-bockers and having my feet pushed into a pair of shoes that were four sizes too small.

'It's OK, you only have to wear them for two days.'

When they had finished dressing me up and I saw myself in the mirror, I felt a complete prat. I didn't want this, I wanted to be Bruce Lee, but I looked more like a character on the Dick Emery show. I certainly wasn't going to tell anyone to watch out for me on TV.

This time, though, I was on my way to be fitted in some beautiful handmade suits, three-button Sixties jobs, and I didn't have a problem with that, as long as the shoes fitted. The window in the taxi-cab slid back and the radio was turned down.

'All right mate? . . . Busy? . . . It's dead out here!'

I was waiting for the next bit.

' 'Ere, ain't you Gary Kemp?'

'Martin.'

'I knew you were one of those Kemp twins . . . I recognized you the second you got in . . . Funny, innit?'

I've been mistaken for Gary all my life. When we were boys my aunts and uncles used to call me Gary and mix the two of us up, so this wasn't something new.

'How's that movie going? You started it yet?'

'No, but . . .'

'Which one are you? The gay one?'

'No, I'm . . .'

'He's in Parkhurst that one, ain't he?'

'No, that one is . . .'

'They were the salt of the earth, those boys . . . there wasn't any of this mugging old ladies in those days, y'know, you could leave your front door wide open.'

I thought to myself, if I had a pound for every time I heard that!

'I'll tell you a story about the twins. They used to live just up the road from my Auntie Doreen, she used to leave her door . . .'

'I know – wide open.'

'Yeah.'

I sat back into the slippery leather seat and tried not to smile.

'Anyway my Aunt Doreen was friends with a neighbour of theirs and she told my mother a very closely guarded secret, something no one has ever mentioned in any of the books . . .'

I thought to myself, you never know, I might be on to something here, it might be a revelation that could change the whole concept of the twins, change the movie. I had to give the man a chance. After all, he sounded sincere enough and I was in the back of his cab. How wonderful it would be to walk into the studio with this piece of information that no one had apart from me . . . How many points would that be worth?

'What was that then?'

I closed the cab window to block out the sound of the West End traffic and I waited for his next few words.

The driver's voice lowered to a growling whisper. 'Do you know where the twins used to get their secret powers from?'

I was bemused but enthralled. 'No . . . Where?'

The driver took a moment, looking out of his window as if he was checking that no one could hear what he was about to say.

'I'll tell you. Their mum, who was a wonderful woman by the way, made them drink every last drop of the water that she had cooked their greens in.'

I tried hard not to laugh, at least until he dropped me in Shaftesbury Avenue . . . Another tale, another myth, that's exactly what the twins are. I could feel the pressure building. It was as if we were making a film that was going to represent Londoners every-where. It had to be right, it had to be good – *I* had to be good . . .

Shirlie had gone through a week of the most unbearable pain leading up to the birth, and like all expectant fathers, the most I could find to say was 'Are you all right, darling?'

I had been in incredible pain with a sympathetic toothache that felt like my head was about to explode with every pump of my heart. Taking care of Shirlie, getting ready for the movie and trying to seem enthusiastic towards Spandau Ballet was really taking its toll. I hadn't been anywhere near the studio for weeks. I really couldn't see the point of going in just to make a toasted cheese sandwich and play pool for two hours – I had other things to do.

On the morning of 18 August Shirlie woke me up . . . 'I don't know how many toes I have.' She was looking at her fingers. 'I can't think straight, I don't know what I'm saying.'

It looked as if Shirlie had some kind of delirium. I thought it might be due to the fact that she had only slept about thirty minutes in the last thirty-six hours. The poor thing had been going through hell the last few days. Men really don't have any idea what a woman has to go through to give us these incredible gifts.

'Martin, help me, I can't see properly.'

We jumped out of bed, I got her dressed and pulled on an old pair of track suit bottoms and a T-shirt. I had just opened the door when, FLASH, a camera goes off in my face. Three Japanese girls had decided to camp outside the house.

'Do you mind if we take a picture with you and Shirlie?' their leader said.

'Yes.'

'Good, can we stand in the middle?'

'No, you don't understand, I do mind.'

'Just one?'

'NO!' I shouted.

Their faces said it all, they more than likely called me every name under the sun and never bought another Spandau record ever again, but this wasn't the time or the place. I squeezed Shirlie into the car, the young Japanese snapping away with their Nikons, and raced down to the Garden Hospital in Hendon. It was a natural birthing hospital for mothers who really wanted to be in touch with their pain. That was a strange concept for me, as I am one of those people who take the view that if there is a drug around, then use it; but that was what Shirlie wanted, so I was willing to run with it. Shirlie was freaking out beside me as I drove the short distance to the hospital.

'What's happening to me?'

'Don't worry, it'll be OK . . . I promise.'

Shirlie had her hand up in front of her face.

'Martin, I can't count my toes.'

'They're your fingers, darling.'

Shirlie burst into tears. I should have played along. I wasn't able to say the right thing all week and things weren't about to change.

The doctor, Yeheudi Gordon, a very big name in this natural pain, I mean, natural birthing treatment, sent us to a friend of his who performed cranial osteopathy. By the time we got there, Shirlie was having trouble seeing out of her left eye. It was scaring me, something needed to be done and fast, before this got any worse. Now, I understood what osteopathy was, I had been cracked and twisted hundreds of times in an attempt to straighten out my back, but cranial osteopathy was something I had never seen. The practitioner lays his hands on the patient and tells them he is busy adjusting the fluids moving around inside the spinal column, while it looks to all the world as if he is busy doing nothing.

I've always been rather sceptical when it comes to 'new age' healing. I've always found it rather like being asked to try on the Emperor's new clothes, that you're obliged to say just how great you feel and how much better you are for having the treatment, before you hand over thirty pounds.

Shirlie was lying on the bed in the middle of the room with her head in the hands of the cranial osteopath. I was sitting on a chair by the wall underneath a huge waiting room Monet poster, and I waited, I waited and I waited for him to do something. He just sat there with his eyes closed. I couldn't believe it. What was the man doing? We had been sent to a fuckin' witch doctor by the man who was going to deliver our baby in the next couple of days.

I could feel myself getting more and more uptight. I knew I couldn't just sit there and watch Shirlie suffer without doing something.

'Are you all right, darling?'

I knew full well that she needed to see a proper doctor – this was ridiculous – then, suddenly, I heard her voice, a quiet whisper at first and then much louder, much stronger.

'Martin . . . Martin.'

'Are you OK? How do you feel?' I said sheepishly.

'Better, my eyesight's coming back . . . yeah, I feel better.'

I looked at the osteopath out of the corner of my eye. I could see a slight smirk on the side of his face . . . he knew what I had been thinking, he had seen my face go purple at the sight of him stroking Shirlie's hair.

'Mr Kemp, your wife's going to be fine . . . It feels like the baby is ready to come . . . She's just experienced a kind of shut-down, everything is getting too much for her tiny body and it just needed a rest.'

I relaxed a little and exhaled for the first time in about an hour.

'I wouldn't be surprised if it came tonight.'

'Are you all right, darling?'

He was right, that night the final bouts of excruciatingly painful contractions pushed our daughter free from her cosy home of the last nine and a half months. That smell I shall never forget. It was almost like I could remember making that same first journey myself. It had fired up a part of my memory that I would not have believed was still there. The warmness, the blood, the security. That pungent odour seemed to envelope every corner of the room with incredible love, and I cried like a baby as Harley was put straight into Shirlie's tired arms. We had decided on the name Harley a couple of weeks back, while we were out taking our Doberman for a walk over Hampstead Heath.

I could hear Yeheudi Gordon say something from behind Shirlie.

'Lots of women struggle at this time of the month . . . It's a very painful time.

'What?'

I looked at Shirlie who was exhausted, beat up, but beautiful.

'What?'

'It's a very painful time . . . A full moon.'

OK, he had my attention.

'Excuse me?'

'It's the pull of the moon on the waters, it causes all sorts of trouble, all sorts of different types of pain.'

I smiled and turned back to Shirlie. 'Are you all right, darling?'

That night as I drove the couple of miles home, back to our house in Muswell Hill, sure enough the biggest harvest moon sat up in the corner of the sky, throwing it's giant gold and silver rays down, lighting up the cold North London streets. The next day we proudly announced to our bemused family that our beautiful little girl would be called Harley Moon.

We started filming in the October of 1989 on the cliffs of Dover. As I waited in my caravan for the skies to clear so that we could make some kind of start, I passed the time by writing in my diary. I had forgotten, or never noticed when I was a kid, just how much hanging about you do when you're making a film . . .

I have just had the ten-minute warning, which could mean anything from ten minutes to two hours, but here I am and here I shall wait. The black crochet tie around my neck is just that bit too tight and my starched white shirt is cutting into my neck. I can't make my mind up as to whether I look like Reggie Kray or a turkey ready to swing from the butcher's shop window. My mouth is dry and my hands seem to be constantly clammy, even though it's cold in this old caravan that I'm using as a dressing-room.

Now I've been in hundreds of dressing-rooms around the world, I have spent hundreds of hours in small lonely rooms waiting to be called, but this one is definitely different. There's a tension in the air that I have never felt before inside one of these small mobile rooms. This is a caravan that has never been used by happy holiday-makers looking for the sun and the nearest Campari and lemonade. A caravan that has never been filled with the excitement of racing towards Canvey Island for the tenth time in ten years. This is a caravan that has the smell of fear. You can almost smell the sweat of hundreds of actors trying to remember the lines that they knew off by heart over breakfast that morning.

I can see out of the scratched Perspex window that the sun is trying to break through the grey skies. It has to be time for me soon. Should I go over my lines, or read The Profession of Violence *to get in the mood? My heart seems to be going much too quick for my liking, I think a meditation, maybe a visualization might help . . . Even a poo might do the trick!*

'Are you ready, Gary?'

I've just been called . . . Well, nearly, they called Gary but they meant me. Well here goes, it's been five years since I first read in the News of the World *that I would be doing this, and now today, here I am about to walk through that tiny door and on to the next stage of my life . . . Wish me luck!*

Filming was spread over nine weeks. Most of the extra shots were taken in Greenwich, and the interiors were in a studio in an old converted water station called the Pump House, just south of the Thames and close enough to the East End of London to be able to smell the pie and mash cooking in the almost extinct pie shops. Every day, old members of the Firm would come down to the set and try to give me advice on how to be more like Reggie.

'No Mart . . . Reg walked with a slight swagger . . . like this . . . know what I mean, son?'

'Mart . . . Reg always sniffed in between his sentences . . . it was a very important habit of his . . . no one will know who you're playing if you don't do it.'

'Listen, boy, if there's one thing you have to do . . . clean your fingernails with a match while you're talking business . . . Reg always did that.'

I had to be polite, so I thanked them for their advice and got on with the job. It was hard, though, because in the middle of a scene, out of the corner of my eye I could see them watching, waiting to see if I had taken their advice on board, to see if I was going to sniff in between every sentence.

Ron, Charlie, the Firm, Aunt May, they had all in turn given me information on how to play Reggie Kray, and thank God they did. Every tiny snippet was fascinating and so important in capturing the essence of his character.

The first half of filming was a strange experience. Some of the violent scenes that we shot in the studio and on location played terrible tricks with my mind, and my dreams were filled with death and murder. So in between that and Harley waking me up six or seven times during the night with her vigorous new lungs, I was exhausted – exhausted but enjoying every minute. I had never felt so fulfilled. For the first time in my life I was responsible for my success or failure; I couldn't hide behind my brother or the four other guys in the band. It was down to me – I was on my own and I loved it. I knew that if I made a good job of the movie, I would at least have something to move on to if Spandau Ballet suddenly came to an end.

We were shooting a scene in Greenwich in which I would drive up to a corner shop and get out to buy some sweets for Frances, my wife in the movie, played by Kate Hardie. When I come out of the shop there are two guys standing around the car looking at Frances. I ask them what they're looking at, but don't wait for their answer before steaming in and knocking them senseless. Peter Medak, the director, had the brilliant idea of filming the whole of the fight from inside the car, so that the audience saw it from her point of view and also felt the pressure she found herself under.

One of the guys I had to hand out a Kray beating to was a close friend of Reggie's. He had spent some time inside with Reg and been promised a small part in the movie. Charlie Kray, who was not this guy's biggest fan, was standing next to me between takes. He came over to me and whispered in my ear in that low, rumbling East End voice, 'Mart, can I have a word in your 'shell-like', son?'

The smell of his aftershave and cigarettes was strong and over-powering.

'What?'

'When you sling your left hook at that geezer over there, it wouldn't be such a bad thing if you misjudged your punch . . . know what I mean?'

'What do you mean, Charlie?'

'Y'know, it wouldn't be such a bad thing if you gave him a real one . . . For me.'

'I can't do that Charlie . . . This is a movie.'

I thought to myself, how weird it must be for him, watching a re-run of his life. Watching small vignettes that he must have seen over and over again in the privacy of his head coming to life in front of his very eyes.

When you're on the set of a movie, things are very confusing. The line between fact and fiction gets blurred, and they blend together, creating a sort of fourth dimension. It all seems very real, and if you have done your job as an actor correctly, you want to believe that it is real. It's very easy to get lost in this land of Narnia.

'But that's Reggie's mate,' I said.

'I know, I know . . . But he ain't mine.'

Charlie obviously wanted me to mis-time my stage punch, which was practised so that I would just miss the guy by a fraction, but it would look as though I hit him clean on the jaw.

'Go on, son, do it for me . . . as a favour.'

I made my excuses, telling Charlie that a real punch just doesn't look good on screen, anyway that really wasn't my style and, besides, I had already taken a black eye from one of the so-called 'expert' stunt men in a previous fight scene, I didn't want another one.

Some of my favourite scenes in the movie are those around the meeting table, where Ron and Reg discuss their plans over tea and biscuits with the rest of the Firm. The meeting table for the Krays was in a room that was upstairs in their mother's house in Vallance Road, in the heart of London's East End. The twins would affectionately refer to the house as Fort Vallance, and during filming that is exactly what the room became for me. It was the only room on the set where I could escape from the noise and the chaos that go hand in hand with film-making. The studio itself was a converted water station, with no sound proofing and none of the luxuries that I have now come to expect. The producers of the movie had even expected Gary and me to share a dressing-room. I felt as if we were back in the bedroom we shared in Rotherfield Street, where Gary's side of the room was covered with posters of Bowie and T. Rex and my side was full of Bruce Lee pictures. So Fort Vallance became my quiet room and my sanctuary over the nine weeks of filming.

During one of the scenes around the meeting table, we were all listening to Ron give a speech about how we were going to take over the rival gangs. We were just supposed to drink our tea quietly and maybe dunk the odd biscuit. The cameras rolled and Peter Medak shouted out 'Action'. Gary stood up and started out on his mammoth speech. He was fantastic as Ronnie Kray, he had worked his socks off to stand in that position, with that much confidence, and to give such a captivating performance, and now, after all that preparation, he was giving the performance of a lifetime.

Then, right in the middle of his big speech, a sound came from out of nowhere.

SHLURPPPPPPPPPPP . . .

Gary tried to keep his concentration, the noise was almost too absurd to be coming from any of the professional actors around the table, Gary continued. He quickly regained his composure and geared up for the end of the speech, and the rallying battle cry that was to punctuate the end. Then once again the strange sound appeared from out of nowhere.

SHHHHHHLURPPPPP . . .

This time everyone stopped and turned to the end of the dark oak table. One of the gang had poured his tea into his saucer and was sucking on it like a goldfish.

SHHHLURPPPPPPP . . .

Some people will do anything to get more camera time! This guy had decided that his part in the movie wasn't big enough, and had made his mind up to do something about it. Peter Medak, always the complete Hungarian gentleman, took him to one side, had a quiet word with him and we moved on.

When I look back at making that movie, it was one of the most exciting times of my life. I was thirty years old, I had my new baby girl, a British blockbuster movie in my hands and Spandau Ballet, which at that point in time was still breathing, even though it was with the use of an iron lung!

The End of the Band and a Slice of Hollywood Humble Pie

When a group of young kids get themselves together and call themselves a band, there is an incredible feeling of togetherness. You all have the same dreams, the same drive. You all want the same things out of life, the same success; you all want to play in front of one hundred thousand screaming fans, all calling your name as your face fills the giant video screen above your head. You have no arguments, you have no track record of disagreements, you're just in there, strapping on your seat-belts, ready for the ride of your life.

So how can a band who have declared their love for one another so publicly then fall out, and to such a degree that at the end of the roller-coaster track is a courtroom, and a judge wearing a white wig staring at you while reading you the rights and wrongs of your publishing agreement?

Women? The Beatles and hundreds of other bands have blamed their break-ups on the wives and girlfriends; on their partners trying to take control or to get their boyfriends to take more responsibility. 'You should be doing this . . . You should be doing that . . . Why is it always him who writes the songs? Why don't you get the front covers?'

That was never really our problem – the girls were really good. I don't think there was a single incident where they interfered with the running of the band . . . well, none that I know of!

178

Touring? The first years of touring are amazing: you discover the world for the first time, you get to live out your childhood dreams of being a rock star, live in the best hotels around the world and get to sample a side of life, that to most people is just a fairy-tale. Later the glamour starts to wear off. Just being away from home for months on end can cause a strain on a band. It puts a tremendous pressure on your friendships. Being with the same people for weeks on end is hard, especially if you find yourself on a tax year as we did, not being able to escape from the other guys at all.

Solo records are another thing that splits bands up. Band members not satisfied with the group success and needing to test the water with their own songs, with their own sound, with their own personality.

So what happened to us? Why did we give up on something that had taken us thirteen years to build up? Fair enough, we weren't selling the same amount of records that we did in the mid Eighties, but we were still capable of playing to sold-out arenas around the world and making good records, and you never know, with the right song we might well have found ourselves back on top!

What split us up in the end was the movie. The other guys in the band couldn't accept the fact that Gary and I were doing something away from them. When we were kids we all wanted the same things out of life, and now for the first time our needs and our goals were slightly different. An outsider might say, 'Just get on with it . . . You don't always have to see eye to eye with the people you work with – but this was deeper than that. A rift had set in and, for the first time in our careers, tremors were shaking the foundations of not only the band, but also our friendships. I don't deny that it was partially my fault for letting my enthusiasm for acting show. All I had been for the previous eight years was a pretty face; now I had a chance to perform and to let the artistic side of my personality, that had been collecting dust for so many years, shine through.

When it came to the premiere of *The Krays*, only Steve Norman turned up; the others couldn't make it. I can understand how difficult it must have been. I mean we all had huge ambitions and

179

huge egos, and it couldn't have been easy to watch Gary and me have all that success on our own.

The movie premiere was one of the biggest nights of my life, far more important to me than when the band reached number one in the radio charts with 'True' back in '84. We drove towards Leicester Square with my parents in a huge black limo – the kind they use for funerals, and which I hate. I always felt fake in those things. The night was damp and foggy. As we approached the cinema, we could see the huge crowd that had gathered around the front entrance, the cameras, the TV reporters, the people who had come just to watch as the hundreds of celebrities arrived.

We pulled up alongside the main entrance and started to get out before life seemed to slow to a snail's pace. A man standing on the pavement pulled a gun out of his coat pocket and pointed it straight at me. Before I could even catch my breath, the man was bundled to the ground by several policemen. I didn't want to scare my Mum and pushed past as quick as I could. What was it? Some kind of underworld vendetta, with someone trying to take out one of the old Firm as they turned up for the premiere, or just some nutter who thought this was the perfect evening for a shoot-out? I'll never know, in all the excitement of the night, the incident seemed to come and go almost as if it was expected, almost as if it had been staged to grab some publicity.

The next morning, the sound of the newspapers dropping through the letter box seemed louder than ever. The noise seemed to reverberate around the hall like it had never done before and up the stairs and into my bedroom, disturbing the quiet sanctuary of my room. My head was heavy from the post premiere party champagne, it was a struggle to lift it off the pillow and open my eyes, but I knew what was downstairs waiting for me on the mat, the reviews that would either make or break the film, and make or break me. If they were bad, my short lived career as an actor would be over in one fail swoop. If they were good . . . who knows! I pulled myself together and out of the bed, Shirlie was still asleep, I could just see her blond hair sticking out the end of the duvet.

My head thumped as I made my way down the stairs and into the hall. I knew I couldn't bend down and pick the newspapers up without experiencing intense pain, so I slid my back down the wall until I was sitting on the floor next to them.

I opened each one in turn and found pictures that were taken outside the Odeon Leicester Square the previous night and laid them all out on the wooden floor in front of me. And then with my stomach churning and my mouth so dry it was starting to become painful, I read the reviews.

I couldn't have wished for more and neither could Gary. There wasn't a bad word to be found in any paper, in any column. They all sang our praises and wished us luck in the future. I might have felt sick and my head might have hurt, but I still managed a smile.

After the success of *The Krays*, acting had stopped being an ambition and become a reality. It had become part of my life once again, it had found its way back into my soul. I remember several conversations I had with Billie Whitelaw in the make-up wagon on the set of the movie, as the condensation raced down the windows and we tried our best to be heard over the four turbo hair-dryers all blowing at once.

'Don't let Hollywood take you too soon,' said Billie one day.

'Hollywood! . . . when I was a kid I used to dream of being Marlon Brando, and of what life would be like living in Hollywood, spending days around a pool under the shadow of palm trees and pollution; but I never thought I would ever make a serious attempt at making the dream come true. I thought that after filming was finished on *The Krays* I would be going back to the band, back to the in-jokes and the security of the familiar surroundings.

We had a tour planned to promote the final album, *Heart like a Sky*, that had been released several weeks earlier to, it has to be said, mixed reviews. There's nothing worse for a band than to go on stage and play songs that an audience doesn't like. When you know they're waiting for you to finish the new songs and get back to playing the songs they have paid their hard-earned money to see you perform.

181

As it turned out, this was to be our last tour. The strain of the movie, the album not selling well and those small niggles that had taken ten years to rise to the surface were all taking their toll.

On the tour bus the atmosphere was tense. Tony, John and Steve would sit at the back watching videos, while Gary would read his book at the front. I would quietly wander up and down the aisle trying to keep the peace, perhaps spending thirty minutes with Gary talking about Shakespeare, then going down the back to watch *Spinal Tap* for the hundredth time.

On one of the first gigs of the tour as we sound-checked in the afternoon, someone noticed that all the chairs in the arena were covered in small posters. They were posters advertising the movie. It was a sore point. I would never say that the other guys were jealous, but the atmosphere was as if we had just asked for a divorce. I found it hard myself, and I felt hurt for them.

The band was splitting up. All of a sudden we didn't have the same things in common. We didn't speak the same language . . . We had different dreams.

We could all see that the band was evaporating before our eyes but no one made an effort to try and stop it from happening. It was as if we didn't want to admit it to ourselves. After all those years of hard work and hopes and ambition we were all prepared to let it slip away from us without even a murmur. No more phone calls asking who was ready to go out on tour, when we were going into the studio next or even when the next pay cheque was due. Nothing. And I for one couldn't have been happier. Ten years inside a band is a life time, living in each others pockets, laughing at the same jokes, the same schoolboy pranks, it was time to move on. I had had enough of the music business, enough of touring, even the thought of buying a CD made me feel sick. So as the ostentatious Eighties turned quietly into the streetwise Nineties, Spandau Ballet would quietly disappear.

As soon as that last Spandau tour was over, I got on to a plane and flew straight out to America to promote *The Krays*. The movie had gone down well out there, so our reception was good. I think it was on the second day that my agent at ICM had asked me to go to a casting. It was for a Bruce Willis film – you know, the one where he saves the world and lives to tell the tale.

I walked into this huge white office on Wilshire Boulevard. It looked more like a doctor's surgery than a production office, apart from the old movie posters on the wall. The girl behind the desk, who had small round glasses and hair neatly pulled back into a ponytail, carried on reading the *LA Times* as she spoke.

'Sign your name at the bottom of the list.'

'What list?'

This was the first American casting I had ever been on, and I didn't know what list she was talking about.

'The casting list. Don't you have that in Britain? Just sign your name, sit down and wait your turn.'

Well, I knew by now she wasn't asking for my autograph. I did as I was told and took my place in the line. I found myself sitting next to a Red Indian. I wasn't sure if I was in the right place. He turned to look at me deep in my eyes. 'How.'

I smiled. It was as if I had been dropped on to another planet. I thought I'd better make sure I was in the right place, so I called out to the girl behind the desk, 'Excuse me, is this the line for the Bruce Willis film?'

'Sir, will you sit down and be quiet, people are trying to work in that office.' She pointed to a set of double doors at the end of the corridor. 'Sit down and wait your turn.'

I wasn't sure if I wanted a turn. My heart was pounding, I felt sick and my nerves were jangling on a thin piece of string. What in God's name was I doing here? I was the cute one in Spandau Ballet – where were the screaming fans, the security guards, the tour bus, the private jet?

Just then a young, good-looking all-American boy came out of the office. Now the girl behind the desk looked at me for the first time.

'OK, English . . . You're up.'

Up for what?

'Have you got your sides?'

'What sides?'

'The script pages they want you to read.'

'No one said anything about . . .'

She handed me the white script pages and said, in a disappointed tone, 'Just go in.'

As I got up, the Indian growled in his native tongue and I made my way to the double doors at the end of the corridor.

My heart was racing and my knees felt as if they were being held together with gelatin. Why was I here? I had just jumped from the top of a very large ladder that took me over ten years to climb and was now waiting at the bottom of a new one, waiting in line to start the ascent once again. The bottom of the ladder was a place I'd forgotten even existed, a place I hadn't been since I left that print factory. Why was I putting myself through this? I felt like shouting out, 'Who knows "True"? . . . Who's seen my band?' Trouble was, deep in my heart I knew I didn't have a band any more. I went into the office.

'Come in, shut the door.'

I turned around again to find eight people sitting behind a long table, all staring at me, waiting for me to say something. This was stress city. I had played in front of tens of thousands of people with my bass hanging in front of me, but this was a whole new world.

'I'll read with you.'

A guy in a pair of faded jeans and cowboy boots stood up from behind the table, and as he did so I could see that he was wearing a Duran Duran T-shirt. A giant Simon LeBon was staring me straight in the eyes. I thought fuck it – Duran were always bigger than us in the States, even though we hated admitting it. This whole episode had been humbling enough, and now I had Simon LeBon staring at me.

I pulled out the pages and went straight for it. I'm a great believer

1985. Some year. Live Aid and my first outing for Melchester Rovers.

Hong Kong provides the back drop to another expensive video and another colourful anecdote!

A gift from a fan ...

1988. Shirlie and I get married in St. Lucia and that night she conceived our first child. There must have been something in the wine.

Cannes Film Festival 1988. Shirlie and Sadie support their cardboard husbands.

The family Dons gather before *The Krays* premiere. My parents on the left and Shirlie's on the right. No one noticed the madman with the gun as we climbed out of the limo!

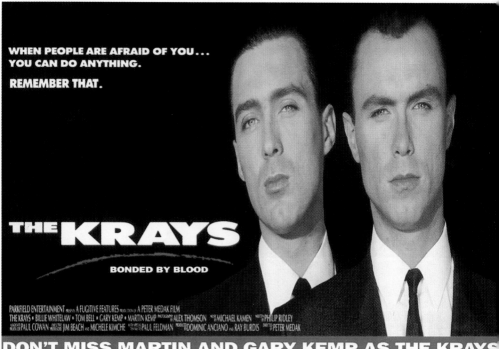

1989. With the Kray twins movie under my belt, the last thing I wanted was to go back out on tour with Spandau Ballet. I had other things on my mind.

Growing Rich, Anglia TV 1991.

1993. Learning to eat Humble Pie in Hollywood was hard, but Harley made things easier.

1993. 'Mummy is having a baby' Harley sang out, as Shirlie tried desperately to hide her contractions as we walked through customs at Los Angeles airport.

1994. Together, just before the brain tumours that rocked my world and changed my life forever.

1994. *Embrace of the Vampire*. I was the last person to see those veins popping out of my head. Everyone thought they were part of the Vampires make up. A telltale sign to the trouble ahead.

1995. Writing the book after my operation became an obsession, a way to flush out my fear and remember the good times. Most of all it was someone to share my darkest secrets with.

And the rest is history … (Photo: © BBC)

in PME – positive mental energy. It was no good trying to fluff around, delaying things. I read.

'OK, you take the right flank, and I'll attack from the left. We can meet up at Fort Avalon.'

I waited for the guy in the Duran T-shirt to read his line. Nothing. A woman from behind the desk spoke.

'I don't think a cavalry soldier would have an English accent . . . do you? Can you do it again in American?'

I could feel my blood pressure hit the warning signals. The guy in the Duran T-shirt sat down, and Simon LeBon looked all the world as if he was laughing at me, as the cloth moved around his oversized stomach.

I was crap at any accent.

'I'll try.'

My effort lasted another two lines before the woman put me out of my misery, and told me to go away and work on it.

I had forgotten how it felt to be that embarrassed. I walked past Simon LeBon, who was enjoying every minute, and out of the door. The Red Indian, who was still waiting in line, looked at me from under his giant plume of coloured feathers and raised one hand. 'How.'

I raised my hand and replied, 'Shit.'

We all have to eat a chunk of humble pie every so often, but coming from a successful rock band where red carpets are laid in front of your feet, doors are opened and champagne is pushed into your hands – boy, is it hard.

The Krays was doing well in the States, not so much box-office-wise, but the reviews were fantastic. Siskel and Egbert, the famous movie critics, gave it two thumbs up, and the broadsheets all had good words to say about my performance. I thought work would fall into my lap, but I was wrong. I was beginning to doubt my own judgement. I was even starting to think that if I had tried harder, I could have kept the band together for another album. I felt as though reality was nipping at my heels. As I slept, I could only dream of being back at the print shop, with Larry getting me to make the tea. In my dream the picture of my face that the printers had decorated with spots and breadcrumbs had the words to 'True' coming from my open mouth.

Gary had rented a house in the Hollywood Hills and had kindly let me stay there with Shirlie and Harley. I worked hard on the American accent. I hated being embarrassed the first time, and I wasn't going to let it happen again. Twice a week I drove down to Silver Lake and handed over my hundred dollars, trying to acquire a movie star's accent.

All that work, and the first job I got was playing Baron Frankenstein in a spoof horror movie called *Waxwork 2*. This meant I had to use my best German accent. It was only a small movie, but it was shot in Hollywood and that was good enough for me!

As I sat in the make-up chair, being transformed into the legendary character, I recalled what my nan had said to my mum all those years ago as I goose-stepped around her high-rise flat in Hoxton.

'There you go . . . He's as German as the day I was born. He's got it in him, I tell you.'

She would have laughed if she could have seen me at that moment.

Next I was sent to Aspen, Colorado, to play in a movie called *Aspen Extreme*. I was to play yet another German, this time a ski instructor. I had lied my boots off to get the part, telling the director that I was a great skier and that for me to play an instructor was almost second nature. I worried myself senseless for several nights, lying in bed wondering what was going to happen when he called out 'Action' on the snow-covered slopes. What was he going to say when he found out that my skiing consisted of a couple of weeks' holiday and a marital argument on the side of a mountain? All kinds of scenarios ran through my brain. What if I was sent home? How awful would that be?

The first day of filming came. The make-up wagon was unusually quiet. There were five guys all in red jump suits, ready to play the part of Aspen ski instructors. This was a movie for Disney, which meant that every spot and blemish had to be covered up, so it was going to take some time. Just then, the director put his head through the door and let the cold wind rush in, breaking the silence and showering everything with pure Colorado snow.

'OK, I want all you guys out in one minute, we're ready to shoot.'

We all finished our make-up, climbed out of the wagon and went over to collect our skis. I carefully slipped mine on, snapping the bindings in place, and slid over to the edge of the mountain where they were filming, concentrating all the while on not letting the tips of my skis get crossed.

Now Aspen is a beautiful place, but the slopes on Ajax mountain are some of the steepest I have ever seen. We all took our places on the mountain's edge and the director called 'Action'. Then, one by one, almost as if it was planned, all the actors slid away down the mountain, completely out of control. Some ended up hanging on to rocks half-way down, others just slid completely out of sight. They had all lied about their skiing ability and some were far worse than myself. After all the red-faced actors were recovered by the snow bikes, the director ended up putting scarves around our heads and using stunt men for all the action scenes.

Shirlie and I stayed in Aspen for four weeks in all before it was time to head back to Los Angeles with Harley, back to the constant round of appointments and disappointments. Life can be hard in LA, even for a much-travelled pop star, and I was always a moment away from completely losing my confidence, giving up the chase and heading back home to London. There's always someone who's bigger than you, better, or just more right for the part. Everyone out there is after the same thing, that elusive winning ticket that will eventually see their name in a gold star on Hollywood Boulevard, to be spat on and spewed over by the junkies and prostitutes who made the same journey years earlier. Sometimes I wondered if I was asking too much from the powers above to expect another wonderful career, a second amazing journey; after all, I had already been blessed with one.

It's a very painful thing to be rejected time and time again, no matter how tough your constitution may be. Every time I walked out of those casting rooms, I believed that the part was mine, that they must already be discussing the contract even as I was driving home. You always know when you get a part, because the phone rings the minute you walk back in through your door. Everyone wants to give you the good news first. If it's bad news you could wait for weeks to find out that they didn't like you or you weren't right for the part; sometimes you would never hear at all. These days I don't even bother to ask what anyone thought, I just do the best I can do in the casting room situation and walk away from it, treating it as a workshop to be enjoyed rather than a trip to the gallows. That doesn't mean to say that I have lost my nerves . . . They'll always be there, but as long as I know I haven't let myself down, then that's all I can ask for!

The sun shone through the huge glass windows and into the living-room, bouncing off the polished wooden floor in the TV room of the house in the Hollywood Hills. It was about three in the afternoon and the heat was getting to everyone. Harley was asleep in the other room. The trip back from Aspen had been a long one, and the change in the weather had taken its toll. The air-conditioner was on the blink again and only came to life when it felt like it – it seemed to have a life of its own. I sat on the sofa as I watched Shirlie drink her hot cup of tea.

'How can you do that?'

'What?'

'Drink tea in this weather?'

'I'm tired.'

'So what's that got to do with drinking a hot cup of tea in a room that must be over one hundred degrees?'

'I need the sugar.'

'If you just need the sugar, you should drive down to the shop and grab a Mars Bar or something . . . They even keep a few in the refrigerator down there, and you could grab a few more Diet Cokes as well, I think we're running low.'

Shirlie hated going to the shops on her own, but I was trying desperately to get her used to life in LA. I knew that the only way forward for us was to make a permanent move out there.

'Tea's fine . . .'

Shirlie walked over to the TV set and switched on the giant tube.

We didn't realize it at the time, but the following few hours would shape the next few years of our life. It was May 1992. The pictures on the screen were hard to take in at first, they seemed so unreal I wasn't quite sure if we were watching a movie, even though I could see the local news station motif on the bottom right hand corner of the screen. I looked over at Shirlie. She was looking down into her tea, both hands tightly cradled around the blue mug. A sick feeling grew in my stomach as I looked back to the TV set, and watched the horror that was starting to unfold. A truck driver lay on the street as a crowd of young LA dudes took it in turns to throw bricks at him, jump on his helpless body and kick any remaining life right out of him. The reporter in the helicopter looking down on the situation was giving a graphic blow-by-blow description. It was like listening to an old Muhammad Ali fight coming live over the radio from Madison Square Garden.

The beating went on for at least twenty minutes. In that time not a single policeman came in to try to get the man out, although they could hardly say they never knew it was going on – by now it was on every TV station. Still the poor man lay on the street, his life draining away by the second. I looked back at Shirlie, who had tears streaming down her face and running in between her fingers as she covered her mouth with her hand. She whispered to herself, 'My God.'

By now the shop on the corner of the street where the man lay had been set on fire, and smoke was pouring out of its windows.

Soon a huge cloud of black smoke started to rise over LA like a Red Indian warning signal.

It was about nine months since a young black guy named Rodney King had taken a vicious beating by the LAPD, and a passer-by had captured the whole thing on a video camera, selling it to every news station across the United States. What we were witnessing on TV was revenge, or at least that's what the downtown dudes in their bandana masks and baseball caps called it.

Shirlie got up off the soft brown corduroy sofa and walked out through the French doors, on to the small balcony which looked out high over LA. That verandah was to be our corner of the world for the next ten hours, as darkness fell and fire after fire was lit across town. In all, over two thousand huge warehouses and supermarkets were set ablaze, and every one of them could be seen from our balcony; it was like looking out over war-torn Beirut.

The commentary on the TV became more and more tense as the fires were starting to be lit closer to the Hollywood Hills, and closer to us. In Hollywood itself, every madman with a gun had come out on to the streets to loot the local shops and to join in with the festivities; weapons were fired indiscriminately from out of their cars, or from the tops of burning buildings.

Smoke filled the house and our eyes were streaming with grey tears. If I had been on my own I could have coped with this, but having Shirlie and Harley with me made me scared.

It was two o'clock in the morning before Shirlie lay down on the bed and snuggled up next to Harley, putting her arms around her tiny shoulders, trying to get some sleep. I couldn't, I wanted to stay awake and watch the news to keep track of exactly where the rioting was taking place. I had this awful fear inside me that I would wake up to find the house on fire or the door being burst open by some lunatic carrying a machine gun making the most of the excuse. Anything could have happened. I thought to myself: is this the place I really want my family to live? Can I really be responsible for bringing them here? When Shirlie had said that she didn't like going to the shops on her own, this was the reason why! This could happen at any time in LA. Tension between black and white, rich and poor, is so high that it affects every corner of society. Shirlie was right to sit at home, and drink her hot tea with two sugars in the afternoon sun rather than go down to the shops and buy a can of Coke and a Mars Bar. This place wasn't London, and it certainly wasn't home.

The riots went on for two days, during which there were no flights in or out of Los Angeles, there was a curfew after seven o'clock, and the smoke from the fires still hung in the air like clouds of mustard gas swirling around the trenches. I wanted to get out of Los Angeles, and I called all the airlines until I found the first flight that was going back to London.

As we drove through town in the back of the yellow taxi two days later, we could see some of the devastation. Parts of the town looked like a movie set: there was nothing left of buildings, shops, whole blocks of homes. I had never seen anything like it.

That morning the airport was packed with people desperately trying to leave town. I had a ticket on a British Airways plane back to London, which happened to be queuing next to a cheap Mexican flight to Mexico City. Shirlie tapped me on the shoulder when I was finished checking in and putting my big black British passport back into its holder.

'Look behind you.'

I pulled Harley down off the counter and she clung to my neck as I turned around.

'I don't believe it,' I said.

Every other young Mexican was carrying a TV or a microwave on his shoulders, or pushing them around on trolleys – not in boxes, just wrapped in paper tied with string . . . It looked as if they had definitely been out shopping for their cousins back home over the last couple of days, or nights.

Our trips out to Los Angeles became fewer and further between after those torturous few days. The fun and the excitement of those once magical streets had disappeared. If I had to go over for a meeting, I would go out there on my own, stay just for a few days and then come straight back. It wasn't the best arrangement – LA's a long way away.

It was on one of these flying visits that I bumped into Waris Hussein, the guy who directed me as a child in *The Glittering Prizes*. He cast me now in a wonderful role in a movie called *Murder Between Friends*. It meant that I was going to have to spend about six weeks in California filming. Fine, that's not so hard. The trouble was that Shirlie was just about to give birth to our second child. She was eight and a half months pregnant and once again the size of two houses. I didn't want to miss the birth. I wanted to be with Shirlie. I had seen the pain that she went through last time, and I wasn't going to leave her on her own to deal with it this time around. There was no alternative, Shirlie would have to come to the States with me. As long as she took her time and did her best to stay calm, the chances of her starting to go into labour on the plane were very slim. After all, Harley was two weeks late, and there was nothing to suggest that this would be any different.

The trip was fine and Shirlie was remarkably calm on the aeroplane going over, a few twinges here and there but nothing out of the ordinary. It wasn't until we were queuing up to go through passport control that the twinges turned to twangs and the twangs started to leave their tell tale signs. America doesn't allow in any pregnant women over eight months. Now I hate that bit of an airport at the best of times. I always feel guilty for no reason, always completely paranoid as I stand at the red line waiting to be called forward. The place was packed; there was a plane-load of Indians in one corner being sniffed by a white Alsatian, and about one hundred Japanese all trying to carry their golf clubs without breaking each other's teeth. The place was heaving with passengers and just as many security guards.

Suddenly I felt Shirlie's back stiffen with a sharp intake of breath. She had started to panic. A guy in a blue hat and official blue uniform came up close to her. Shirlie was huge – she looked at least ten months pregnant. I grabbed all our jackets and Harley's small rucksack and sat them on top of her stomach. She looked at me, and I could see she was far from OK. Her eyes were starting to water and her bottom lip was quivering slightly. I tried to calm her down with some meaningless chat, but at the same moment Harley had decided that she wasn't going to wait in line; she had rushed through the crowd and was talking to one of the guards. I could feel him asking her where her mother and father were, and why she was standing on her own on the other side of the red line. I jumped forward, called her back and smiled nicely at the guy behind the desk, as Harley once again climbed up into my arms. I looked back at Shirl. She was sweating – something wasn't right. I moved along to the middle of the line.

'Martin . . . I'm having contractions.'

'You can't,' I said.

'I know . . . but I am!'

'Can't you wait five minutes until we're through to the other side?'

Shirlie's eyes grew smaller again, her gaze drilling a hole through my head.

'How close are they?'

'Every three minutes.'

'Christ . . . You're kidding.' I knew she wasn't, I just couldn't believe it was happening.

Harley could see something was wrong. 'What's wrong, Mummy?'

Shirlie replied without thinking, a reflex reaction. 'I'm having a baby, sweetheart.'

Harley started to sing out, 'Mummy's having a baby, Mummy's having a baby.'

I put my hand over Harley's mouth.

'Mummy's having a ba . . .'

The young couple behind us smiled, and for a horrible moment I thought the guy was going to try and shake my hand and congratulate me.

We were now at the red line, and the guard called us over. I tried to stay in front of Shirlie, with Harley on my hip. I was praying that Harley didn't want to tell the guard that she was expecting a baby brother or a baby sister. He looked at our passports. I looked at Shirlie. She was purple and cross-eyed. I could see her face shaking under the contractions.

The guard spoke in a rough West Coast accent. 'Come for the big one, have you?'

'Er . . . that's right.'

'That big old 'quake is gonna hit soon. If you feel a tremor, do you know what to do?'

I answered him – we had to get out of there fast! 'Find the nearest door, right?'

He looked at me right between the eyes. 'And stand underneath it . . . OK . . . you got it. Have a nice day now . . . Next.'

We started to move off, I could hear Shirlie breathe out for the first time. We had only taken a couple of steps when the guy called out, 'Hey, wait up.'

I thought to myself the game was up. I had visions of Shirlie giving birth under guard and us being deported.

'Hey, little girl, you dropped your Winnie the Pooh.'

I looked down at Harley. 'Go and get it, darling.'

As soon as we got to the house in Hollywood Hills the contractions stopped, and thankfully didn't start again for another four weeks. Our second child was born in Los Angeles, in the Cedar Sinai hospital. A beautiful blond-haired baby boy. We named him Roman. Two weeks later Shirlie took him home to show our families and I started work. It was to be a busy period for me, as I went from one film to another. None of them changed the world, but at least I was working.

I was only home for a few weeks before I had to fly off to Brazil, to start work on a small independent American movie called *Boca*. I was to star alongside Ray Dawn Chong. I had never been to Brazil, so I didn't know what to expect. All I heard was that you shouldn't wear your best watch in the streets, as the crime rate there was phenomenal.

All the location stuff was to be shot in the 'Favelas', that are up on the hillside overlooking Rio. The Favelas are a world unto themselves, entirely run by the drug barons. In these small villages – the largest holds over two hundred thousand people – the only thing missing is the police. That's the deal. The drug barons and their people keep themselves to themselves on the hillside, and the police let them get on with their trade.

The movie was based loosely on the life of a modern Brazilian folk hero – a gangster called Boca d'Oro who stole from the rich and gave to the poor . . . blah, blah, blah. So the local drug lord had agreed to us filming up there for a couple of days.

The first thing that hits you as you turn the corner, and drive up into the hillside is the stink coming from the open sewers that run down the middle of the tiny streets. The pungent, purple fumes find their way into everything. Your clothes stink, your hair stinks and, after a couple of days, the sweat falling out of your pores in the morning heat stinks like the sewer itself.

Everyone in the Favelas has a gun. For men, they're like a part of the body, a third arm that's carried around with a strange sense of pride and a frightening smile. Women too carry them around, tucked carefully inside their heavy black shawls, like newborn babies being taken out for their first glimpse of the world around them. I saw a seven-year-old boy kicking a ball around on a small patch of gravel next to the makeshift church, with a pistol tucked down his shorts. I say makeshift, but to the people of the Favelas the church was a permanent building. Everything there is built by throwing a few red bricks and a handful of home-made cement together and hoping it will stick.

It was only my second day in the Favelas when I saw first hand just how cheap life is. It was a grey overcast morning, as the sun hadn't yet found its way through the giant black clouds. I was being taken to the set in the back of a tiny Fiat Uno along the main roads that lead to Rio's beauty spots, like Ipanema Beach and

Copacabana, then through the smaller side streets that led up into the Favelas. As we approached, out of the corner of my eye I saw a young man lying in the street, he must have been about the same age as me. He had his hands tied behind his back with a thin piece of string and what looked like sticky tape around his ankles, and a pool of thick red blood seeped from the side of his head. My stomach turned.

'Christ, shouldn't we stop and see if we can help this guy?'

The Brazilian beside me in the car, who had just lit his fourth cigarette, threw his match out of the open window and growled, 'He's dead.'

It was the first dead body I had ever seen, I couldn't take my eyes off it. I was overwhelmed with sadness – not for his death, strangely, but for his life. I felt like I was on a different planet a billion miles away from home. As the car passed the body, I turned to look out of the back window. An old woman walked around the young man and barely glanced down. She, like the driver, had seen it too many times. We drove on, I was lost for words! The driver's words were spat out.

'He's from the Favelas that's their justice . . . They don't have police up there but they have guns.'

When I first read the script to *Boca*, it was a standard low-budget American thriller based loosely on a true story. By the time I eventually saw the finished product, it resembled nothing of the original screenplay. It had been changed so much in post-production and the edit suite, that the movie was almost unrecognizable. Still, that's the trouble with being an actor: you have no control over the finished product. You turn up, do your job the best you can, and then walk away from it. To me it felt hugely different from working on an album with the band. With Spandau, we had complete control over every aspect of a record from the beginning to the very end.

Early one morning, as the night sky was starting to brighten, we drove in the tiny Fiat back down the loose stone track out of the Favelas, and back into the centre of town. I was tired. It had been an all-night shoot, and we had been on the set for something like sixteen hours, a fair day's work by anyone's standards. After seeing that first dead body on the sidewalk, however, it was hard for me to close my eyes and relax on the short journey back to the hotel.

The scene we had just been filming was a shoot-out among carnival floats that had been stored in an old warehouse for the winter. Earlier during the day, the armourer had come to me with a selection of guns, all empty of course, and laid them out on a table in front of me. As usual when the guns come out on a film set, all the blokes gather round and tell their tales of near misses and narrow escapes. It's funny how guns bring out the macho side of even the quietest man.

Out of the several guns available, I chose to use a small Berretta. It was easy to carry, and certainly easier to hide than the giant Magnum. I picked it up and felt the weight of it between my hands, I pulled back the safety catch and cocked the gun. Now when a gun is cocked, you hardly have to touch the trigger to fire it; in fact, with some you only have to breathe on it for it to explode.

The guy sitting next to me in the car was the dresser, an American who had been in Rio about a week longer than myself. We had both become so accustomed to the stench of the Favelas over the last week, that by now we only noticed it on the way in or on the way out; while we were up there . . . nothing. As the Fiat reached the last bend in the road, and was held at a stop by a small pedestrian red light, I noticed a man jump out in front of the car. He was wearing dirty old jeans, not expensive Levis, but those cheap light blue stone-washed imitations that you can buy down the local flea market, and a grey T-shirt that had been stretched around the collar. His hair was shoulder length, greasy and had that Brazilian beach bum style about it.

A second man came from the other side of the road. I didn't see him until the last moment, as he was hidden behind a parked car. At first, I didn't realize that they were coming towards us. I gazed down at a can of Diet Coke I had grabbed from the craft service table the minute I was wrapped for the night. The empty can was buckled and twisted; the edges were sharp as I had been playing with it on the short journey home.

Just then I heard a voice screaming at me in Portuguese. I looked up and right in front of me was the beach bum holding a huge silver Magnum pistol, pointing it straight at me through the windscreen. My first reaction was strange: I thought to myself, 'Now that's a nice gun.' The fact that we were in real life, and not still in the land of make-believe, hadn't quite sunk in. He screamed at me again. This time I saw his face turn purple with rage as he made his way around to my side of the car. My stomach was already starting to turn as I looked over to my American friend sitting next to me, but I wasn't going to get any moral support there; he already had a black Berretta up against his temple.

'Christ, what's going on?' I said.

How I managed to speak was beyond me, but the words seemed to come from nowhere, up from the very pit of my churning stomach.

I watched as the man in front of me made his way around to my open window, screaming all the time at the top of his voice. I closed my eyes and waited to hear the gun go bang . . . it would be a short escape from the horrible reality of the situation. Just then I felt the cold steel of the Magnum being shoved up against my temple. I opened my eyes and, in a natural reaction, turned slightly to get a better look. The fucking thing was cocked, and the man with his finger on the hairpin trigger was screaming at me, ready to pull it, the veins in his forearm pulsating with anticipation. If I only knew what they were saying – I never had a clue if he wanted me to stay in the car or get out. If he did want me to get out of the car, I wasn't quite sure if my legs would even hold me up.

Was this it, I thought to myself – was this how my life journey was going to end . . . a bullet in the head, I felt the cold steel dig into my skin as he pushed me forward with the blunt nose of the gun. At that moment a loud noise made me jump and close my eyes – for a terrifying moment I thought that my American friend had been shot. In fact, his Brazilian bandit had opened his car door and started to drag him out.

It was then that I took an educated guess that what they were screaming in Portuguese was 'Get out of the car.' My hand started to move towards the door lock. I looked down towards the floor, I didn't want to make eye contact with this madman, I didn't want him to think that I was challenging him in any way. I kept my eyes down, away from him and his silver Magnum, as I pulled back the handle on the door.

He grabbed my hair, and in one move pulled me out of the Fiat and up against the trunk. I could feel his garlic-saturated breath on my neck and the nuzzle of his gun just above my left kidney, but every moment I remained in the land of the living, the more faith I had that I wasn't going to die. If he was going to shoot, surely he would have done it by now.

He turned me around and for the first time I could see deep into his dark brown, expressionless eyes. I looked over at my friend, who was now lying over the hood of the car having his pockets turned inside out. The Brazilian spoke in English for the first time.

'Turn out your pockets.'

I saw him un-cock the gun and slip it down the back of his waistband. I felt myself breathe for the first time.

'Polizia . . . You buy drugs?'

'No . . . I'm English.'

'I don't give a fuck who you are . . . You buy drugs from Favelas?'

'No . . . I'm working on a movie . . . I'm an actor.'

'An actor . . . like Richard Burton?'

'And a musician.' I don't have a clue why I said that, but a smile started to form on his face.

'You play music too?'

'Yes, in an English band.'

He stepped back and reached in his pocket for a lighter and a packet of cigarettes.

'What's it called? Do I know them?' He smiled to himself as he spoke out of the corner of his mouth. 'Duran Duran?'

Even in the heat of the moment, I was strangely disappointed that he had chosen them as the most famous of British bands.

'No . . . Spandau Ballet,' I replied.

'No . . . You joke with me?'

'Yes.'

'I love Spandau Ballet . . . "True", "Gold", "Only When You Leave".'

I could have done without the discography. Then suddenly, his smile dropped as quickly as it had formed and once again he glared at me from under his brow.

'Me, drug squad.'

He lit the cigarette and blew the grey smoke into my face, I wanted to cough but I didn't want to look as weak as I felt. He stared at me for a moment and then spoke in a slow rumbling voice as he searched through his pockets.

'You give me autograph.'

I wanted for all the world to tell him to fuck right off, but I signed his piece of paper and they both went back on to the sidewalk from where they had come from.

We drove back to the hotel in silence, both of us in complete shock . . . but an anecdote richer.

I was called back to LA to shoot another independent movie called *Desire*. The movie was about a character who has an incredible sense of smell and who uses it to perverse ends rather than professional gains within the perfume industry. The script wasn't great but it kept me working, and there's no better promotion in that town than to be able to tell people that you're working. The first thing people ask you in LA, whether you're out to dinner or in the gym, is 'What are you working on at the moment?' If you answer with 'Oh, nothing, I'm just doing castings' it's the social kiss of death. People in LA only have time for people that are successful – it's hard but true.

The production office on the *Desire* movie booked me into a room at Le Parc Hotel. It's a small hotel off Santa Monica Boulevard, and I knew it well. I used to stay there with the band when we gigged in LA. It was only small but the service was always first class and the roof terrace with its pool and jacuzzi was fantastic. It was decorated like most small LA hotels in the Eighties, in green carpets and dark brown wood, obviously a taste left over from the Seventies when Starsky and Hutch were hip.

The hotel held some fantastic memories for me. Great gigs, wild parties, afternoons recovering from hangovers around the pool, having to be led out through the kitchens so that the fans couldn't jump on you as you got into your long black stretch limo – all the usual things that went with being a rock star on tour.

All of these memories came flooding back as I walked into the small foyer from the street outside. I was exhausted, dehydrated and miserable at having again had to leave my family back in London. I hated leaving them behind.

'Ah, Mr Kemp . . . Come in.'

It was Nasa, the hotel manager, an Egyptian with a smile as wide as the Nile and a hairstyle that looked remarkably like the great pyramids.

'Gonzales will take your bag up to your room. How are things? I haven't seen you for a long time . . . How are the other guys?'

All of a sudden I felt very alone. Where *were* the other guys? Why was I standing in this hotel on my own? A wave of panic ran through me. I missed them. I missed Steve's corny jokes, I missed nagging Tony about his smoking, I missed John's mood swings and the security of having Gary around.

'The actors are waiting for you in Room 101 for rehearsals,' said Nasa, as he took my credit card. 'Sign here.'

'Room 101?'

'Yes, you remember that room!'

I certainly did, that was the room that all our after-show parties were held in. The party room at the end of the corridor.

'Thanks,' I mumbled as I wearily walked up the flight of steps leading to the first floor.

As I got to the top, I could hear the Californian tones of the other actors rehearsing some of the scenes from the movie. The double doors to Room 101 opposite the top of the stairs were wide open. I took a deep breath of the malodorous hotel odour and made my entrance.

'Hello,' I said, trying my hardest to smile.

The room answered in unison with a resounding upbeat 'Hi'.

Oh my God, this was so weird! It felt like a dream being back in this room. I felt almost naked without the boys swigging from bottles of Jack Daniels and popping champagne corks by the side of me. The room was exactly the same, its green carpets, the small bar in the corner that had held Tony upright as the sun started to break through the heavy green cotton curtains, and the en-suite loo that I had been sick in more than once in my life. I could almost hear the music being played so loud on Gary's portable stereo that it distorted as it came out of the tiny speakers. There was a table at the back of the room that now held an automatic coffee-maker and small packets of biscuits. Five years earlier, almost altar-like, it had held aloft our small flight case with a bottle of champagne and a bottle of vodka cut into its inner foam protection, just in case you were caught lacking in stamina and needed an immediate 'slammer' to pick you up. Everything was so different, but then again exactly the same. I thought of those party nights when I had left early and gone back to my room to go to bed. Why did I waste those moments?

The director, who must have been about forty with his hair pulled back into a pony tail and small round glasses on the end of his nose, held out his hand. He looked pleased to see me, but I got a nervous vibe from him as he stubbed his cigarette out in the heavy glass ashtray.

'How was your flight?' he said as he blew out a lung full of thick grey Marlboro smoke.

'Fine thanks.'

I sat down at the table that was in the centre of the room. The five other actors had obviously been there for some time, judging by the dirty coffee cups and crushed Diet Coke tins. The flight over had been anything but fine, in fact it had been decidedly crap. Harley had thrown up on me just as I was giving her a kiss and saying goodbye to her at the airport, so I stank of sick while I was checking in. Then a baby sitting next to me decided to cry for the whole five thousand miles, and the air-conditioning had broken so the plane had been boiling hot for most of the trip. I hate lying to anyone, especially within seconds of meeting them, but I was too tired to go through the trip in detail. Besides, he didn't really want to hear – he was just being polite. The director took his glasses off and stuck them into the top pocket of his denim shirt.

'Martin . . . do you want to act out some scenes with us?'

I didn't – that was the last thing I wanted to do. What I really wanted to do was to go to my room and get into a hot bath.

'I'd love to.'

I acted out several of my scenes, and I was terrible. I couldn't remember a single line of the script that I had spent hours learning the week before. My insecurity was at an all-time high. I looked around room 101. Jesus, I missed the other guys – the band, the roadies with their disgusting jokes, the life I knew. I felt out of my depth. My insides felt like they were crying out for the safety and security of ten years back. I wanted to be back in the band so much it hurt!

I worked on the movie for three weeks. I remembered my lines and played the part as well as I could, but if a script isn't that great to start with then it's hard to turn out an Oscar-winning performance.

It was the summer of 1995, and I had been asked to fly out to Minnesota to start work on a movie called *The Embrace of a Vampire*. There wasn't much time to get myself together, I had to catch the plane two days later and be on the set working twenty-four hours after that. It always amazes me that production companies leave it so late before they cast the roles, especially the leads. It would be better for everyone involved if they were given more time: better for the director to have a chance to get to know the actor, and better for the actor to have time to prepare and to get comfortable with the idea of the role and the character that he or she is going to try to play. For this role there wasn't much imagination needed, admittedly. I was going to be a vampire, the tried and tested Count, and as long as I hissed in the right places it was going to be a breeze. The last time I was a Count was in the early days of the band, when I used to check into hotels under the pseudonym of Count DeNiro, which in English means count the money.

Counting the money was exactly what I was doing here. I knew that the film wasn't going to be another *Kray Twins* classic, but the cash was much needed, and I was working on the old Michael Caine principle of three for the money and one for me. And how true that is: it's always the films with the dodgy scripts that pay the money, and then, when you do come across one that is written well and you'd give anything to do it, that is exactly what they expect, and the wages are minimal.

It was the first day of filming and I was stripped to the waist, crawling around the floor of an old bell-tower, hyperventilating as I growled and snorted beast-like straight into camera. I had been shooting the scene for well over an hour now, and for a low-budget movie that's a lifetime. I was tired, my jet lag was terrible, and I had a headache that hit the back of my head every time I moved. One of the runners handed me a can of Coke to clear the dust out of my mouth and to help me wake up. It was the same guy that had picked me up from the airport the previous day. He looked too old to be doing that job; he had thick brown hair that was slightly greying at his temples and a moustache that hung well over his top lip. He looked like a cowboy in his snake-skin boots and massive silver buckled belt.

As we drove through town he pointed out the front of an old theatre and said, with a beautiful Southern drawl that fitted his image, 'You see that place there? I see you guys play in there back in eighty-four . . . Man, you were awesome.'

I couldn't work out if the theatre was on the way to the film set or if he had taken a detour to give me the guided tour. Either way he was quite excited, he had obviously been a big fan . . . and was having trouble hiding his enthusiasm.

'Thank you,' I said awkwardly.

'Man, they were good times.'

'It was a long time ago, though.' I was almost whispering to myself, hoping that he would give it up. I didn't feel up to having a full-blown conversation, but he heard me none the less.

'Jeez, man . . . why did you guys ever stop? You had the world at your feet . . . I would have given my back teeth to be in that position.'

'I like acting.' My answer seemed so weak, even to myself. I sounded so grown-up, so fucking English. Why would anyone in his right mind give up being in a successful band?

'Well, all I can say is you must *really* love it. The last time you were here you stayed in the best hotel in town . . . This time you're staying in the pits.' He sighed and blew out his stubbled cheeks. 'Man, you must really love it.'

Usually I wouldn't be able to recognize the outside of any theatre. They're not places that you ever get to see when you're in a band. When you arrive at the venue you go in through a side door, and when you come out you have to keep your head down as you make your way through a screaming crowd of kids all wanting autographs and a piece of skin.

But this theatre was different; the front of it did hold some memories. I remembered walking outside the glass swing doors and into the afternoon sunshine to lay my hands in a slab of wet cement, leaving my mark in front of the main entrance.

As we drove past, I glanced down to where the pavement held my name. I could see it clearly indented in the grey slab. I was mesmerized. I sucked in some of the cold air-conditioning and some of the cowboys' musty aftershave that the car was recirculating. I was seriously having an out-of-body experience. I felt as if I was looking down at myself from another life, or from a distant planet.

The cowboy spoke and brought me out of my private thoughts.

'Do you smoke?'

'No.'

'Do you mind if I do?' He was just about to light a Marlboro that was dangling from his pursed lips.

'Yes, I do . . .'

The cowboy was taken aback. 'Er . . . OK . . . I thought you rock and rollers didn't care about stuff like that . . . all the drugs, women and boozing you must've done.'

I snapped a little, I was sharper with my reply than I had intended.

'But that was rock and roll, this is acting. My sinuses are already blocked up by the flight . . . I won't be able to breathe if you light that thing.'

I knew I had disappointed him. I could tell that he had thought he was going to be picking up the rock and roller from Spandau Ballet.

He took the cigarette from his mouth and put it back into his box. He sulked for a moment before licking his lips and making a fresh start to our relationship. He felt the tension but he carried on smiling as he spoke to me.

'This college that we are going to work in was where Marlon Brando studied drama. You can see his name carved on one of the wooden beams, they say he put it there . . . but I couldn't say for sure.'

He was right. As I crawled around in the dirt, howling like a wolf on heat, taking my role as a possessed vampire far too seriously, I could see above me a carving on one of the bell-tower beams . . . M. Brando. Whether or not it was done by the man himself was a matter of contention, but it did give me the encouragement to dig down into my energy reserves and to get through the rest of the day's work.

When I had finished the scene and had got up off the floor, a photographer stopped me. His black, wiry hair stood up on end as if he had seen the devil himself, and an unlit 'roll up' drooped from the side of his mouth.

'Hey, buddy, do you mind if I take a few shots before you get changed? Would you lay back on the floor for me?'

I was too tired to argue, and went back down and took up my position once again. He spoke to me as he snapped away, capturing the creepy images.

'It's amazing what they have done to you, dude . . . I love the make-up.'

'Thanks,' I said, wanting to get this over as quickly as possible.

'Are those veins on your forehead prosthetic?'

'What veins?' I had never noticed any veins on my head before.

'Those huge veins . . . Are they stuck on?'

I felt my head with the tips of my fingers. It felt strangely bumpy. I hadn't ever felt anything like this before.

I looked over to the slide, where there was a mirror leaning up against a wall. I could see from a distance that my forehead looked like a relief map of the Rockies. I was shocked, and a sick feeling ran through my body and sent a cold shiver down the back of my spine. I could feel my scalp break out into a sweat and a bead of perspiration run from underneath my heavily gelled hair.

'OK, that's enough,' I said.

'Yeah, thanks man . . . good luck with the rest of the film.'

The photographer left me, and I got up and walked over to the mirror to get a better look at my head. What was going on? I had never seen anything like this before in my life. The veins in my head were swollen to such an extent that I could count my pulse just by looking at them. I didn't want to touch it again – it all looked too delicate, as if they would burst with the slightest touch. I thought to myself that I must just be overly tired, I knew that day's work had taken its toll, but this was freaking me out. I felt an overwhelming urge to lie down right there and then and relax, to meditate, but that had to wait until I got back to the privacy of my hotel room, which really was as nasty as the cowboy had told me. I got my things together, put my baseball cap on my head, pulling it down low to hide the mass of veins, and made my way back to my dressing-room. I didn't know it at the time, but what the photographer had pointed out to me was the network of veins that were supplying the hidden tumours with blood. It was my first real clue, and I missed it!

*

The second clue, that was also missed, was when I landed in Los Angeles to start work on a small independent film called *Cyber Bandit*. I was really racking up the bad films now, I was starting to wonder if I would ever be offered a good movie again. But this one seemed like it might be fun, because Adam Ant and Grace Jones were also lined up to take part, and Robert Hayes, the actor from the *Airplane* movies, was to play the bad guy. I had never met Adam, but I had met Grace before on an indulgent night out in London with Steve Strange. I knew she was fun and might make the time in LA pass quickly. The storyline was basic, but the film has a kind of *trash noir* quality that gives it some breathing space.

Here goes . . . I play a sailor called Jack Morris who has been given a CD rom containing the data needed to make a weapon that could . . . wait for it . . . destroy the world. Now to get rid of the CD rom, I have the data ingeniously tattooed on to my back, hidden inside a giant, beautifully decorated Japanese snake. When Grace Jones and Robert Hayes (the bad guys) find out, they also discover that the only way to get the information from my back is to feed the skin itself into a machine that will decipher its hidden code . . . Phew! I wish real life was as straightforward as that.

Adam, who played my friend in the film, was a nice guy. He reminded me of a young Sid James, in the way he laughed and the way he played his role, but there was something very rock star about him. He had that unmistakable wall built up in front of his emotions and behind his ego and protective pseudonym that was hard to break through. I could tell that he was finding the transition from singing to acting hard work, and that looking at life from a much more humble point of view was hurting his ego in exactly the same way as it had affected me over the last few years. Adam was a much bigger star than I ever was – when I looked at him it was hard not to see the white strip across his nose and the tassels in his hair. I always think of him on the cover of the *Radio Times* the week our first record came out. The headline was 'Would you let your daughter marry this man?' I thought we had been beaten to the post, that Adam and the Ants had stolen our thunder. I was wrong, of course – it only opened the doors wider for us to make an entrance of our own.

I knew only too well what pains Adam had gone through in the last few years as his career as a rock star slipped and reality started to sink in. It wasn't pleasant and it wasn't spoken about, but we both had that in common.

Grace was different; she was a star, and wanted everyone to lay their jackets down in front of her step. I loved watching her, from the moment she got off the plane wearing her JPG all-in-one commando outfit with full headgear, including flying goggles and accessories. She played hard to get with the director, coming out of her trailer two hours late and making the whole crew, me included, wait for the first shot of the day. But Grace is Grace, and she was outrageously good fun.

When I got off the plane at LAX, I was asked to go straight to see the local doctor, as I had to go through an examination for the insurance company. These examinations are more like a check-up than the real thing. They sit you down, ask you a few questions about old injuries and get you to roll your sleeve up so that they can take your blood pressure.

The room on Wilshire Boulevard was huge and was decorated with travel pictures and posters of Hawaii showing perfect sandy beaches and wonderful blue skies. In the corner was a tacky electric fountain that needed its water refilling. You could hear it sucking the water out of a half-empty bowl and desperately trying to push it up through the mouth of a stone leprechaun. I sank into the black leather sofa and waited for the nurse to come out and get me. The door opened at the far end of the room and a sweet-looking nurse with red hair and bright red lipstick came out and called my name.

'Mr Kemp . . . come in. This won't take long.'

She must have been about sixty, but her face had been pulled into a knot behind the back of her head, giving her the classic Californian smile.

As I stood to get up, I felt dizzy, my legs felt weak as if they were going to give way from underneath me. Christ, what a time to feel like this! What am I going to say when she says 'How are you?' What would she think if I said, 'Oh just a little bit dizzy . . . stand back, I might fall over?' I bet she wouldn't sign my insurance release then.

She must have sensed that something was wrong, for as soon as I got into her office she asked me to lie on the bed.

'Mr Kemp . . . you look flushed . . . are you OK?'

'Yes . . . fine . . . never felt better.'

She started to wrap the blood pressure cuff around my arm and squeezed on the little black rubber ball as she spoke to me. I could feel myself starting to panic. I knew what the result was going to be. I could feel something wasn't right and that my blood pressure was high.

'Just relax, Mr Kemp.'

The band around my arm started to tighten and I saw her eyes bulge from over the top of her small reading glasses.

'Oh my God!'

I knew what she was talking about straight away. I didn't have to look at the reading on the chart.

'Your blood pressure is incredible, Mr Kemp.'

'Thank you.' I tried to ease the moment by making her laugh.

'I want you to try to calm down . . . Think of a nice place for five minutes . . . er . . . we must get that blood pressure down.'

As she held my hand and made me breathe slowly in and out, I wanted to tell her about the swollen veins on my head that had happened a few months earlier, but I had to stop myself – this was after all an insurance medical.

It took half an hour to bring my blood pressure down before she signed the papers and let me out of her office. I should have put the two things together and realized that something was wrong with me. The bulging veins on my head, the high blood pressure – this wasn't normal, but I was just about to start the movie, so it would have to wait.

I had only been in Los Angeles a week when I called Shirlie and told her to get on the next flight out with Harley and Roman to come and join me. I hate being away from them for longer than a few days. It feels as if my whole body aches and I can't think straight. I need my family around me all the time, they give me the encouragement and the strength to keep going and to hold on to my ambitions.

After Shirlie and the kids had been there for a few days, making the compulsory trip to Disneyland and the ride through Universal Studios, she was exhausted when she woke up next to me on my first day off. We were staying in a hotel in West Hollywood, and it was nice. We had a good-sized living-room with a small kitchen at the far end, and a bedroom that had the biggest bed I've ever seen. That morning the kids had been awake since five. They don't understand jet lag, they just have to get up and go. They were watching a re-run of *Casper the Friendly Ghost* on the cartoon network, and eating egg and chips that Harley had ordered from room service. Harley has been travelling with us since she was a baby, and she knew the international code for room service was '2'.

Shirlie looked fantastic. It's amazing how a suntan can make you look great even if you feel exhausted. She was telling me how easy it was coming through passport control now that she had an American son with an American passport. At the same time she switched on the massive television that was at the end of the bed. Channel Five news popped on, and pictures of a small earthquake somewhere in the Valley were thrown up on to the giant screen. That wasn't unusual; there are small earthquakes every day in California. I laid my head down on her lap and let her stroke my hair as she always does. I let the warm feeling of safety and security flow through me. At that moment I had everything I needed: I was working, and I had my family around me.

Then Shirlie spoke, and I could hear a strange tension in her voice. I thought she was going to tell me that she was worried about the earthquakes, as she had done a million times over the last few years. She didn't.

'Martin . . . Have you felt this?'

I was just about to drift off back to sleep, I slowly opened my eyes. 'What?'

'This . . . on your head.' She moved her hand over my hair. 'Have you bashed your head?'

I thought back over the last few days. 'No . . . Why?'

'It feels like you have a bump on your head.'

'What?'

'A bump . . . It feels like there's a bump on the back of your head.'

I brought my hand up and ran my fingers through my hair. I couldn't feel a bump, my head felt the same to me as it had always done. Shirlie spoke to me again, I could tell she was concerned.

'Can you feel it?'

'No.'

'Look, give me your hand.'

She took my hand and placed it on the back of my head. It did feel slightly different, but it wasn't sore and it didn't feel like a soft swelling – it was my skull.

Shirlie spoke again. 'There, can you feel it now?'

'Oh, it's nothing,' I said. 'I must be getting old. Do you know that some people have their cranial bumps read to tell their fortunes? Don't worry . . . it's nothing.'

Shirlie got up out of bed and made her way into the *en suite* bathroom and shouted at me as she sat down on the toilet, 'Well it wasn't there a couple of weeks ago.'

I didn't say anything, distracted by the news report of another drive-by shooting. Another two young kids shot dead on the streets of LA for no apparent reason. The shooting had taken place about a block away from the place we were filming the day before.

Shirlie called out again. 'Did you hear me?'

I ran my fingers through my hair once again and felt the back of my head. It felt the same to me, there certainly wasn't a lump, and it definitely didn't hurt, but there was an odd feeling in the pit of my stomach that I couldn't explain, that hadn't been there before Shirlie had mentioned it. I can't believe that I never put all the signs together: the veins, the blood pressure and now the bump that Shirlie was so positive she could feel. She came out of the bathroom and jumped back into bed.

'Will you get someone to look at that?'

'Shirlie, it's nothing, I promise you . . . it's always been like that.'

The news reader took our attention once again, there was panic in his voice.

NEWS READER

There are horrific fires burning out of control through the Malibu hills. Already several homes and cars have been destroyed and fire fighters are struggling to get the blaze under control. So far no one has been injured, but the devastation to the community is, I'm afraid to say immeasurable . . . And all this after this wealthy part of LA has just recovered from the terrible mud slides we experienced only a few weeks ago!

Shirlie and I looked at each other. Each of us knew what the other was thinking: we couldn't have Harley and Roman growing up in Los Angeles. However, life carried on as normal, and I finished the movie while Shirlie and the kids sat around the pool. Two weeks later I said my goodbyes to Adam and Grace and we all flew back to England.

I had only been home a week, hardly enough time to unpack my bags and dig out my dirty washing, when I was sent to Canada. I was going to work on an episode of *The Outer Limits*, playing a demented scientist. It was there, as I sat in my trailer, looking at myself in the mirror wearing a ridiculous bald cap, that I saw that the small bump that Shirlie had found on the back of my head had grown into a fucking mountain.

Eight Hours Later

'MARTIN . . . *Martin* . . . *Martin* . . . You're back with us now, you're in the recovery room. Everything went fine.'

'My head hurts.'

The nurse gave me a shot in my leg. My head thumped. I managed to open my eyes for a moment before drifting in and out of a strange sleep. I felt as though someone had stuck me down to the bed with super glue, I couldn't move. I could just about open my mouth to mumble a word or two.

'I need a drink.'

I was more thirsty than I could ever remember being. The nurse smiled at me and stroked my face. The skin on her warm hand felt soft, and I could smell the hand cream as she gently pushed a plastic straw between my cracked lips. I would have paid a million for that one drop of water.

'How long was I out?'

'Nearly eight hours . . . just lie back and relax.'

'More water,' I said.

She held the straw up to my mouth once again and I pulled hard on the water. The injection was starting to take hold, and my body was starting to tingle around the edges like the boy on the Ready Brek advert.

*

'Martin . . . Martin . . . MARTIN . . .'

I opened my eyes again. I had been moved to the intensive care ward. I could just about see Shirlie at the end of the bed, her face was red, distraught with a pain that was far worse than my own. I was still in the bizarre world of anaesthetic and opium-based painkillers. Shirlie's reality hurt far more as she held my hand and whispered 'I love you' in my ear. My only response was to pull a funny face to try to let her see that I was OK, to reassure her that everything was as normal. Of course it wasn't – nothing would be the same again.

I could feel the huge bandage on my head and the pipes coming out of every corner of my body.

'I need a drink.'

Shirlie gave me some water and kissed me on the cheek. I could feel her face was wet and hot from crying, but the comfort she gave me was enough to send me back into my dream world.

'Martin . . . Martin . . . MARTIN . . .'

This time as I opened my eyes the pain was intense. A nurse came over before I could say a word and dumped two big bags of ice either side of my head, then rolled me over, sticking me with yet another barrel of opium. Dr C stood at the end of the bed with Shirlie. I had been moved again, this time into a private room on the top floor.

'Martin . . . It went very well, we got all of the tumour out . . . but we had to remove most of your skull.'

'No wonder I've got a headache.'

'Yes, I'm afraid that's par for the course.'

Dr C pulled back the thickly starched sheets and looked at my legs.

'Can you feel this?'

He dragged the sharp end of a pin across both of my feet.

'Only on my right foot.'

'Try and lift your left leg for me and wiggle your toes.'

I tried, and I tried again, but there was no response at all. My leg wasn't working. For the first time in my life it wasn't responding to a simple message. A wave of panic ran through my body. Christ, what if I can't walk? What am I going to do? What will the rest of my life be like? These were trying times, to say the least, and my head still thumped like crazy.

'The lump had grown up into your skull, that's why your head was so out of shape. It was as if the bone was protecting itself, rather like when your bone is broken and it reinforces itself around the weak spot . . . When we threw it away it weighed over two kilos.'

Wait a minute – did Dr C just say he threw my skull away, or was I hearing things?

'If you threw my skull away, what's holding in my brains, apart from the bandage?'

'Oh, they won't drop out, I assure you of that . . . but you will have to be careful when we send you home. You're going to need a metal plate and that won't be ready for three weeks . . . So you won't be able to roll around on the floor with the kids!'

'Damn! I wanted the lump in a jar so that I could put it on the shelf in my local boozer.'

Dr C smiled. I liked it when he did, it was reassuring and made me feel like we were a team, and in this mess together. Suddenly I heard myself yell, almost as if I was listening to someone else, as if the sound was coming from across the hall. It was intense and frightening.

'NURSE!'

The pain had overtaken my body and my 'Ready Brek' feeling had worn off. It was time for another bowl.

Sleep came and went in that following week. The blinds in my room were permanently closed. It was hard to decipher day from night.

My dreams turned into hallucinations, and when I closed my eyes to escape them, they just turned from black-and-white into Technicolor. There was one interesting hallucination. I was travelling around the inside of the Wimbledon ladies trophy. I could see every scratch, the smallest speck of dirt that had been hidden in the grooves of this prize piece of silverware. The hallucinations kept me awake for days. The only time I ever seemed to sleep was when Shirlie or my parents would come to visit. Only in the safety of their warmth would I let myself drift off.

Every day I tried to move my toes, willing them to move, slapping my leg, trying to get the blood moving and my reactions back. The nurse had told me that my leg would work, the feeling would return when the bruising on the brain had gone down. Thank God she was right. Within a week I was up and walking. I can't tell you my relief – every step was a pleasure.

Shirlie took me home and looked after me like a baby. I never moved from my chair in the living-room, not even to make a cup of tea. Having no skull was like being asked to carry around a freshly laid egg. By this time I had no bandages, just the skin sewn together holding the whole thing in place. Every time I moved I could feel the water in my head roll around, I could see my pulse pump and watch the top of my head move in time.

It was hard to look in the mirror, I looked like Frankenstein . . . A giant letter 'H' had been carved on to the top of my head and my scars showed clearly where I had been opened up like an envelope. I told Shirlie to keep the house lights down low in case a helicopter tried to land on me.

I didn't recognize the person I saw in the mirror. I tried to remember the face that was on the front of the *Record Mirror* and *The Face*. I held no resemblance to anyone I knew. I was frightened that I might scare Harley and Roman, that they might have nightmares over the way I looked, but being children it worried them less than it did me. In fact, by the end Harley would sit behind me while we were watching TV and pull out the stitches.

'Dad, you need a haircut,' Harley said, as she was busy picking. I had to laugh. I only had this tiny tuft that stuck up on the front.

'Why don't you cut that silly bit off?'

She was right. The next day I went to see my friend Claire, who smuggled me into the back of her shop and went at it with a razor. Now that was a strange sensation as she moved the electric razor around the soft part of my skull, and between the tram lines, sending ripples through my CSF (brain fluid).

Somehow, during this period even I had forgotten about the second little fellow – the other, smaller tumour that Dr C didn't want to talk about. It had to be dealt with at some point. I knew it was in there, but now wasn't the time to worry about it, and besides, in the back of my mind I was positive that it wouldn't grow.

The tumour wasn't the first time I had been in hospital for an operation. A few years earlier I had to go in to have another piece of metal put into my body. A screw had to be put into my left shoulder, basically to hold it together. I have always joked with Shirlie that after I've gone to that great gig in the sky, she will be able to get it back and hang it around her neck as a memory to the 'Last Screw'.

It was in Andorra in 1980 that a fall down the side of the French Alps ripped my arm from its socket. I carried the injury for the next couple of years, not wanting to go through with the operation that my doctor had told me I had to have. As the months rolled by my arm got steadily worse, it was popping out of its socket at every opportunity – playing snooker, swimming, even once on stage.

We were on stage in Japan, and two thousand Japanese girls had gathered in the local theatre to scream their lungs out and throw thousands of flowers up on to the stage. The Japanese were great audiences, if slightly different. They would scream and shout after every song, but as soon as you spoke a word into the mike they fell deadly quiet, all putting their hands over their mouths and giggling in silence. We soon found out that it was better not to say a word from start to finish of the concert.

We were in the middle of 'To Cut a Long Story Short', when I had wandered too close to the edge of the stage. I was enjoying the buzz of throwing those rock and roll shapes, with my bass guitar slung low around my young shoulders. The crowd were responding, feeding my ever-thirsty ego with cheers and yet more carnations.

At the point where I had taken in enough of that wonderful sound, I turned to go back to the drum riser. I could see John behind his now massive drum kit, smashing his cymbals as he laughed at me. I smiled back. This is what we had dreamed of, this is what we had worked towards, but this wasn't a dream; we *were* actually rock stars . . . and it felt fantastic.

I had only taken a single step towards John when one of the kids at the very front of the stage grabbed on to my leather jeans. I tried to keep my balance and to continue hitting the notes of the song. If you hit a bum note on a bass guitar it booms out like a giant foghorn. I tried to remain upright, but my other foot came down on a bunch of flowers. They slipped from under my foot. The girl on my other foot let go of my jeans, as she realized I was about to lose the struggle and fall to the floor. I could hear her call my name as twelve stone of pretentious rock star fell to the floor.

'Martin . . .'

As I hit the deck, my bass guitar boomed out a horrible, low, brassy feedback. I realized that the whole audience had their white gloved hands over their mouths. They were silent, all waiting for me to get back up.

I looked slowly around. I had taken a bit of a whack on the head, as well as a dent in my ego, and slowly started to get back on to my feet. The other guys all looked at me in a strange way as they carried on with the song. It was only when I was back on my feet that I realized that my arm was sticking out of my body at a right angle. It had been wrenched out of its socket and jammed in the up position. I couldn't move. If I tried to walk, the weight of the guitar pushed down on my shoulder and the pain was excruciating. I could feel the blood starting to drain away from my face, and a sick feeling was rushing through my body. The last thing I wanted to do was to faint in front of the audience. How stupid would that be?

In the wings was a guy called Nicky Sibely. He was the first person we ever employed to help us, a kind of roadie, as well as a friend. Thank God he was watching me. He ran out on to the stage, grabbed hold of me and turned me around to face him. He then went behind my back and snapped my arm back into its socket. My arm fell from its heavenly position and the quiet crowd roared its approval.

The concert finished, Keeble gave me his own bottle of Jack to numb the pain and to get me through the party that followed the gig, but the next day something had to be done. When the hotel in Tokyo said they were going to get me a doctor, that's what I expected – a doctor with a shoulder support and pain-killers. The doorbell rang at about eleven, when I was just coming out of the morning's hangover. I couldn't quite work out what hurt the most, but I thought that if the doc did give me some pain-killers for my arm, they were bound to have a good side-effect on my head, and kill two birds with one stone.

I opened the door. A small Japanese man in his late sixties walked into my room. He would have been great casting for a Bond movie. He wore a small pair of thick round glasses on the bridge of his nose, and his blackened teeth stuck out at me from between his dry lips. I was worried about my breath until I smelt his; it stank of seaweed and he had every intention of blowing it all over me.

He laid me down on the bed and opened his small brown case. He got out a white envelope and tore it open. Inside was a piece of linen, which he unrolled. I looked on, fascinated. He hadn't said a word to me yet, but I wasn't that worried – in the state I was in I don't think I could have held a conversation together anyway. He unrolled the piece of linen and pulled out a set of about thirty or so tiny needles.

'Just welax.'

Acupuncture for a dislocated shoulder? . . . How?

'Look, I have a bad shoulder!'

'I know . . . just welax and turn over on to your front . . . face down.'

I felt his cold tiny hands on my tender joint, pulling at the skin that was gingerly holding it all in place.

'Ouch!'

'Just welaxxx.'

'Ouch!' I couldn't believe that wasn't an international word for pain. He completely ignored me and carried on with his job. I stayed there on the bed until he had every tiny needle in place around my shoulder. I watched as he went for his bag once more, this time taking out a huge sticking plaster.

'Bweathe in.'

He rolled the plaster over my shoulder and on top of every needle, sticking them firmly in place.

'OK, I must go . . . I will see you again tomorrow.'

I sat up, and the pins dug deeper into my skin.

'Ouch . . . er, look you can't leave me like this . . . I have a show tonight.'

He didn't have a clue what I said, and didn't even turn to look at me as he let himself out of the door.

'Bye . . .' And as quickly as he had come in, he had left. I was right about one thing, my hangover had completely gone, but what was I going to do tonight? The pins and plaster were exactly where my heavy bass guitar hangs from its black leather strap.

I gave myself the afternoon to rest, feeling more relaxed than I had been for a long time. A couple of the boys called, asking me to go into town for lunch, but even with my insatiable hunger for Japanese food I declined. It was as if I had been given some kind of happy drug.

The show that night was fantastic. The lights were brighter than usual, the sound was sharper, but every time I tried to throw a rock and roll shape, I would get a sharp pain in my arm from the thirty or so pins that were still under the sticking plaster. Maybe that was his cure: to calm me down on stage so that I wouldn't be in any danger of falling over. Whatever it was, it worked for a while. As soon as I got home I went into hospital to have it mechanically fixed in the comfort and safety of St John's Wood.

Three weeks had passed since my meningioma had been removed. I was still at home, taking care of my exposed brain. I'd had no major mishaps and even had a trip to Kipling's, my local curry palace.

Before I could say brain salad surgery, I was back in the hospital ready to be fitted with my new metal skull.

'Hold out your hand . . . You're gonna feel a sharp prick . . . That's it . . . Now count to ten for me.'

Just as I was going under the anaesthetic, Dr C appeared in his green face mask and little green surgical hat.

'You're OK, Martin, I'm gonna look after you. This won't take long, we're just going to pop you under and put your new head in place.'

His words as always were warm and he spoke with that soft Irish accent that I had learnt to trust. I started to take that journey back down the spinning twister, into the land of nothing, where time stands still and where the world stops turning. The pictures on the walls of the giant twister were back again. This time I tried to look deeper into the frames. I wanted the security of knowing that I was with the people I love and wasn't on my own in this mess. I started to panic as I realized that the frames were completely empty. For a moment I had a terrible thought – I thought I was going to stop breathing and suffocate. I could taste the anaesthetic in my mouth. I had coped with so much pain over the last few weeks, putting a brave face on my darkest of moments, but now for the first time I was really scared. I felt my hands jump and the needle in my arm dig further into my vein.

'It's OK, Martin, just try to relax.'

I could feel myself fighting this . . . I knew I needed a head, but all of a sudden I found myself in a giant panic.

'Martin . . . Listen to me . . . Count to five.'

'One . . . two . . . threeeeeeeeeeee.'

This time there was no great vision, no pictures, no smells, nothing, just a darkness that seemed to last for a click of the fingers.

Going under the anaesthetic must be the closest thing to death that a human being can experience before the big day itself. It's as if all systems close down around you, only starting up again when the doctor tells you softly that it's all over.

*

'ROLL CAMERAS.' . . . I opened my eyes . . . Where am I?

'ACTION.' . . . I looked around. Shirlie was sitting at the end of my bed, fast asleep. What was going on? Was I still in some weird dream brought on by the remains of the drugs. I had been up from the theatre for about six hours. I tried to lift my head off the pillow . . . WHACK! It felt just as if someone had hit me across the back of the head with a blunt hammer. I noticed that there was a strange light in my room, a surreal glow that looked artificial. I closed my eyes, I must be dreaming.

'CUT.'

That was no dream. I definitely heard someone say that. I looked back at Shirlie. She had woken up and was now standing next to the nurse at the foot of the bed.

'Hi, darling . . . Are you OK?' she said.

I didn't have a clue what was going on. I could feel my head thump underneath the bandages that held it together. I tried to speak but my mouth was far too dry. Shirlie held some ice up to my lips as the nurse spoke to me.

'Just suck on the ice, we don't want you to be sick.'

I sucked. It felt like heaven.

'CHECK THE GATE.'

'What's that?' I asked.

Shirlie smiled and stroked my hand.

'They're making a movie outside the hospital in the street below the window. The assistant director must be using a megaphone.'

I licked my lips . . . 'Thank Christ for that, I thought I was dying.'

My head seemed to hurt more than ever. The bandages seemed to be tighter. The tubes and pipes that drained my head of excess fluid seemed to be placed in the centre of my head, stopping me from lying down comfortably on my back. Everything was sore. The only thing that would stop the constant thump was the wonderful pain-killing injections. The fluid levels in my head weren't settling down, sometimes it would drain quicker than it should and then at other times it would swell, making the back of my head pump like something from a different galaxy.

Time passed ever so slowly over the next six weeks. I had been in the same position since they screwed on my new metal head. Not once had I been able to get my head from off the bed, or even raise the back of my bed a couple of notches to a more upright position. I began to wonder if the pounding headaches would ever go, if I would ever get my body into an upright position again. I hated eating and drinking lying down, and as for using the bedpan, my embarrassment had long left me but it was excruciatingly painful. I knew that Shirlie was getting ever so worried, and my mum and dad were already at their wits' end. I had to get through the pain barrier and sit upright. One of the nurses had told me that as soon as I could do that, my fluids would re-arrange themselves accordingly, but the pain barrier was unbelievable; it was like trying to ignore someone ripping out your spinal column.

One evening, when I had been in bed for nearly seven weeks, I had finished my plate of macaroni cheese and was about to make an attempt at my pudding before settling down for the night. Shirlie and my parents had gone home about half an hour earlier and I was left alone, just myself and the hit-man standing behind me with the jack hammer, ready to pounce on my slightest movement.

EastEnders had just finished on the television that was suspended on a bracket hanging down from the ceiling in the corner of the room, and the titles to the next programme had just started to roll. It was presented by David Frost and was one of those shows about the unexplained. Where good old Uri Geller will claim to bend the BBC cutlery, and all sorts of mind-readers will be wheeled out to fill the hour-long show, all claiming to see into a complete stranger's thoughts. This was all no different from shows that I'd seen a million times before, but just as I was coming to the end of my jam and semolina pudding and was about to switch off, a man appeared and started to take his shoes and socks off. He was going to walk over a bed of hot coals, burning at over one thousand degrees. There was something different about this guy. He certainly wasn't any kind of Tibetan monk, and he definitely wasn't a greasy new age traveller. He was just an ordinary bloke, someone you might bump into down the local pub. David Frost spoke to him. You could tell that the guy was concentrating on the task ahead – making good television chatter wasn't one of his immediate priorities. He walked to the edge of the burning hot coals, and after a deep breath walked out on to the furnace. He got to the other side with nothing more than a scratch. I pushed my empty tray to one side and closed my eyes for a moment. What that guy had just done was all about willpower, mind over matter. He had just given a perfect example of mind over pain.

I felt so useless. This guy could walk out on to a burning bed of red-hot coals, but I couldn't lift my head from my pillow and face my own pain barrier. I *had* to do it, I couldn't stay in this bed any longer. I turned off the television in disgust, then I closed my eyes. I had to do it . . . and do it now. I grabbed hold of the side rails that ran along the edge of the bed, and slowly started to pull, an inch, two inches, three inches . . . and then, as if Thor had thrown a lightning bolt directly at me, a pain of mythological proportions ran up my spine and into my head. I lay back down and stared up at the familiar ceiling. I thought to myself that the guy on television hadn't walked out on to his coals slowly, he had made a decision to do it, set the task clearly in his mind and gone for it. There was no option to him, he was going to reach the other side. I held on to the rails once again. I knew that Thor wasn't going to be any happier now than he was the last time, but now was the time to meet my opposition head on. I took in a deep breath, counted to three, and pulled . . . I made it!

At first there was nothing, no pain at all, I thought maybe I had been too fast for him and that he had missed my trick all together, but then . . . WHACK . . . WHACK . . . WHACK. It was incredible pain, I didn't know if I could take many more blows before giving in. I thought to myself that I would let him hit me three more times before I lay back down in my bed and gave in to the greater force. I counted the blows.

WHACK . . . one . . . WHACK . . . two . . . whack . . . three . . . I stayed there . . . the last blow was definitely smaller . . . it was as if the power had drained out of his hammer . . . four . . . five . . . six.

My door opened, and the Indian dinner lady pushed her caring face into the gap. She saw me sitting up in my bed.

'Oh my god . . . Martin.'

I was grey, drained of blood and enzymes, but I was up!

The dinner lady called the doctor, who then called the nurse, who then called Shirlie on the phone. I think she broke all records that day for the journey from Muswell Hill to Queen Square.

For seven weeks I had been badly beaten into submission, but now, thanks to the guy on the television giving me that perfect example of mind over matter, I was up, and one week later was on my way home from hospital, and with a metal head to go with my metal screw.

Within a year I was back at work, in an episode of the American cable television show called *Tales from the Crypt*, and a small low-budget English movie called *Monk Dawson*. They weren't classics, but I was up and getting my confidence back. Every day that passed was a step away from the darkest moment of my life. I was starting to relax as well, taking the family on holiday to Ibiza to visit Steve Norman, and making several trips down to the Dorset coast to stay with my mum and dad. Life was starting to return to normal. It was taking time, but it was slowly returning.

The Second Brain Tumour

'Martin. Can you come into the surgery some time tomorrow.'

It was a cold Friday afternoon when Shirlie and I walked down past Lord's cricket ground and into the Wellington Hospital in St John's Wood. The clouds hung in the sky, like giant lumps of cotton wool filled with old make-up that had been removed after a night on the town. Dr C had called me that afternoon and asked to see me following a scan that I had two days earlier. I could tell by the tone of his voice that everything wasn't all OK. I had come to know Dr C's voice patterns only too well. I could tell if he was smiling on the other end of the phone and had called to give me the good news on my recovery, or if what he was about to tell me was serious and would affect the rest of my life. This time his voice was slow, deadpan, and growled slightly at the end of all his sentences.

I answered in a bright, almost happy, high-pitched voice, 'Sure . . . How are you?'

'Oh, I'm fine . . . but I want to go over your scans with you.'

'Sure . . . Is everything OK?'

'We can go over that tomorrow when we meet . . . Look, can you make an appointment with my secretary.'

My voice now dropped a tone or two and slowed down to match Dr C's. 'Sure . . . I'll see you later then.'

I put the phone down. I knew exactly why he wanted me in the

227

office and why he wanted to talk to me face to face. I'm not that stupid. My knees felt like jelly as I sat on the chair behind my desk, my mind racing with a million thoughts. The screen saver on the computer was flashing up pictures of Harley, Roman and Shirlie caught in happy moments over the last two years: the four of us over at the park with our dog during the long hot summer, and Harley and Roman with Mickey Mouse at Disneyland. It had been two years since I had been out of hospital, the hardest two years of my life. I was now starting to see the light at the end of the tunnel. The last thing I wanted now was to go back into hospital and have my metal lid removed for another mammoth operation, and yet another two-year recovery.

I had always known in the back of my mind that it was coming. I knew it had to be done at some point. A brain tumour isn't something you can ignore and hope that it might just evaporate. It isn't like a spot, if you leave it alone it will just heal itself. These things get bigger every day, it's just a matter of the speed at which they grow. If you're lucky and they grow slowly like the one I had removed, you could have ten years, but if they decide to grow fast, then Bob's your uncle.

It was funny, but in the last two years I must have heard of at least sixty people who had brain tumours. Anyone who knew someone with a tumour wanted to tell me their grisly story. Everyone wanted to pass on their knowledge, sometimes to reassure me that every-thing was going to be all right, and sometimes to show me how lucky I was that my tumour was benign. Other people would tell me their stories almost as if they were cleansing their own heads, as if by telling me they were ridding themselves of their own fears.

It was always the second little fellow, as Dr C had lovingly called it, that frightened me the most. It was the second little fellow that made me feel as if someone was really out to get me. OK, you can have a brain tumour, cut it out and get on with life and accept the consequences along the way, but to get two was really unfair. Whoever dealt me that hand didn't want me to move along the board any further.

The first tumour had grown on the meninges which wrapped themselves around the outside of the brain. The problem with that and all tumours is that the bigger they get, the more pressure is put on to the brain, sometimes even cutting off vital blood supply. I had my first one growing inside my skull for years without feeling the slightest effect, apart from a blocked sinus, and even though it was huge I was lucky: it was sitting between my brain and my skull, and was relatively easy to get at.

The second little fellow had decided to latch itself on to the centre of my brain in the space right at the top of the spine. Now you don't have to be a brain surgeon to know this meant trouble.

When I was in the hospital recovering from the first operation, everyone would come in to visit me, telling me that the nightmare was all over and how I could start to look ahead. Only I knew that the nightmare was only half the way through. I always knew there was the second little fellow to deal with, a second tumour sitting there, growing quietly in the warm confines of my brain.

Shirlie and I walked into Dr C's office. He already had my scans up on the light box that was hanging on the wall. The pictures of my inner head were throwing weird, contorted shadows in the darkened room.

'Come in . . . Martin, Shirlie, come and see what we have here.'

I walked up to the light box. I knew exactly what I was looking for and where to look. Shirlie took a deep breath and held my hand.

'Well, it's growing! I think we have to get it out.'

'Shit.' My heart had missed a beat and my hands started to sweat.

'We always knew we would have to take it out at some point, and I think that point is now.'

A wave of emotion passed over me and for a moment I thought I was going to faint. Shirlie felt my hand go cold, and I heard her cracked voice.

'Martin, sit down in the chair.'

I sat down with my head in between my legs and let Shirlie do the rest of the talking.

'When? . . . I mean, how soon?'

'Well, not tomorrow.'

'What's the risks with the operation . . . is it dangerous?'

'Let me show you. Look here on the scan.'

Shirlie moved in closer to the light box. Their voices were spinning around in my head, every word making me weaker by the second.

'The tumour is in the centre of the brain, sitting next to the regions that control his eyes and his memory . . . Now, as careful as we will be in getting in there, there is still a risk factor . . . We will have to pull the two sides of the brain apart and work our way down the central canal to get at the thing. In doing that Martin will, no doubt, suffer a lot of bruising.'

'You said we don't have to do this tomorrow, so we have time for a second opinion.'

My ears pricked up. What? Shirlie was asking for a second opinion. I had to admire her. I hated asking for second opinions about anything. I always feel like I'm saying 'I don't trust you', or 'Let me speak to your boss' . . . Dr C replied without the slightest hesitation, 'Of course . . . There's a doctor in America that might be able to help. Professor Black . . . Let's send the scans over to him and see if he can come up with an alternative, but whatever way we use, we need to get this little chap out of your head.'

I felt physically sick. I thought for a moment that I might have to get to a bathroom.

'Martin, do you want a drink of water?'

I remembered sitting in the same chair two years earlier feeling exactly the same, being asked the same question – if I wanted that glass of water. It was like a recurring nightmare, only I couldn't wake up. I couldn't believe it was happening again.

We left the office and made our way along the corridor and to the lifts. We waited in silence for a couple of minutes before I found enough breath in my body to squeeze out some air . . .

'Thanks.'

'What for?'

'Everything.'

Shirlie's eyes filled with water as she tried hard to hold back the tears. The two metal doors slid open and Shirlie and I moved into the empty elevator.

We waited about a week before Professor Black answered our letter and found time to take a look at my scans, but when he did it was quite encouraging. He suggested that the tumour might be treatable with 'tactical radiation'. It was a relatively new form of therapy, but one that had been quite successful on people with malignant tumours in awkward places. He told me in his letter to call him at some point to go over the procedure. I tried for several days with no luck, until finally his assistant put me through to him while he was working in an operating theatre in Boston. I could almost smell the anaesthetic and rubber gloves. The conversation was punctuated by the sound of the life-support machines and various faceless people asking for surgical instruments. It was like being in on an episode of *ER*.

BEEP . . .

'Professor Black . . . Is that you?'

'Martin . . . Nice to speak to you at last.'

BEEP . . . *More light over here.'*

'I can't talk for long, Martin, but the letter I sent you covers just about everything . . . Are you feeling OK at the moment?'

'A little scared.'

BEEP . . . *'Pass the scalpel.'*

I had to get off the phone, I was starting to feel woozy.

BEEP . . .

'Martin, I must go, I'm in the middle of something, but I'm glad we touched base.'

'Professor Black . . . What side-effects are there from the procedure? I can't believe I'll walk away from this scot-free!'

BEEP . . . *'Clamp it for me!'*

'None, we hope . . . Anyway, like I said, I'm a little busy right at this moment . . . Bye.'

'Yes . . . Bye.'

Well, it looked to me as though there was no choice. There was either surgery or the radiation, and I had definitely had enough of the surgery. There were only two places in Britain that had the stereo-tactic-radiation machines, and one of them was St Bartholomew's, which was only a few miles from my house. I had already made up my mind that I didn't want to go back into the National Hospital and be opened up again, no matter how nice the food was, and no matter how sweet my little Irish nurse could be. There was really no choice.

The whole procedure was going to last for two days. The first would be spent letting the doctors take measurements of my head. They were going to make a head frame that would screw directly on to the giant radiation machine, locking me in place, keeping me perfectly still while the tumour in the centre of my brain received a massive dose of X-ray, killing off any living tissue it touched. You can see why they were going to such great lengths to make sure that I was screwed in place, unable to move. If they misjudged the shot by a fraction of a millimetre, I could end up blind or unable to speak. It had frightened me to be told by Doctor C that the tumour lay among the area of the brain that controlled the eye movement. This was one time in my life I was going to sit still.

The morning of the treatment was strange. Even though I was relaxed, I felt a strange tingling in my arms and legs in anticipation. I had waited to come face to face with this moment for the last two years. The pressure of knowing I was carrying around a brain tumour for that amount of time had worn me down. I was tired, irritable and felt that I was carrying the world on my shoulders. With the first tumour, I never knew I had it until the day before they cut it out. This one I had had to live with, watching it grow silently at every MRI scan. This was a very different ball game.

I had spent the previous two years trying to keep it quiet. I didn't want it getting into the press that I had another tumour, or no one would have hired me to work on a movie ever again. I denied any rumours, only letting my closest of friends in on my terrible secret. *'Don't mention it to anyone'* became my favourite catchphrase.

The hardest part of all was listening to people congratulate me on my recovery, asking me how it felt now that it was all over. I wanted to pour out my heart to everyone and tell them that I was only half-way home. I desperately wanted their support. I smiled politely and lied, and said how happy I was now that it was all over.

I was told that the side-effects from the radiation wouldn't show themselves until about six months later, the side-effects being if any of the brain was hit by the high dose of X-rays and died along with the tumour. Still, it was either that or death . . . No contest!

The streets outside the red-brick hospital were busy by the time I arrived for my nine o'clock appointment. The smell coming from the meat market on the other side of the road hung heavy in the air, and its workers, proudly displaying the dark red blood on the front of their white cotton coats like medals of endeavour, were busy loading the huge sides of cow on to a fleet of butchers' vans lining the pavement.

Shirlie and I made our way through the giant blue metal hospital gates that had welcomed the sick for over eight hundred years, and into the cancer ward where they were expecting us. The cancer ward in any hospital is a world where nightmares are made; where men, women and children alike are told that they have the sometimes incurable disease; where people are told that they have months, weeks, sometimes just days to live and to make their peace with the world. It made me step back for a moment and appreciate just how lucky I was that my tumour was benign. If it had been malignant, I would have been dead a long time ago.

We made our way down the long corridor, past an old couple who were sitting outside a doctor's office, squeezing each other's hands reassuringly, then past a young mother with two children playing by her side. One of the little boys had no hair from the radiation treatment and looked a strange shade of yellow. She kissed him on the head and whispered something in his ear that made him smile.

'Stand back.'

I looked up, an elderly woman in a bed was being pushed straight down the small corridor towards us. The old woman's eyes were closed and her mouth hung loose at the jaw. Her hair was white, a lifetime of worry having taken its toll. I wanted to look longer, but a strange feeling of guilt overtook me and made me look away. I felt as if I was stealing her silence.

We reached the room at the end of the corridor, I rang on the small plastic doorbell, and Shirlie and I waited outside the room. I felt odd, I didn't want to sit in the chairs outside. I didn't want to be a patient in a cancer ward, it frightened me too much. The door opened.

'Martin, come in, old chap!'

Shirlie and I followed the young doctor into the room. There was a table in the middle and on it what looked like some strange medieval torture contraption.

'How do you like it? It's your head frame. We finished it last night after you had gone home,' he said proudly.

'Nice,' I said under my breath. I didn't mean it to sound sarcastic, but that's how it came out.

The young doctor walked around the back of me and quietly slid a wheelchair up behind my knees.

'Take a seat.'

As soon as I sat down he placed the metal frame over my head. He slid a gum-shield into my mouth and up around my teeth.

'Comfortable?' he whispered to himself. He then pulled out a tool from his pocket and bolted on the Perspex sides that were covered in markings and measurements that had been meticulously made the day before. In a matter of moments my head was completely encased in this see-through box.

'How does it feel?' He smiled to himself, pleased with his work.

'Alllriiiighht.' I couldn't talk, the most I could do was dribble.

'Don't worry, Martin, this whole thing won't take long. We're going to wheel you over the road to the stereo-tactic-radiation department. That's where they'll do the surgery.'

'Over the road?' Shirlie said.

'Yes. It's not far, just about two hundred yards.'

Before I knew it I was being pushed along the pavement outside the hospital. My Perspex box keeping me out of the cold, but making me the centre of attention. Some people stared, others found it just too embarrassing to look at and, like myself with the old lady moments earlier, shot me a quick glance and then looked the other way. I had to laugh – I had spent months worrying that people were going to find out that I was having treatment on a second brain tumour, and here I was being pushed up the high street in a wheelchair with this Perspex box on my head. I had never felt so conspicuous in my life. Even in the mad monk's dress I had never drawn so much attention.

I was wheeled into the radiation theatre and met by the sight of two young girls, both wearing head boxes similar to mine. We sat opposite each other, waiting our turn to be zapped. After a few minutes I found myself looking into the eyes of one of them. I tried to smile, but a long strand of dribble just swung from my bottom lip. It was best if I shut myself off and stayed inside my box until this episode was over. All I needed now was a nurse to ask for my autograph.

'Are you OK, Gary?' The nurse had crept up on my blind side.

'Martin,' Shirlie said.

'I'm sorry, it's just that I was watching *The Bodyguard* the other night . . . He was awfully good in that . . . Did he meet Kevin Costner?'

'I should think so somehow!' Shirlie replied.

'Kevin's my idol . . . Anyway, this won't take long.'

She took hold of the handles at the back of the chair and pushed me through two giant rubber swing doors. Shirlie followed.

'Yes, I've got all his movies.' The nurse carried on talking as Shirlie and I got our first glimpse of the colossal machine that was going to save my life. *The Untouchables* was my favourite . . . Yes Kevin's the one for me. OK, let's have you out of there, Gary . . . Ooops!'

Gently, two other nurses helped me out of my wheelchair and up on to a bed. The bed was then slowly pushed into place beneath the enormous radiation machine which looked as if it belonged inside a Fritz Lang movie.

The head frame I was wearing was bolted on to the main frame of the machine until we became one. I bit down hard on the rubber gum-shield that was to help keep me still and in place for the next thirty minutes.

'OK, Gary . . . I mean Martin, we're starting the treatment now, we will just be in the room off to the side, your wife can come and watch on the monitor in there with us.'

Shirlie leaned in and whispered in my ear, 'Stay still won't you?'

I gurgled back, 'I can't bloody move!'

A noise came from deep inside the X-ray machine, a deep, growling sound, it wasn't friendly, you could hear that this piece of equipment meant business. The giant X-ray gun started to move around my head, stopping at the points that had been meticulously typed into the computer programme.

BANG . . .

I heard Shirlie's voice saying, 'What was that?'

'Oh . . . it's the machine . . . it's a few years old . . . it plays up every so often.'

I couldn't believe this. Here I was, lying on my back, screwed on to a machine that was going to burn out the inside of my brain. The smallest of errors could leave me in a rather sticky position for the rest of my life, to say the least, and the day I decide to use it, it starts to play up . . . Great!

The nurse came over to me. 'Mr Kemp . . . That's easier, isn't it!' – she laughed quietly to herself – 'Mr Kemp, we're just going to start the programme again . . . it's an old machine.'

What did she want me to do – feel sorry for it! The nurse and Shirlie walked off into the protective room, and watched through the Perspex glass as the machine went into action for the second time that morning. This time it seemed to cough and splutter a little, but within a couple of minutes it was working properly and moved around my head in giant sweeps. The noise of the machine was almost 'new age'; it had a tone to it that made me drift off into a deep state of meditation, half-way between my conscious and my subconscious.

The nightmare was nearly all over for me, but I couldn't help feeling that in some ways a new one was only just beginning. What was I going to do now? I had lost the brash confidence that I had in Spandau Ballet. The incredible power I had experienced while I filmed *The Krays* had long since left me. The vulnerability of life was all too clear; it was far too fragile ever to take for granted again. These thoughts were making my fists clench as I lay on the bed. I wanted desperately to relax and help the healing process, but it was impossible.

Over the last few years I had become comfortable with being a victim, comfortable in sitting back and letting things just happen around me. The idea of having to get back into reality, to take on the responsibilities of life again frightened me.

Shirlie, in her unstoppable devotion to getting me better, had enveloped me in the softest cotton wool imaginable, and now it was time to unwrap myself and once again feel the cold winds. I was frightened, I had to think about working, about mixing with people, about real life. A friend of mine who had spent most of his life in prison once told me, that in a strange way he felt secure inside, and how not having to face the real world was one of the perks of being locked up. I laughed at him at the time, but now, all of a sudden, what he had said made enormous sense to me.

Over the previous three years, I had suppressed so much pain, so many fears of dying, so many thoughts of leaving behind my children and letting them grow up and face the world on their own. Watching the agony I put Shirlie through and not being able to do a thing about it had left a scar on my heart. I was terrified. I knew that when this giant machine had done its job, it would be time for me

237

to face the music. I finally relaxed into the rumbling hum and drifted off.

I was out in LA for a quick visit when a friend of mine suggested that I should try a flotation tank, it's supposed to relieve you of all kinds of stress and tensions. I certainly needed it, the pressure of the castings was really getting to me, and I hadn't seen Shirlie and the kids for at least four weeks. They were back in England because Shirlie's mother had been taken ill. I went along to this small house in West Hollywood near Sunset Boulevard where a plaque on the door said 'flotation centre'. I wasn't alone – I wasn't that brave! I was with Gary, Steve Dagger and Marco Pironi, the guitarist from Adam and the Ants, all of us in need of some kind of relief.

It was everything my friend had told me it would be. I found it a truly amazing experience, after getting over the initial claustrophobia. The tank is small, just a little bigger than your average coffin, and made from a thick light blue plastic. It's filled with about ten inches of warm salt water which is kept at body temperature. The idea is to close the door behind you, locking out any sounds and light, and then to lie down in the water and float on your back for about an hour: complete sensory deprivation. For me it was amazing; within seconds I was in a world of dreams and was already vowing to do it again. It was the heaviest form of meditation I had ever experienced. I felt as though my conscious state had closed down for a while, and my subconscious was running wild in its temporary moment of freedom. When my hour was over, a little red light went on inside the tank. I got out feeling refreshed and with a sense of smell and taste that I had forgotten I had.

Fifteen minutes later we were all sitting in a restaurant on the other side of Sunset Boulevard, talking about our wonderful experiences, when Marco broke away from his four-cheese pizza.

'I thought it was fucking amazing, it was like a wonderful trip. At one stage I thought I could hear "Sergeant Pepper's Lonely Hearts Club Band". It must do incredible things to your head.'

Steve Dagger looked up. 'That's funny, I thought I could hear that as well.'

'Really . . . That's weird.'

Gary, who was only eating a small salad as usual, broke the moment: 'Look over there!'

On the other side of the road, right next door to the flotation centre, was Groove Records, a retro record shop. In the front window was a giant advertisement for the old Beatles album at a knock-down price.

Marco hid his disappointment in another bit of pizza and called for the bill.

I drifted out of one dream and into another with complete ease as the machine carried on with its delicate work inside my head. I started to think about a party we were at once after the premiere of *Backbeat*. It was at the Waldorf Hotel, and everyone was there – the cast, celebrities, movie stars, rock stars, the usual party crowd. I was standing by the ornate golden bar, drinking with Derek, Pepsi's long-standing boyfriend, knocking back my twentieth glass of champagne when a girl came over to me and stood by my side. She held out a pen and a small piece of paper. Her lipstick was deep red and her perfume was dangerously flammable.

'Excuse me, could I have an autograph?'

I signed her paper napkin and gave it back to her, my ego having just scored another ten points. She took it from me and stared at it for a moment. Her glass jewellery tried desperately to sparkle under the glass chandelier that hung from the ceiling. She looked puzzled.

'What does that say?'

Before I could answer she looked at it again and breathed out the remains of her Silk Cut.

'Oh, I know, you're in Duran Duran.'

'No no no . . . I'm in Spandau Ballet.'

She looked at me again. 'Oh, that's right, I'm sorry, I saw you in *The Bodyguard* . . . You're Gary Kemp.'

My ego had just been punctured and I could feel Derek enjoying the moment . . . I laughed politely through my gritted teeth.

'No, that's my brother.'

She looked again at the crumpled paper napkin she held in her black lace gloves.

'Oh, of course, I am *so* sorry, but I couldn't read your hand-writing.'

'That's OK, don't worry about it.'

Derek tried to rescue me. 'Fancy another beer, Mart?'

The girl got the message and started to walk away.

Derek leaned in closer to my ear. I could hear him laughing under his breath.

'Can you believe it . . . Some people!'

Just then the girl turned around, and as the music died out she shouted back at me, 'Thanks a lot . . . I'll see you then, Tony!'

The X-ray machine took nearly half an hour to scorch out the brain tumour. I came around as they were unscrewing my head and detaching me from the main frame.

Shirlie was the first by my side as usual. 'How are you?'

'Not too bad, I had some weird thoughts, I was at a party.'

'Well that makes a change!'

I don't quite know what I expected, but I sniffed the air to see if I could smell burning . . . How embarrassing! The nurse smiled at me as she spoke.

'Are you OK . . . Martin.'

I could tell she had gone out of her way to get my name right this time. I could tell she had been rehearsing for the last half an hour behind the Perspex glass.

'Yeah, I'm fine.'

'Do you want to sit down? A glass of water?'

'No, I'm fine, thanks.'

I wanted to get out of that room as quick as I could. For me the whole nightmare was now over. I was finally on the home straight after all that time, after all that worry. I wanted to go home, sit in front of *Richard and Judy* and, for the first time in two years, know that my head was free from brain tumours, that there was no time bomb ticking away inside my skull. I wanted to hold Shirlie and tell her it was all over, tell her not to worry any more, and for the first time mean it. I knew I had to wait the six months to see if there were any side-effects, but I was sure in my heart that I was home and dry and that it was time to move on with my life. I felt as though I had just run the marathon and Shirlie had caught me at the winning post just before I collapsed from exhaustion. Life is so sweet when you've tasted the bitter side.

I got into the car and before I could put the seat belt around my waist, I burst into tears. Maybe I was jumping the gun a little, but I had waited two years for this moment and now it had arrived without any fanfare. Shirlie held my hand. We couldn't speak, we didn't have to, each of us knew what the other was thinking.

It was a blustery afternoon as Shirlie and I drove away from St Bartholomew's and back up the New North Road. The grey pavements were strewn with giant golden leaves from the horse chestnut trees. It was cold outside, and although there wasn't a single blemish in the sky that day, the wind had turned distinctly icy, but inside the car the heater blew out its comforting warm air. On the way home I got Shirlie to take a small detour around Old Street. We passed my old grammar school, that sat proudly on the west side of the roundabout, and then drove down a small back road that led to the old print shop I had worked in years earlier as an apprentice. It looked the same – nothing had changed – and it still had the brass plaque on the side of the door that said 'Adrepro'. I looked gingerly out of the car window in case Larry or any of the guys I had worked with came walking out. I couldn't face them. I couldn't face anyone. I could almost smell the stale air that used to fill my lungs. The ink and the putrid fumes from the hot metal being cast into hundreds of tiny letters, ready to be jammed into the heavy printing presses.

We moved on up the New North Road and into Islington. The area has changed since I lived there as a small boy. It's far more affluent now, far more middle-class. We turned right off the main road and then left by a small playground, where several boys were kicking around a well-worn football. One of their dads had been chosen to play referee and was having trouble keeping up with the game. We finally turned into Rotherfield Street. We drove slowly past the entrance to the original home of Anna Scher's Children's Theatre. The giant red-brick building that had frightened me as a child, and had seemed so daunting, now looked very different. It seemed smaller than I remembered it, but still just as uninviting.

I glanced over to the other side of the street to the house where I grew up. A little girl was kneeling down on the pavement drawing a picture of a beautiful white palace with a piece of chalk. Behind her was the dark blue door of the old Georgian house where I was born, where the queue of people waiting to pay their rent in the hallway below could sometimes be heard over the black-and-white television. Looking up, I could see the window of the bedroom that Gary and I shared and where my mother had given birth to me a lifetime ago. She had struggled to keep me alive in those early minutes, I could almost feel her pain and hear her cries. Life isn't easy at the start, and the older you get the tougher it becomes.

In my head I could see the torn Bruce Lee posters that decorated my walls as clear as day. I could see Gary's guitar that hung above his bed and vibrated to the sounds of 'Roll out the Barrel' coming from the Duke of Clarence next door. I could see the huge Batman picture that my dad had painstakingly painted on the back of our bedroom door, and the small opening to the side that he had built high up into the wall that separated my mum and dad's bedroom from ours, so that they could hear us crying and take us into the comfort and safety of their giant bed.

Shirlie looked at me. 'Are you ready to go?' Her soft voice brought me out of my dreams and back into reality.

I thought for a moment before taking one last look at the past.

'Yeah . . . Let's move on.'

Albert Square 1998

A small jet flew high above my head and into the evening Californian sky. The deep blue of the day and the dark purple of the early evening were merging, twisting together like acrylic paints on a well-used palette. I followed the plane as it punched its way through the evaporating heat and above the low grey cloud of smog. Just then the jet started to leave behind a small trail of pure white smoke, spelling out letter after letter as it made its way across the virgin canvas.

I . . . LOVE . . . LA.

The letters hung in the air like a message from the gods.

I looked down at the twinkling city lights below me. I couldn't help but remember the horrific night when we watched the city burn from our balcony above Sunset Plaza, but now, at that moment in time, it was once again magical. A land of dreams and opportunities, a place where everyone including the bin man has a plan, a way out of the monotony that rules their existence. I watched as the thousands of gas-loving cars moved around the city. It looked wonderful from my vantage-point, way up in the Hollywood Hills.

'Are you ready, MK?'

A Birmingham accent brought me out of my dream state and back

243

into the land of the living. It had been a long day, slaving away, trying to make yet another movie on a shoestring budget.

'Ready when you are, JT.'

For some reason which I was never quite sure of, John Taylor and myself only ever called each other by our initials. John's Birmingham accent has softened over the years, and his cute boyish Duran Duran looks were now starting to hide themselves under the onset of middle age. I've always liked John, I always felt that we were like two peas in a pod, made from the same mould. Both of us not great at anything, but both of us capable of everything. John always had that certain charisma that seemed to cling to his shadow wherever he went, and I for one loved to sit back and watch it slide along with him.

JT and I were making a movie called *Sugar Town* with Rosanna Arquette. It was a black comedy based on a successful band from the early Eighties trying desperately to put it back together in the late Nineties. It was JT's first shot at acting on the big screen, but it went without saying that he could pull it off.

Just then a young runner in a pair of well-worn yellow Caterpillar boots and knee-length army shorts, with the pockets on each leg bulging at the seams, came up to me and put a letter into my hand. It's always an immediate worry, getting passed messages on a film set. My mind always races through the worse scenarios . . . Are the kids okay? . . . Is Shirlie all right? . . . My mum and dad? . . . Shirlie's mum and dad? . . . It's like getting that phone call in the middle of the night, when your heart skips a beat fearing the worst. I could feel my hands sweat and my stomach jitter as I started to open the small white envelope. Being that many miles away from home is scary when you have a family.

'MK . . . Let's get the last shot.'

John was right, I put the letter into the pocket of my tight black 'rock and roll' Levis and tried to forget about it for the moment.

We were trying to get the band's press release picture – we being John, myself, Michael Desbarrs, who played with JT in the Eighties supergroup The Power Station, and Larry Kline, a local musician, who also got the job of writing the musical score for the movie. We were on the veranda of this beautiful Hollywood home.

I lined up alongside the other three chaps and smiled my best rock star smile. It had been a while since I had last used it, but none the less it was still there.

SNAP! . . . SNAP . . . SNAP . . . SNAP . . . SNAP!

I looked around at my new band. Our faces thick with make-up hiding the heavy bags under our eyes and the deep lines that were working their way across our faces . . . I thought to myself . . . Thank God . . . Thank God that this isn't real . . . Thank God this isn't Spandau's reunion tour and that I'm walking away from this in a few moments. I realized, probably for the first time, that I was too old for this, physically and mentally. I was glad to feel that I had moved on. Maybe a year earlier I would have jumped at the chance to get back together with Tony, John, Steve and Gary and try to re-live those hedonistic years that are indelibly etched in our memories, but now, on top of this West Hollywood hill, on this wonderful September evening, being given this free taster . . . Forget it!

The letter was starting to burn a hole in my pocket as the last glimpse of scarlet sun dipped down behind Coldwater Canyon.

'OK . . . Let's call that a wrap, everyone . . . Thank you for today. I know it was hard work, but I'm sure it will be worth it.'

The soft Californian voice that had just brought the curtain down on the shoot was that of the director, Allison Anders, a beautiful West Coast woman in her early forties, whose ethics and manner-isms were stuck firmly in the days when flower power and peace and love ruled California.

After the hand shakes and the hugs and kisses and swapping of e-mail numbers I slipped off into a quiet corner of the veranda to read my note.

September 1998.

Martin . . . Call me first thing in the morning . . . 'British time' . . .
Matthew Robinson wants to do a screen test with you for a great
recurring role in *EastEnders*. A character called Steve Owen. I've read
the character breakdown and it couldn't be more like you if I'd
written it myself . . . The only problem is you have to catch the first
flight out of LA.
   Call me a.s.a.p. and I will explain more.

   Derek Webster.

Now *EastEnders* . . . It was never something I saw myself doing. In
fact even during my favourite days of 'Den and Ange' I never once
saw myself walking into the Queen Vic to order a pint. Not once,
when I was watching the show with the rest of the band cooped up
in a hotel room in some corner of the world, did I ever see myself
causing trouble in Albert Square. Our special DHL delivery of video
tapes from England every Thursday broke the monotony of a jet-
setting lifestyle. It was the high point of the week, an excuse to
down tools and walk out of the confines of a sterile studio and settle
down to our Chinese takeaway in front of the television. To us
EastEnders was both real life and a kind of escapism. Most people
would watch the big American soaps, *Dynasty* or *Dallas*, to dream of
being involved in a lifestyle beyond their means; we would watch
EastEnders as a way to touch base with the lifestyle we had so eagerly
left behind.

I hadn't done that much work since my operation, just a small
student film to find my feet and to see if my brain was working well
enough to even remember lines, and a small part as a policeman in
Lynda La Plante's television drama *Supply and Demand*.
   When I took the role of DS Eddie McEwen I was just on the end of
a massive course of steroids that were keeping at bay the side-effects
of the radiation treatment the year before. They were working a
treat, but my weight had ballooned up to a massive sixteen and a

half stone. I looked like a caricature of myself. A nasty cartoon you might find in the *Sun*. I wasn't used to carrying that kind of weight, I felt as if I had been wrapped in bubble wrap. The first thing to gain weight on a course of steroids is your face. Your face seems to explode into a big ball of fat, and your eyes become set back into your head. I was grotesque. I felt as if I should be floating above Wembley Stadium on the end of a rope, a decoration that was to be released to float freely away before the kick-off. Neighbours were talking, friends were laughing, everyone had noticed – I was the talking point of Muswell Hill, and all for the wrong reason.

My appetite was enormous. People would invite me to dinner and be astounded at how much food I could put away. An ordinary chip tasted as if Anton Mosimann had been in the kitchen slaving over it all morning, and the desserts were definitely made by the angels themselves . . . But hey, the steroids were doing the job . . . and I had to 'roll' with it.

It was after the read-through for *Supply and Demand*, where all the actors had brought the drama to life for the first time and Lynda and the producer had made their final notes, that I felt the most conscious about my weight.

Lynda had laid on a massive open buffet for lunch, and I was tucking into my third plate of chicken satay when I saw her watching me from across the room. I smiled and politely waved my half-eaten skewer in her direction before turning around to finish my lunch. A moment later Lynda tapped me on the shoulder.

'Martin, can I have a word?'

I wiped the peanut sauce away from the corner of my mouth with my free hand and swallowed the last chunk of delicious 'cluck'.

'Sure.'

'We were thinking that you, well Eddie McEwen to be precise, could have some kind of . . . some kind of eating disorder.'

Shit, I knew straight away that there must have been some kind of discussion about my size.

'Yes, I thought it might be an idea if your character eats when he gets nervous.'

'Right,' I said.

'Some cops smoke, some cops drink . . .'

'And I eat.' I beat her to it.

'That's right . . . think about it!' she said as she moved away.

I was, and it was depressing me. For the first time, I wasn't the love interest, or the action hero, or even the villain. I was to be the obese joke. The fat boy in the 1970's TV show 'The Double Deckers' who couldn't quite get through the fence. Who stuffed his face with cakes each time he took centre stage.

The whole thing was so depressing. More so because the only people who knew I was on steroids were my closest family: my mum and dad, Gary, Shirlie. I didn't want everyone to know that I was still on medication to stop the side-effects of the 'tactical radiation' even though it had done its job.

After *Supply and Demand* finished I quickly fell into a depression. Not only because of my huge size, but because all the fear I had suppressed over the last three years was ready to come to the surface and show its ugly head. One minute I would be fine, the next I would be in tears. It was the extreme changes in mood that finally got me down, that finally made me face my demons and finally got me to see someone about it.

SESSION ONE

I never thought therapy was the answer to any of my problems and would never have been there in the first place if I wasn't almost tricked into it. Three years earlier, directly after the first operation when everyone around me suggested that I needed some kind of counselling, I didn't go. I found it far easier to deny the whole thing. To live life, as much as I could, without acknowledging the fact that it had ever happened. I wanted to suppress the episode and lock it away in some corner of my head where no one, not even myself, would go. If I spoke about it, it just reminded me that I had another tumour, a far more dangerous tumour, floating around in there, living and growing.

I also had an intense fear directly after the operation that I was being tricked, that everyone was keeping a dark secret from me, that everyone knew that the tumour was malignant apart from me. I became so paranoid about it that even when I spoke to Shirlie about appointments with doctors, or simply about mundane things like what we were going to have for dinner, I would try to look deeper into her eyes to see if she wanted to tell me the bad news. I was obsessed. It hurt me to think that I didn't trust anyone and that they in turn were lying to me. When I spoke to my parents or Gary over the phone I was waiting to catch them out, waiting to see if they would slip up and I would find out the truth.

Looking back on the situation now, the first thing that I should have done after my recovery was to get myself some professional help and talk to a therapist – but everything is easy in hindsight. I thought the best way to deal with my problem was not to burden others with it. I could see first hand how it was tearing Shirlie apart, and I didn't want to make things worse. I thought to myself that if Shirlie and Gary don't want to tell me I have cancer, then that's the way I will play it. I wondered several times if I was going truly mad, if Dr C had cut out the part of my brain that made me see common sense . . . I was completely paranoid.

The whole episode had jumped up on me, not giving me any time to prepare myself. From finding out about the tumours to finding myself on the hospital table was only twenty-four hours. It was rather like being in a car crash, and now I was suffering the delayed shock. How could I go to a complete stranger and tell him that I doubted my brother, my mum and dad and even my wife? I felt that this was my problem and that only I could sort it out.

The belief that I had brain cancer lived with me for about six weeks after the operation, until I found the strength in me to talk to Shirlie about it and to pull myself out of that shock. It was a dark time, and it hurts me to take myself back there.

I first came across cranial osteopathy when Shirlie's gynaecologist introduced me to it during her first pregnancy. He said it was good for relieving stress and worry, and off and on over the last two years I have found that this was excellent advice. I had my first session with a young cranial osteopath called Simeon.

Simeon has a practice in Highgate Village. Highgate is a beautiful place, but ruined by too many cars and lorries travelling through it, making their way north and leaving behind them a thick black cloud of pollution that sticks to the walls of the two hundred year old buildings and turns the green summer leaves on the chestnut trees a dark shade of grey.

I went along to this Simeon's practice after a huge lunch with some friends in Café Rouge, the restaurant next door. The garlic chicken baguette and the half-bottle of Chianti were finding it hard to make their way down into my stomach, and were repeating on me every time I made a move. My digestive tract hadn't made a very good job of the French food and I felt dehydrated and uncomfortable.

Simeon is only young, but his presence is that of someone much older. You feel you can trust him, can let him into your world and your quiet thoughts without him walking away with your dreams. I noticed that his wire-framed glasses looked tiny on his round face, and that his white coat had several black and red Bic pens protruding from the breast pocket.

The room was small, decorated by his new wife in pretty découpage and designer crackle glaze. The shelves in the alcove at the far end of the room held a computer and a small amount of well-read books. I put my hand over my mouth and apologized for any smell of garlic that might be emanating from my stomach as he led me on to his couch.

The first ten minutes were as I expected. I lay on my back and dozed off as he held my neck and rubbed my temples. The only thing that woke me up from time to time was the sound of my own snoring that seemed to jump out and shake me by the head from time to time. Then out of the blue he whispered to me in a voice that was caring and full of warmth.

'I want you to imagine that you can see into your body.'

I opened my eyes, I was surprised to hear him speak. 'What?'

'Close your eyes for me and imagine you are taking a journey into the centre of your body.'

I thought I should do as he said. I had nothing to lose.

'Martin, I want you to think of yourself as only an inch tall and you're inside your chest. I want you to take a look at your heart, the way it pumps and pushes the blood through your body, keeping you alive. Look at how big it is and how hard it works for you.'

He went quiet for a moment to allow me to think, to allow the visual image he had strategically planted in my brain to sink in. Within seconds, the sound of the traffic passing in the street below had metamorphosed into the sound of the blood running through the veins leading into my giant heart, and every lorry passing over the bumps in the road made it sound as if it was alive and beating. Then he continued.

'In front of your heart there is something obstructing your view. Something you need to climb over or push out of the way to see properly.'

There was silence. The images were so vivid, so clear, it was as if it was right in front of me. I noticed that the taste of garlic and red wine had disappeared from my mouth and the lump of warm bread in my chest had dissolved. I was completely involved in this strange visualization. I swallowed, and then told him what I could see.

'I can see giant black rubber bands in front of it, crossed and unevenly nailed onto a black wooden door frame,' I said cautiously, half waiting for his response. When it didn't come, I carried on.

'There are giant metal staples holding the bands together where they have snapped several times over the years. The bands look fragile, as if they are disintegrating . . . Some of the pins are rusty and look dangerous.'

'I want you to get a pair of shears in your hands and cut away the bands until you can walk easily into the room.'

It looked dark behind the rubber bands. I didn't want to walk into

251

that room. I felt like a child needing to be hugged and told that everything is going to be okay.

Simeon didn't have to ask if I had done what he had said. Tears were rolling freely down my face. I had no embarrassment; I felt like a child as I wiped them away. He waited a moment, let me regain my composure; it was the first time I had ever experienced that kind of inner shock.

'What can you see?'

I waited a moment. 'The derelict basement in the house where I was born . . . 138 Rotherfield Street. I hated that place.'

'I want you to go in there, I want you to walk into the room, I want you to throw open the dirty windows to let the sun light in . . . Can you do that for me?'

I nodded my head. I couldn't get the words that I wanted to say out.

'Now I want you to take a pot of white paint and decorate the room until it's unrecognizable, until it looks clean enough to lay down a brand new white carpet . . . I want you to look around and see just how stunning that room is, how happy it feels in there. I want you to walk in there and sit in your favourite armchair and let the fresh air from the open window rush over you as the clean white cotton curtains flap in the breeze.'

I sat up and swung my legs over the end of the bed. Simeon passed me a tissue from the box on the shelf behind him.

SESSION TWO

My second appointment with Simeon was for two thirty on the following Monday. It had been a strange weekend. I had reflected on my first session in awe. I couldn't believe the effect it had on me. It was the strongest, most powerful form of treatment I had ever experienced. It not only left me shell-shocked and in a state of constant reflection, but also in a state of emotional turmoil. For the first time I realized that I was walking on eggshells. I wasn't as strong as I thought I was. I wasn't as strong as I wanted to be. I held so much fear inside that had been locked up over the previous three years that it had unconsciously worn me down. It has to. It has to go somewhere. A force that powerful doesn't just dissipate.

Highgate Village was as busy as usual, the heavy traffic was rattling the roads and leaving a film of black oil on top of the cappuccino's that were being sipped on the pavement outside Café Rouge. It wasn't quite as hot as the previous week, a wind was blowing up the Holloway Road, keeping the temperature unusually low for this time of year.

I was lying on Simeon's couch with my head resting firmly between his hands when he spoke to me. It was different from last time. This time I wanted him to speak to me, in fact I would have been disappointed if he had just let me lie there and sleep. He spoke with the same voice, it was the same voice he had used last week and the same voice that my mum used to wake me up with on my birthday. It was soft and mellow but had an air of excitement to it.

'Martin . . .'

I smiled, to show him I was listening and to show him I wanted to go on.

'I want you to take a walk. In front of you there is a wonderful green field with a path that leads right down the centre. There are flowers on either side of the path and their scent drifts across the field and attacks your senses. There's a stream of running water at the far end of the field and the path turns into a small bridge that traverses the stream. I want you to walk down the path and smell those flowers, maybe even pick one on your way, I want you to listen to the running water and make your way to the bridge.'

He left me for a while to let this picture settle into my brain. It did, and I felt wonderful. I even added the sun and could feel its warming rays.

'Martin . . . As you walk over the bridge you can see a small group of boys, you can't see their faces, but you can see that they're only young . . . maybe only six, or seven.'

Suddenly I felt my chest tremble, a lump appear in my throat and my mouth dry up. What was happening?

253

'Can you see the boys?'

'Yes.'

'Now, very slowly they are going to turn around.'

The group of boys did as Simeon had asked, but I still couldn't see their faces. I couldn't see their faces, but I had an overwhelming sense of grief, as strong if not stronger than I had ever experienced in real life.

My fists clenched and my neck started to tighten as once again I started to cry uncontrollably. I sat upright, and once again Simeon handed me the tissues from the small box on the side in exactly the same way he had done last week.

I couldn't explain what was going on. I only knew that there was something deep inside of me that needed to be flushed out. I knew that I had started something that had to be finished. If I let go of it now it might scar me for the rest of my life.

'We're moving in the right direction,' Simeon said, and patted me softly on the back.

SESSION THREE

There was a downpour outside. It looked as though a cloud had burst specifically over Highgate Village. The sky was black and the rain rattled the tiny windows inside the small room. I could hear it as I lay on the couch and drifted off into a state of relaxation that was very new to me.

I had always doubted people who spoke about how visualization had worked for them. In fact, I doubted any form of 'alternative' help. I had always been a firm believer in the kind of medication that comes in tablet form.

I was asleep when Simeon woke me up. In the middle of a dream that left me feeling wonderfully happy and satisfied. It was all I could do to stop myself from laughing out loud.

I was back on stage with the band. We were playing in front of a huge Italian crowd, a football stadium packed from top to bottom with screaming fans. We were in the middle of an encore and every pair of hands were up in the air clapping along to 'Fight for Ourselves'. I looked over at Gary, who was down the front of the stage sharing the mike with Tony, singing along to the choruses. John was in his regular place on his podium with what looked like the biggest kit I had ever seen, and Steve was blowing his sax, his white fringe being blow around in the wind machines that were placed at the front of the stage to cool us down. I was playing my bass guitar with ease, it wasn't one of those dreams where I can't find the notes and I'm just waiting to be revealed as a fraud. This was perfect, in fact everything was perfect, it was exactly how it was supposed to be. We were the band that loved one another and that cared for one another like the closest of families. It was the feeling we started out with all those years ago.

'Martin, I want you to take that same path that we took last week, over the fields and down to the little bridge that crosses the stream,' Simeon said.

I remembered the path and the field and the smell of fresh flowers. I also remembered the group of young kids on the other side of the stream. How could I forget? I had thought about little else the whole week. I wondered what on earth made me cry like a baby at the sight of these small boys. There was no obvious solution to this, and the harder I tried to sort it out, the more of a muddle I found myself in.

I was scared as I walked down the path and started to cross the bridge. I could see the stream running underneath the bridge through the cracks in the wooden floor.

'Martin . . . Have a look over to your right . . . What's there?'

I took a deep breath and replied to his question.

'The same boys as yesterday . . . The young kids.'

'Can you see their faces this time?'

'No.'

'Walk closer to them . . . I want you to see who it is.'

I walked over to the group of young kids. I only saw one face clearly, but that face bit deep into my heart. I couldn't hold back my tears any longer, they started to stream down my cheeks and roll into my mouth. I could taste the salt, it was stronger than I had tasted it before.

'Who is it, Martin? Who can you see?'

'It's a boy who lost his dad while we were at school. He was my best friend when we were kids. We did everything together . . . played football, went to one another's houses after school, saw each other at weekends . . . everything!'

'And what happened when his father died?'

'It happened just as we were finishing school and I never got a chance to tell him how sorry I was.' I was crying uncontrollably.

'Martin, I want you to go over to your friend and take this opportunity to tell him how sorry you are. I want you to put your arms around him and hug him and tell him everything is going to be OK . . . because it is . . . Everything is going to be OK . . . Tell him.'

I held back my tears and swallowed down hard to get a grip on myself. I spoke out loud . . . repeating the sentence slowly several times.

'Everything is going to be OK . . . Everything is going to be OK . . . Everything is going to be OK.'

Simeon stopped me . . .

'Martin . . . Martin.'

I opened my eyes . . . I could see him looking down at me through his small glasses.

'Martin . . . Are you OK?'

'I think so . . .' I thought for a moment before answering his question. 'Yeah, I'm fine.'

Simeon didn't have to tell me what all these visual images meant, it was pretty obvious. I was still scared of death, I was still scared of leaving behind my children, Shirlie, Gary and my mum and dad. I still needed reassuring that I wasn't going to die. Deep down in the centre of my body, I still held the greatest fear of all.

END OF SESSIONS

I knew it was too late to get the last plane out of Los Angeles, so I breathed a sigh of relief. It had already been a long day, and I could feel the effects of standing out in the Californian sun for the past twelve hours. My skin was starting to get hotter, even though a cool wind was now blowing down the canyon.

I said my last goodbyes to JT, the producers, directors, grips, cooks, lighting crew, runners, make up girls, hair girls, wardrobe man and the dog that had wandered on to the set during one of my earlier scenes, and walked over to my hired Ford Mustang. The smell of the hot plastic seats came rushing out and hit me in the face as I opened the heavy black door. I climbed in, switched on the five-litre engine and pushed a button that sent the electric roof sliding back into the trunk. It reminded me of being at Southend watching the caterpillar ride speed into the tunnel of love and hoping that my dad didn't want to take me on it.

The wind felt good on my sunburn as I made my way down the hill and on to the Pacific Coast Highway back to West Hollywood. I was tired and sunburnt, but a satisfying glow was still with me and my brain was buzzing at the prospect of working on *East-Enders*.

I stopped at the main junction. In front of me was Malibu beach, and beyond that the glistening Pacific Ocean. LA is a beautiful place to be, but at that moment in time I desperately wanted to swap it for the grimy streets of Walford. The prospect of working on a show that I have loved for years, and being able to do that without having to travel six thousand miles away from my family, was a tantalizing prospect.

The lights went green and I took the left turn off the Canyon Road and up Sunset Boulevard. I knew Derek my agent had said that I had to test for the role, so it went without saying that I wasn't the only actor in the frame. There had to be several other actors chomping at the bit, salivating at the prospect of such a plum role. My problem was I could already see my name on that end credit, and hear those famous end-of-episode drums that leave the nation in suspense until the following week.

Jumping the gun with excitement has always been my problem; that's why disappointment has always hit me so hard. But this time my mind kept flashing back to my note, and Derek's words, 'It couldn't be more like you if I'd written it myself.'

Just past Jayne Mansfield's pink Hollywood home on the winding tarmac strip there is a strange-looking house with several statues on the front lawn. The brass statues are of ordinary people doing ordinary things. One is cutting the grass, one sitting on a bench and one picnicking on the lawn. I have watched the statues grow in numbers over the years and have always tried to work out what could be coming next. It always seemed to me that the people inside the huge mansion beyond the statues were living ordinary lives vicariously through the bronze works of art. I mean life in Beverly Hills is far from ordinary at the best of times. My mum has always said that the grass is always greener on the other side of the fence . . . And how right she is!

I finally made it to the beautiful house I was staying in, which belongs to George Michael. It's really more of a home than a house. A small part of paradise, perched on top of a canyon ridge that looks out over Los Angeles. A home that smells of vanilla candles, wood floors and sweet jasmine that gently blows in from the garden. It's always hard to believe that a mate of mine owns such a wonderful piece of the world.

I put the car in the garage and walked up a small flight of stairs and into the kitchen.

'Martin . . . Hi.'

Christ, I had forgotten about my session with Christian Dion. Christian was an ex-pat whose bright red hair and long white fringe reminded me of my nights at 'The Blitz'.

'Martin . . . The maid let me in.'

Christian was our local psychic healer. He was – and still is – the man the stars in Bel Air trust with all kinds of personal secrets, and who they hope will give them a glimpse into the future.

'Christian . . . I completely forgot you were coming over.'

Christian replied in his sweet, camp Northern accent, 'Well, thank you, darling . . . That's boosted my ego no end.'

'I'm sorry, I didn't mean that, it's just that I'm knackered . . . It's . . .'

'*Been a long day.*' Christian has a strange knack of finishing your sentences for you.

'Martin, why don't you get washed up and come and lie on the sofa. I can do your healing at the same time as we chat.'

That sounded like a good idea to me. After my experience in Highgate anyone who wanted to put his hands on my head and tell me he was healing me was more than welcome, and before long I was lying on the couch with my head in his hands meditating on the sound of the fountain hitting the swimming pool outside.

I could feel the heat from his hands travel up the back of my neck and into my head. It was as if the energy was jumping from his body into mine. I took a deep breath. The idea that a relative stranger was ready to show me such warmth and affection was overwhelming.

Christian began to talk and talk and talk. He doesn't expect answers to his questions, he just likes to ramble on and say what's in his mind.

'Now Martin . . . Are you thinking of moving? I can see a plot of land, a plan of something that's not even built yet. Does this make any sense to you?'

Shirlie and I had talked about moving, but we always do. Five homes in twelve years. I always think it has something to do with my days on the road – itchy feet, living out of a suitcase, moving from one hotel to the next. But Christian was right: we wanted to move again, to move away from the house that held difficult memories of my struggle back to good health after my operation, the struggle to get back on our feet financially, and the struggle back to happiness.

*

'The fact is Shirlie is looking at houses now, because I feel she has made her mind up . . . She's putting the "hebeegeebees" on a place as we speak. Oh, she has really put a spell on it. Tell her to look out for a river . . . That's a good sign!'

I had to smile – that was Shirlie all over. Whenever she wants something, she writes it down on a piece of paper and keeps it in a special place. Through the bad times I would find hundreds of her little spells all round the house. I secretly read the ones I came across, folded them back into their neat squares and put them back into their hiding places.

'Anyway . . . you will be moving in six weeks. I know that doesn't give you much time, but that's how things are . . . Are you with me, Martin?'

I nodded. I was enjoying his words.

'Oops . . . I'm with Shirl again . . . She's having trouble with the trees . . . They're blocking the light . . . Still, she'll sort that out for you, don't you worry. She doesn't want you to worry about a thing . . . Shirlie's a strong woman, but listen to me, Martin, sometimes she needs looking after as well, you know, don't you ever forget that . . . She has been through more than you could ever imagine caring for you. You have pushed her to the limit, she's cried more tears than she knew she was capable of . . . Oh, you have taken a lot out of that young lady. You have to start thinking about giving her back some of that love . . . You can't just carry on taking now that you're better.'

Christian had hit the nail on the head. My illness had drained Shirlie, I wanted things to go right for us so much – not just for me, not just to satisfy my own ego, but for my wife, who would have quite happily swapped places with me during the worst moments and the darkest times of my illness without even flinching. I wanted some success, and soon, to give her back some of that enthusiasm for life that I had fallen in love with so many years ago.

'Those trees are a problem, though . . . it's very dark in the garden.' He moved on again.

'You will be back here, Martin . . . Not in this house, but in a home of your own . . . I can see you all sitting around your pool . . . This film you are doing at the moment isn't the big one! But I do feel that everything you are about to touch is going to turn to gold.'

I was always sceptical when a psychic said that, but Christian was on a roll, and I was ready, and more than willing, to believe him . . . So gold it was!

'That's the way it's going to go for you, Martin. You are going to do something that is going to let everyone know that you are well and truly back. It's time to forget about your illness, forget about Spandau Ballet. This thing, whatever it is, is going to take you right back into the spotlight again.'

I smiled to myself. I felt good, and why not!

'Now your son, he is the psychic one, you know, he has got it in him. You had it, Martin, but it wasn't encouraged enough! Please let the boy develop it. He is so artistic, I think he's a painter who sees everything through his psychic vision.'

Full marks . . . Gary was always pushed to be the artistic one, with his music and his songs. I was the son who played sports and football, the far more traditional North London route. I wouldn't have had it any other way, but it was true!

'Now listen to this, Martin . . . I see Shirlie healing, tell her not to be afraid when she starts seeing pink . . . It's not to be afraid of.

'Oh hang on, your brother's back. Tell him to let go a bit, he gets a bit too tense, it's time for him to stop trying to control everything.

'Now Martin . . . I do see you and your brother doing another movie together. I think it would be good for both of you . . . to bring you back together.'

I would love to do another movie with Gary, and people have always talked about making a sequel to *The Krays*. In fact there have been a few scripts come through the door, but until everything is right, I wouldn't even consider it. *The Krays* is my finest moment on screen, the thing that I am the most proud of. The movie has become a 'British classic', and I for one wouldn't want to trample on that by making a second-rate sequel for a few quid. I know that Gary feels the same because we have spoken about it several times, usually after a few beers at the end of a night. We discuss all permutations . . . 'The Krays in glorious 3D' . . . 'The Kraysies' (a musical version) . . . Or what about 'The Krays versus Godzilla'?

I'm not saying there's not another film to be made, I'm just saying it has to be right.

'Shirlie's back . . . Do you know she's seen this house twice?'

She had.

'But those trees are winding her up rotten, but trust me, the garden will look beautiful . . . Martin, do you want more children?'

I would love more children, but I wouldn't want another baby. I don't think I could go back to steaming the bottles, sleepless nights and worrying over every cough and cold. As much as those memories are dear to me, I couldn't do that again.

'More children, yes . . . because I see three lights around you . . . How many have you got now – two? . . . Well there's definitely three lights over your head . . .

'What's this . . . 'ang on . . . I can see a courtroom . . . Are you or your brother going into court soon?'

Christian was spot on. I tried to make a small gesture with my face.

'Stay still and relax . . . PLEEEEEASE.'

My brother was just in the process of being taken to court by John Keeble, Tony Hadley and Steve Norman, in an argument over what they claim are 'unpaid publishing royalties'. If you had told me that this was going to be the final chapter in the Spandau Ballet story I would have laughed for a month of Sundays. We were the best friends anyone could ever have, a close family that saw each other nearly every day for twelve years. We discovered life, found our personalities, experienced the highs and lows of success and failure together and explored the world.

The tears that were being shed over the court case were a long way from the tears that were shed as we hugged and kissed each other in a Nottingham hotel on the wonderful morning that 'True' went to number one on the BBC charts. Those memories were some of the sweetest in my life and were now starting to sour with every thought of my brother being sued, and having to defend himself in court.

Gary had worked harder than anyone in the band, taken on the responsibility of writing over one hundred hit songs spread over several hit albums. I watched him over the years as the pressure of that task took its toll – on his personality, his enthusiasm and his relationships. Without the songs there wasn't a band, it's as simple as that. We all relied on Gary to come up with the goods – without his work there would be nothing.

But Tony, John and Steve have their reasons for bringing this lawsuit and they're not for me, at this moment in time, to go into, or to condemn.

For me the whole thing was extremely sad. Not only were my closest friends in court with my brother, but it was also the closing of the Spandau book. Would there be a Spandau reunion at some point? Would we ever get back together in the years to come and play a couple of shows, or even to make the odd record? After this, the answer is definitely no.

'Those bloody trees . . . They're blocking *my* way now . . . She's got to do something about them, she's not happy, you know,' Christian blurted out.

'Your brother's going to win his case, you know . . . Oh yes, there is no doubt at all. He is going to win . . . But tell him from me that he has to be there, in court, every day. Don't just send a flunky . . . make sure he goes himself.'

'Now let's see about you, shall we? Have you been up to no good?'

I felt my pulse quicken slightly as I started to scan my mind. I couldn't think of anything offhand.

'Mmmm . . . Very weird.'

OK, Christian had my attention, now get on with it.

'I can see bars . . . bars all around you.'

That was nothing new, I've spent half my life in bars around the world. He went on.

'I'm not talking about licensed bars, I'm talking about prison bars . . . I keep getting an image of you being locked up behind bars, you spending time in a prison . . . Don't worry, though, it's not here, it's at home in England . . . Martin, you're sweating . . . Just relax.'

What does he expect? Here I am trying to meditate and he's telling me that I'm going to prison.

'Oh no . . . Things are getting worse!'

My eyes opened quickly and I saw a blurry Christian looking down on me. He wasn't aware that I was looking at him, his eyes were closed and a pained expression tore at his face as his nostrils flared wide open.

'Christian . . . Christian,' I said. 'What is it?'

'It's those bloody trees . . . They're in the way again . . . They've completely blocked out my light . . . Shirlie will have to get a specialist in for those.'

I lay back down and tried to relax.

'Don't look so worried, I'm telling you this so that you can change things that are about to happen . . . Alter your own destiny.'

Christian was right, my destiny was mine to control. It's amazing how sometimes we forget that simple fact and blame others for our own failures. I decided to think positive thoughts about the impending *EastEnders* test and imagine myself in an episode with the rest of the cast . . . You never know, it might just work.

The sound of the fountain hitting the top of the pool once again became my focus, and the jasmine once more became apparent drifting in through the french windows. Gradually my pulse started to regain its composure, and slowly but surely I had drifted into a wonderful, well-earned sleep.

It had been a week since I had performed my two audition scenes in front of Matthew Robinson and his tiny digital handicam. A week filled with the usual post-casting trauma of waiting for the phone to ring, wishing and wanting, trying to forget, and lying to myself, making out I wasn't really that bothered if I got the part or not.

As long as I feel I have done my best in any casting and grabbed the moment by the horns, I'm usually happy. This time, I didn't' have a clue what I'd done, I was so jet-lagged and tired from the overnight flight that my brain felt like a milk jelly, struggling to remember lines and hold my concentration together. But with thirty years of casting experience behind me I got through it, and walked away with my self-esteem intact.

It was on the following Friday that Derek called me and told me I had got the part.

I can't tell you the relief an actor goes through when he hears those incredible words coming form his agent . . . THEY WANT YOU! . . . It's like a giant weight being lifted from off your back; all your anxiety and stress immediately turn into joy and elation, and a smile finds its way on to your face that only seconds earlier had been filled with worry. Your stomach unties itself and your stiff neck starts to loosen as he reassures you that you did actually make a good job of that casting, when by now you've convinced yourself and everyone around you that you were crap.

I was no different. I was as pleased to get the part as I was relieved that I didn't have to tell people that I didn't. This was my mum and dad's favourite show, and by now word had spread through the whole of the family that I was possibly going to work on Albert Square. Even my aunts and uncles in deepest Islington were waiting for that phone call, waiting to see if they were going to watch me on television three times a week. The pressure had been enormous, but after Derek's phone call it was time to relax and enjoy the congratulations that came with it, before starting work three weeks later.

My fading suntan felt out of place as I drove through those Elstree gates for the first time since the morning of the casting. The security guy on the door in his BBC uniform waved me through. There was a welcoming smile on his weathered face, as if he had been expecting me. I smiled back and tried to seem relaxed.

I had spent the previous three weeks shopping for clothes that were going to make Steve Owen the man he is, doing a couple of press calls and learning pages and pages of dialogue. I had never seen so many scripts come through the letter-box in my life. It was then that I realized for the first time just what I had agreed to do. I wasn't about to work on a nice relaxed movie, or even a six-part television drama where time is that much more valuable. This was a soap opera, where they shoot one and a half hours of film every five days, sometimes even two hours if the storyline needs an extra Friday night episode. This was going to be hard word, but I was looking forward to it.

I always found my first day on any new film to be traumatic, but it has to be said that this one took the biscuit. I was more nervous starting *EastEnders* than anything else I had ever done, and by the time I was through the gates and being led up to my room, where my costume was hanging on its rail, my stomach had that familiar queezy feeling, and my heart was pounding so hard I could see my T-shirt jump in time. The grey BBC phone in the corner rang.

'Martin, we're on the scene before yours . . . Can you come down on to the set?'

I quickly got dressed and pulled on my new shoes. My hands were shaking as I did my laces. Why, after all these years, after all I had been through – my years as a child actor, my years living the life of a rock star with Spandau Ballet and my years working in Hollywood – was I scared of walking onto the set of *EastEnders?*

Deep down I knew the reason, I knew the cause of all that anxiety. This was a new beginning, a new start for me, a chance to forget about the horrors of the last three years and finally move on.

The phone rang again.

'We're ready for you.'

I coughed and gently cleared my throat.

'OK . . . I'm coming!'

I walked out of my dressing-room and down the small flight of stairs to where the corridor widens into a small reception area, and where the artists meet up before their scenes to run through their lines together for the first time. A young PA, who would have looked more at home in the Indian outback with a rucksack over his shoulder than at the BBC, was waiting for me at the double doors that lead on to the Square.

'Martin . . . All right?'

I wasn't. I was as nervous as hell. Remember my lines? At that moment I don't think I could have remembered my address.

I followed the PA out the double doors and into the parking area and then up a small flight of stairs. There was rain in the air and dark clouds hung overhead. I didn't mind, the damp air cooled me down slightly and clung to my cheeks, taking the redness away. Suddenly his walkie talkie sprang to life.

'Matthew . . . Come in! . . . Is Martin with you?'

He put his radio to his mouth.

'Travelling!'

I was, and with one small turn of a corner I was in the middle of Albert Square.

The market was heaving. Ricky and Bianca were going through their lines with Phil and Grant by the clothes stall. Frank Butcher was sitting on one of the chairs outside the café playing with a freshly made 'roll up' and studying his script. Dot Cotton was lighting up one of her famous cigarettes outside the launderette, sending the sky above her a strange hazy grey; and, sitting on top of the damp skyline in all her splendour, looking down over her domain and all her famous subjects, was the glorious Queen Vic.

I was just simply dumb-struck. I felt as if I had somehow been sucked into my television set on a Sunday afternoon. A free *EastEnders* episode happening before my eyes. To say this was one of the most surreal moments in my life doesn't do it justice.

In some strange way, I felt as if I had come home. The small terraced houses around the Square, the market, the pub on the corner. The familiar deep cockney accents that rang in my ears like the sound of Bow bells. I could quite easily be back in Islington, back in Rotherfield Street, where this whole incredible journey started. Where my dreams and ambitions were still just boyhood wishes, and the game was still only minutes old.

A warm feeling surged through my body on that cold October

morning. A feeling that I had come a full circle, that I was ready to throw the dice for my second turn around the board. That I was ready to collect two hundred pounds and pass go!

And, with a smile from one side of my face to the other, I walked in front of the camera, feeling that the best was yet to come.

Index